A Tale of Two Fronts

A Tale of Two Fronts

A German Soldier's Journey through World War I

Hans Schiller

Translated by Karin Wagner

Transcribed by Otti Kiraly

Edited by Frederic Krome and Gregory Loving

Foreword by Brian K. Feltman

University Press of Kansas

Published by the University Press of Kansas (Lawrence, Kansas 66045), which was organized by the Kansas Board of Regents and is operated and funded by Emporia State University, Fort Hays State University, Kansas State University, Pittsburg State University, the University of Kansas, and Wichita State University.

Names: Schiller, Hans, 1897–1945. | Wagner, Karin, translator.
Title: A tale of two fronts : a German soldier's journey through World War I / Hans Schiller ; translated by Karin Wagner.
Other titles: German soldier's journey through World War I
Description: Lawrence : University Press of Kansas, 2024 | Includes index.
Identifiers: LCCN 2024013573 (print) | LCCN 2024013574 (ebook) |
ISBN 9780700638000 (cloth)
ISBN 9780700638017 (ebook)
Subjects: LCSH: Schiller, Hans, 1897–1945. | World War, 1914–1918–Personal narratives, German. | World War, 1914–1918–Campaigns–Eastern Front. | World War, 1914–1918–Campaigns–Western Front. | Germany. Heer–Military life. | Germany. Heer–Officers–Biography. | BISAC: HISTORY / Wars & Conflicts / World War I | BIOGRAPHY & AUTOBIOGRAPHY / Military
Classification: LCC D640 .S43295 2024 (print) | LCC D640 (ebook) |
DDC 940.4/1343092 [B]–dc23/eng/20240620
LC record available at https://lccn.loc.gov/2024013573
LC ebook record available at https://lccn.loc.gov/2024013574

British Library Cataloguing-in-Publication Data is available.

Contents

Foreword

Brian K. Feltman

The First World War centenary (2014–2018) led to an upturn in academic and general interest in the events of the conflict that shaped the course of the twentieth century. As scholars approached the study of the First World War from new perspectives, local communities and national governments sought to bring the war, its effects, and participants into the public consciousness. Despite a new wave of scholarship and broad public interest in the events of 1914–1918, the centenary and the years that followed saw the appearance of few previously unpublished war memoirs. In the English-speaking world, the German perspective on the war has been predominantly molded by two accounts: Ernst Jünger's memoir *Storm of Steel* and Erich Maria Remarque's renowned novel *All Quiet on the Western Front*. More than seventy-five years after his death, Hans Schiller's memoir, handwritten in 1928 and found in a drawer by his granddaughter decades later, offers a new and accessible window into the life of the German soldier of the First World War.

Schiller's memoir is more than merely an account of the combat experience. His writings reveal the excitement he felt, like so many other university students from his social background, at the prospect of going to war and serving as a volunteer. Schiller's status as a one-year volunteer (*Einjärige Freiwilliger*) elevated him to a position of privilege above many of his peers, but his rank did little to quell his envy for contemporaries who made it to the front before him. The pressures to serve were significant for the men of Schiller's generation, and he naively believed that the worst possible scenario would be that the war might end before he reached the front lines. When Schiller's time at the front finally began in January 1915, he disembarked his train not in Belgium or France but behind the Eastern Front. The considerable time during which Schiller served in Russia and Poland as an artilleryman is among the elements that make his memoir so valuable. The trenches of the Western Front dominate histories of the First World War, and Schiller's memories of war in the east provide rare and poignant insights into life on the "forgotten front."

Although generally seen as a sideshow to the more lethal Western Front, death was an ever-present threat in the east. Schiller's first depictions of Russia are characterized by destruction and devastation. He recalls burning villages whose inhabitants' lives had been ruined by war and walls of enemy dead. Schiller's descriptions of death are vivid and haunting. He writes of comrades who "folded like a pocket knife" after being hit by shrapnel, a lieutenant with "blood encrusted eyes" who had lost the entire back of his skull, and lying alongside the dying, covered in freshly turned earth, as they begged for water. This was not the adventure Schiller had imagined as an eager volunteer. His candid recollections of the First World War's carnage will remind contemporary readers of the psychological baggage carried by the soldiers who managed to survive their time at the front. Schiller's proximity to death made it impossible for him to forget his own mortality and impermanence. When observing the graves of the fallen marked with helmets, he reasoned that only weeks after their passing the men were a distant memory to their comrades who no longer "seemed to care about them." With time, Schiller surmised, all vestiges of the soldiers' earthly remains would be gone, and the same would be true if he were to find his final resting place in a foreign field.

The infamous trenches of the Western Front had no counterpart in the east, but Schiller and his comrades were not spared from the attacks of parasitic lice infestations, debilitating dysentery, or the suffering brought on by supply shortages. Schiller's account of battle in the east exposes how soldiers lost themselves in the enormity of the event in which they were participants, perhaps as a means of coping with their daily realities. Surrounded by death and longing for sustenance and comfort, Schiller and his fellow soldiers became "machines" who lost all sense of time and space as they marched across the vast expanses of the east. They were no longer troubled by the corpses and scorched landscapes they encountered; they had become an army of "living corpses." Yet war is a human endeavor, and Schiller's memoir demonstrates that we contain the capacity for both destruction and compassion. Even after having participated in fierce fighting against the Russians, Schiller and his comrades observed an Easter truce during which they exchanged vodka and cigarettes with the same men they would fire upon the following day. Schiller also showed compassion for the enemy by refusing to fire upon the wounded, a practice he believed to be unfair. The war had transformed Schiller into a machine unbothered by the butchery of modern warfare, but it had not managed to completely strip away his humanity.

Schiller's transfer to the Western Front came at a pivotal moment in the defeat of the German army. With Russia's withdrawal from the war following the Bolshevik Revolution of 1917, Germans anticipated final victory on the Western Front, as the military would no longer have to fight a two-front war. Schiller's recollections show that despite the optimism felt by many of his countrymen, the spring offensive of 1918 was a last gasp for the German army. Upon arriving in the west, he encountered young soldiers whom he described as "undernourished and childish," with bodies incapable of filling out their uniforms. Readers will sense joy in Schiller's words when he and his men stumble upon abandoned French sausages, wine, and delicacies that they had not enjoyed for months. He must have realized that his enemy had access to far better provisions than those available to the German army. Nonetheless, the Germans managed to put together an impressive push in spring 1918, and Schiller was present for what his comrades believed to be some of the war's most intense fighting. He also witnessed the German army's collapse. The victories of the spring offensive came at a high cost, and Schiller realized that he was part of a "frustrated effort against an overwhelming superior force." Like so many German units, Schiller's had taken tremendous losses, and he understood that the war could not be won.

Schiller's account provides significant insight into the confusion that reigned in the war's final days and poisoned the postwar political climate. He saw the German army's resistance as heroic, but the enemy's superiority in manpower and munitions rendered all efforts to continue the fight ultimately futile. Schiller acknowledges that the German soldiers' morale was irreparably damaged, and he indicates that the home front likewise understood the military's fragile state of existence. In other words, his writings expose his belief that the German army had been thoroughly defeated across the front. Schiller, writing his memoirs a decade after Germany's defeat, "held it for cowardice that the liberal leftists had taken advantage of the fatherland to fulfill their own aspirations." He accepts that the German army was vanquished but insists that in "battle we had not been beaten." This paradoxical logic was embraced by millions of Germans like Schiller who supported the stab-in-the-back myth that blamed the German army's downfall not on its leaders or soldiers but civilian elements on the German home front who betrayed the armed forces. For men like Schiller, who had given so much of themselves to the war, it was difficult to accept that the war experience had ended in defeat. They readily accepted counterfactual narratives that soothed their egos by offering an explanation for their failures.

One of the distinctive elements of Schiller's memoir is the record it provides of his life in the immediate postwar years, most importantly his service in the east with the Freikorps. Schiller survived the war, but he returned to a German homeland racked with hunger, instability, and political strife. Back in Bromberg in Prussia, Schiller imagined that "shirkers, deserters, and rear echelon pigs" who had sabotaged the army and induced home front revolution now controlled affairs in his hometown. The radical myths to which Schiller gave credence found an eager audience among extremists, some of whom would become early National Socialists. When he signed up for duty with the Freikorps in the east, he undoubtedly found himself in the company of men who shared his views. Schiller's reasons for joining the Freikorps may have been influenced by ideology, but they were also practical. He was unemployed and had few prospects. Serving in the east allowed him to resume the occupation for which he was best suited at the time—soldiering. In many ways, Schiller's time with the Freikorps was a continuation of the war for which he had volunteered in 1914. He saw himself as a defender of Germany and its resources, just as he had as a young student in 1914. When he volunteered for the Freikorps, though, he did so with a full understanding of war's horrors.

Schiller's recollections of life with the Freikorps expose his distaste for communism. In view of his relatively privileged upbringing, he was likely repulsed by the ideas of the far left even before he became a veteran of the First World War. He saw communists not as revolutionaries working to create a better world for the proletariat but thieves bent on plunder and murder. Schiller was not alone in his loathing of Bolshevism, and his musings on their aims help us to understand why some Germans would eventually accept Nazism as an acceptable option to the threat of communism. Schiller's record of his service with the Freikorps conforms to what we know about the type of men who sought to continue their military service in the postwar east. Far from casual soldiers, the men Schiller found himself among were ardent fighters who could be molded into what he referred to as fighting machines. Those who "had no appetite for battle" were culled from the ranks. Months after the armistice of November 1918, one could still talk of dying a hero's death in the east. The men with whom Schiller made his postwar life were fighters by choice, those who felt comfortable among the hazards of the front. According to his family, Schiller never approved of Nazism, but the war had been one of the formative experiences of his life, and he internalized many of the distortions of history popularized by postwar extremists. The indignation he felt over the way that the war came to an end stayed with Schiller. It was no coincidence that he chose to end his with a denouncement of the Treaty of Versailles.

The journal entries that formed the basis of his memoir reflect Schiller's understanding of the significance attached to the event that had transformed his life. A self-described "history buff," his attention to detail creates visual imagery that allows readers to imagine that they are observing Schiller's experiences, albeit from a safe distance, and many of the visuals created are difficult to remove from the mind's eye. Like his contemporary Ernst Jünger, Schiller would go on to serve in the Second World War, but he would not achieve the status of a German literary icon. Instead, he made use of his military experience and pursued a career as a police officer. His memoir of the war is thus unpolished when compared to those of professional writers like Jünger and Remarque, and that distinction lends considerably to the memoir's appeal. Nearly a century after its writing, Schiller's memoir, pulled from the dark recesses of a drawer, sheds light on a common soldier's experience in a war that continues to impact our present.

Not all memoirs found in drawers are worthy of publication. Most are of interest only to the author's family and find their way back into the darkness after a cursory reading. Schiller's memoir of the First World War and its aftermath, however, deserves a place on the bookshelves of both historians and general readers.

Acknowledgments

On a beautiful early autumn day in 2013 my mother, Ingrid Kochmann, asked me to look over family heirlooms that she wanted me to keep after her death. Many of these things were displayed around the family home as I grew up, yet I knew little about them. Nothing was ever spoken of that world my parents lived in before they came to the United States from Germany in 1956, when I was only three years old and my brother, Thomas, an infant of just six months. Now my mother had just turned ninety, cancer eating her from within that she refused to acknowledge. I did not know on that gorgeous autumn day that she would be gone before her ninety-first birthday.

During this visit I opened a drawer in an antique desk and found my grandfather Hans Schiller's memoir. I couldn't read it because it was handwritten in old German script, but I could make out the cover sheet, "Memories of War." My mother told me it was his account of the Great War, based on diaries he had kept. I asked my mother if she had ever read it, and she said no. Again, forbidden subject. But there was a portrait of Hans Schiller hanging in our home, painted during the Second World War by an unknown artist in Russia. Over several months my aunt, Gisela Nuernberg, would read the memoir aloud, and I would then translate as she read. We spent many a weekend working on this, but when my mother became seriously ill, everything stopped, except caring for her. During this time, both my aunt and mother finally opened up about their lives in Germany. The trauma of the Nazi era had haunted them all their lives, and because of this, I realized that much of my own personal history was also a blank.

After my mother's death, I contacted the German department at my alma mater, UC Berkeley, to inquire if anyone there could transcribe the journal. They recommended a lovely lady in her seventies,

Otti Kiraly. Though she had transcribed and translated many things, including postcards from concentration camps, my grandfather's manuscript was something she couldn't get out of her head. She felt it should be shared with the world and not kept private, so I dove in and started translating in earnest. During this process, I began to get to know my grandfather and what a remarkable human being he was. He was compassionate, fair, and without pretension. He ate with his men and not with the officers. He enjoyed a good smoke, good wine, good company, and good laughs. He loved animals and was an excellent horseman. Well before I knew this, I started a foundation named Neigh Savers that rescues, rehabs, retrains, and rehomes primarily off-track Thoroughbreds. I now know my grandfather would approve and is smiling down at me every time we help another horse.

Many of my relatives died before and during World War II. Coming to the United States during the mid-fifties and being of German heritage was not exactly popular, and my grandfather had been an officer in the German army. I didn't want my friends to see that portrait of my grandfather in his German uniform, swastikas on display. But now I feel at peace. I know enough about my grandfather and the kind of man he was that I can imagine the internal conflicts he must have gone through in World War II and how this contributed to his untimely death.

There are many people to thank for this project, starting with my late mother, Ingrid Kochmann, and my late aunt, Gisela Nuernberg. My cousin, Ingrid Nuernberg, not only supported me through the process but unearthed a photo album of Hans Schiller's military career put together in 1941, which included many of the images seen here. Thanks to our transcriptionist Otti Kiraly and to my longtime friend and horse rescue supporter, artist Sally Cruikshank, who proofread the first draft translation. My longtime friend in rescue, Jenny Whitman, encouraged me to never give up and wrote an article years ago connecting me and my grandfather through horses. Thanks to Rachel Satterfield-Masen, who has been with me since almost the inception of Neigh Savers, for years of support and friendship. Rachel photographed much of the Schiller archive for this book.

My good friend Gayle Loving, whom I met years ago when we worked at the same company, connected me with her husband, Professor Gregory Loving, who then brought in his colleague, Professor Frederic Krome. Professors Loving and Krome put untold hours into this project. Thank you from the bottom of my heart! I hope this book will give readers something to think about as well as a window seat into what it was like fighting on the German side during World War I.

We would like to thank Jack Humason, who created the maps with the support of a UC Clermont College Faculty Development Grant. Technical assistance with issues such as image scanning was provided by Mark Sanders as well as the IT staff at Clermont College. Lori Vine, program director for the social sciences department, made sure the grant money and other purchases were handled properly. Academic leave from the university also allowed time to complete the project. Gayle Loving and Claire Krome often acted as enthusiastic research assistants. Many other friends and colleagues have given us advice and feedback along the way, including Dean Jeffery Bauer's in-laws in Germany and retired technical editor Brant Evans.

Thanks to Joyce Harrison and the team at the University Press of Kansas for shepherding us through this process and to the referees who read through the manuscript and provided excellent feedback. We are especially grateful to Brian Feltman for writing the foreword. Without such academic publishers recognizing the value of projects like this, much would be lost.

—Karin Wagner
Walnut Creek, CA

A Tale of Two Fronts

Introduction

While helping her dying mother comb through family possessions in California, Karin Wagner came across a large folio, handwritten in German, in the back of a dresser drawer. When Karin asked her mother, Ingrid Kochmann, what the document was, Ingrid replied, "Oh, that is your grandfather's Great War memoir." Ingrid, in her nineties at the time, had never told Karin of this document. Karin set out to translate the memoir with assistance from her aunt, Gisela Nuernberg, Ingrid's older sister. The memoir documents the Great War experiences of Hans Schiller, born March 4th, 1897, the only child of wealthy industrialist and architect August Schiller. August married very late in his fifties to a woman in her late thirties, Adele. Hans was born when Adele was thirty-nine. At the outbreak of the war in August 1914, Hans was a seventeen-year-old student in Bromberg, Prussia, now part of Poland.

Schiller's memoir of his wartime and immediate postwar experience is an important contribution to the study of World War I, or the Great War, as it was known at the time. While historians have reached a consensus that the conflict was a watershed in modern world history, the experience of soldiers on the Western Front still dominates the historiography. The majority of Schiller's service, meanwhile, was on the Eastern Front. In the aftermath of the war, he also served briefly with the notorious Freikorps in the Baltic, both in Latvia and Poland. Given that the Freikorps era is less studied and less settled in historical understanding, Schiller's documentation of his service adds significantly to the available material.

Schiller's memoir is part of what historians now refer to as "ego documents," a category of sources that range from wartime diaries to postwar memoirs.[1] Written after the war in 1928, Schiller's

1. For an analysis of the various types of ego documents relating to World War I, see Richard Bessel and Dorothy Wieling, "Inside World War One? Ego Documents and the First World War," in *Inside World War One? The First World War*

memoir challenges many of the conventional assumptions of the war. Not only do wartime accounts trend toward both the Western Front and, in English, the Allied side; an assumption is often made by historians that the unique circumstances of the war led to a sense of alienation between the soldiers on the war front and their families on the home front. This alienation, so eloquently expressed in Erich Maria Remarque's *All Quiet on the Western Front* (1928), is perhaps the single most consistent theme among historians trying to understand the mindset of the soldiers and their postwar activities.

Yet, just as the war was more than the Western Front, the experience of the soldiers cannot be universalized, and their actual response to events, therefore, can defy generalizations. Schiller's memoir, like many such ego documents, can easily be understood as part of his effort to make sense of his experience.[2] Thus, reading the memoir and comparing it to the current historiography can help us determine where the need for revisions may lie. As Jay Winter argues: "The stories soldiers relate tell us something of what they have been through, but the act of narration tells us who they are at the time of the telling."[3]

A generation of scholarship has revised the old image of thousands of exuberant young men marching off to war. Recent research on German reaction to the declaration of war in August 1914 by scholars such as Jeffrey Verhey demonstrates that many men either joined their reserve regiments or volunteered with something of a fatalistic patriotism. Indeed, Verhey argues that the group most enthusiastic for war were secondary and university students.[4] It is in this group that Hans Schiller belonged, and he commented directly on this dynamic in the narrative. He heard about the assassination of the Archduke Franz Ferdinand in Sarajevo while he was on a hiking trip in the Bohemian lands of the Hapsburg empire, and by the

---

and Its Witnesses, ed. Bessel and Wieling (New York: Oxford University Press, 2018), 8–13.

2. See Bessel and Wieling, 8.

3. Jay Winter, *Remembering War: The Great War between Memory and History in the Twentieth Century* (New Haven, CT: Yale University Press, 2006), 116.

4. Jeffrey Verhey, *The Spirit of 1914: Militarism, Myth and Mobilization in Germany* (Cambridge: Cambridge University Press, 2000).

time he returned home, Germany was at war. Schiller describes his decision to enlist as "a marvelous prospect."

Schiller's description of the process he had to undergo to join the army—first taking his completion exams to receive his diploma immediately and then enlisting—provides some of the mundane details that are often overlooked in the broader story. After enlisting and qualifying as an artilleryman, Schiller departed for the Eastern Front, a place that many Germans regarded as so primitive that it was likened to a "journey back in time."[5] Schiller first served on the front in January 1915 against the Russians in what is now Poland.

To Germans of Schiller's generation, the east was a quasi-mystical place, inhabited by semi-primitive Slavic people who were placid, lazy, and easy to rule and yet "barbaric when aroused."[6] The east was usually described by German officials as a territory in disarray, with crumbling infrastructure and in need of a firm hand for development. Schiller's description of the east—primitive forests alternating with open country—was shaped by this popular mythology. Schiller was one of more than two million German soldiers who served on the Eastern Front during the war, and his account of his interaction with the indigenous population aligns with the stereotype held by many that it was a region without "European culture."

From 1915 to 1917, Schiller saw action in what is now Poland, Latvia, and Lithuania. Schiller's depictions are often vivid, and he neither glorifies nor fetishizes combat. *Ober Ost*, or the "Upper East," as the German authorities called it, was first a war front and then a conquered territory. Schiller was part of a grand project that sought to remake these regions as a military state to both modernize the region and to have it serve the *Kaiserreich* as a source of natural resources.[7] He indicates that many of his fellow soldiers dreamed of settling the territory after the war. Throughout his memoir, Schiller provides cogent details of his daily activities, demonstrates awareness of the wider issues of the war, and describes his activities in often vivid detail.

It is also worth mentioning what Schiller does *not* discuss. Although

5. Vejas Gabriel Liulevicius, *The German Myth of the East, 1800 to the Present* (Oxford: Oxford University Press, 2009), 136–37.

6. Liulevicius, *The German Myth of the East*, 135–36.

7. Vejas Gabriel Liulevicius, *War Land on the Eastern Front: Culture, National Identity and German Occupation in World War I* (Cambridge: Cambridge University Press, 2000).

the memoir contains references to his family life and the packages and letters from home, there is very little about the German home front in his memoirs. Schiller had home leave on a number of occasions, but it did not seem to cause him to experience alienation from the civilian world, at least based on the evidence of the memoir. He always looked forward to his time at home but rarely commented on the conditions or attitudes there. Absent much personal correspondence aside from a handful of extant postcards, this subject is one of the blanks in Schiller's story.

After the October 1917 Bolshevik Revolution and Russia's withdrawal from the war, Schiller was transferred to the Western Front. He arrived in time for the Michael Offensive, Germany's last great attack in the west in March 1918, where the attempt to break the Allied lines included what is believed to be up to that point the single greatest artillery bombardment in human history. Like other soldiers who spent the bulk of their time on the Eastern Front, with a battle line over twice the length of the Western Front and conflict characterized by greater movement than the elaborate trench system found in France allowed, Schiller was appalled at the conditions his comrades had endured against the western allies.

Schiller depicts those final days before the armistice as a valiant effort in a lost cause. The German army had expended its resources, its lines were thin, and political upheaval at home meant the war was basically lost. While Schiller sees the leftward political shift in Germany at the end of the war as populated by opportunists and "shirkers," neither does his account easily align with the later "stab-in-the-back" picture that the Nazi Party both fomented and exploited. As Schiller returns home at the end of the war, he is still a German patriot, though a skeptical one. He was most critical of political ideologies that used unrestrained violence as a tool for "world improvement," as odd as this may seem coming from a willing soldier.

As Robert Gerwarth has documented, the ethnic and political violence that followed the collapse of the Central Powers in the fall of 1918 meant that the war did not really end in November 1918. After the German retreat and armistice, Schiller was one of thousands of demobilized soldiers without prospects yet possessing unique combat skills, and who reentered military service in the "Freikorps" or "Free Corps," German mercenary groups fighting in former German territory in Eastern Europe, where the conflict dragged on even after the Treaty of Versailles.[8] The shifting alliances and fighting between the Freikorps and various nascent national groups, fueled by support from both Russia and the Allies, contributed to the overall chaos as new national boundaries were drawn. Schiller gives life to this chaos, even including his own rare account of the friendly-fire death of Latvian colonel Oskars Kalpaks.

Conventional wisdom sees membership in the Freikorps as part of the radicalization of veterans, often making a linkage to later membership in the paramilitary of the Nazi Party.[9] As with his enlistment in 1914, however, Schiller does not describe his decision to join the Freikorps in ideological or excessively patriotic terms. Although his personal ideology is anti-Communist and aligns with the cultural interests of the German aristocracy, it was not ideology that led to his participation in the fighting in the Baltic after the war. Instead, it is best to consider his decision in personal terms. Schiller was part of a generation of young Germans who had their life plans irrevocably altered by the war. He had been set to go to university at the outbreak of war. After his war experience, Schiller considered it too late to go back to those plans. He was part of a generation that had become inured to violence as well. As such, continuing the fight after November 1918, after the armistice was declared and without official government sanction, caused little cognitive dissonance. Lacking options and having served in the war zone for all his early adult years, Schiller did not seem to find committing himself to more violence as anything other than something to occupy his time.

This is one of the intriguing questions that the memoir raises but cannot answer. Research on the long-term impact of the war demonstrates that many Great War veterans, especially those who joined the Freikorps, developed a willingness to use coercive power as a "symptom and constitutive element" of their approach to social issues.[10] Was Schiller therefore one of those who embraced a casual approach

8. For some context on Schiller's post-1918 service, see Robert Gerwarth, *The Vanquished: Why the First World War Failed to End* (New York: Farrar, Straus & Giroux, 2016), 69–74.

9. See Robert G. L. Waite, *Vanguard of Nazism: The Free Corps Movement in Post-War Germany, 1918–1923* (Cambridge, MA: Harvard University Press, 1952).

10. Although it focuses on the ending of World War II in the east, Bastien Willems raises a number of interesting points about the long-term impact of World War I and the Freikorps on those who held administrative and military positions

to violence in the service of the state? It is important to take note of Schiller's description of both his Freikorps service and those with whom he served. Schiller expressed a healthy dose of contempt for both the leadership and the mercenary cadre. He is subject to the stereotypes of his day and his culture, no doubt, but is not controlled by blind obedience to any person or structure, so often the justification for violence. His signing on to the postwar Freikorps and his decision to leave are described in a matter-of-fact tone—simply as a job to do and a job done. Schiller was one of those veterans who receives less attention in the historical literature—a man whose reintegration into society was not necessarily hampered by alienation or proclivities toward further violence.[11]

Hans Schiller left military service in May 1920. Did Schiller suffer from psychological issues such as post-traumatic stress disorder? The record is largely silent on this matter, and of course our contemporary understanding of these dynamics is far advanced compared to the early twentieth century. Family accounts of his behavior as his life progressed, especially during World War II, are consistent with such a diagnosis. Still, it is interesting to compare Schiller's experiences and thoughts with those expressed by Remarque in his lesser-known book *The Road Back* (1931), which some scholars describe as a sequel to *All Quiet on the Western Front*. The novel describes in vivid imagery the efforts of veterans to reintegrate into a German society that was vastly different from the pre-1914 world. Remarque's narrator summed up many a veteran's attitude to the war when he asks his mother: "What was the good of it all . . . ?"[12]

Before the Great War, the Schiller family was comfortably middle class, and yet after the war, they found themselves on the wrong side of the postwar territorial realignment where significant parts of East Prussia, such as Bromberg, became part of the reconstituted Polish republic. The Schillers were forced to relocate, allowed one suitcase each, stripped of most of their possessions and assets. As

---

under the Nazis. See *Violence in Defeat: The Wehrmacht on German Soil, 1944–1945* (New York: Cambridge University Press, 2021) 144–45.

11. See Richard Bessel, *Germany after the First World War* (New York: Oxford University Press, 1993), ch. 3 passim, for a discussion of returning soldiers.

12. Erich Maria Remarque, *The Road Back*, trans. A. W. Wheen (Boston: Little, Brown, 1931), 111.

noted near the end of the memoir, Schiller had begun a courtship with a woman he had met on leave. On May 31st, 1921, Schiller married Margarete Zeisler and raised a family—Gisela and Ingrid, born in 1922 and 1923, respectively—in Unruhstadt, in the province of Grenzmark-Posen, West Prussia. His parents had no other choice but to join them, so Hans was responsible for supporting his parents, his spouse, and their two children. Due to his military experience, along with his postwar service in the Freikorps, Schiller went into the police force as a captain and worked in several different cities in both East and West Prussia, settling in Koblenz in the Rhineland in 1938. A number of Great War veterans who served in the Freikorps later became policemen; thus Schiller, at least in part, once again fits into a pattern.

The memoir is based on diaries Schiller kept during the war, since lost. In many respects, the memoir contains an incredible amount of detail, certainly due to the diaries. Such diaries were common on both sides of the war though often discouraged by military leadership should they fall into enemy hands. In 1928, Schiller contracted scarlet fever and was quarantined for six weeks. He took advantage of that time to write the memoir, originally titled "Kriegserrinerungen," or "War Memories." As far as we know, nothing was done with the manuscript for almost one hundred years after that.

The time at which the manuscript was written is critical for several reasons. First, the memoir was written soon enough after the events themselves that Schiller's memories were still vivid, bolstered by the diaries, which certainly comes through in the reading. Second, the memoir was written before Germany descended into the grip of National Socialism. A significant amount of Great War material written subsequently was colored by the lens of Nazi ideology, one way or the other. Schiller's account is free from the retrospective lens of World War II politics and the aftermath of the Holocaust. Schiller did not express any motive for writing the memoir. And once written, he apparently simply put the manuscript away and continued supporting his family as a police officer. According to his granddaughter, he had a fondness for literary imagery, and even years later, Hans's widow remembered that her husband's favorite subject in school was creative writing. He very well may have found that writing his account helped to exorcise some of the demons from the war.

Though the manuscript is not colored by the rise of Nazism, Hans

Schiller's life was certainly affected subsequently. In 1935, Hitler reconstituted the full German military, the Wehrmacht, in violation of the Treaty of Versailles. Former members of the military were conscripted as part of this effort. In 1938, as part of a general militarization of the police, Schiller reentered military service as a lieutenant.[13] Photographic evidence puts him in Artillery Regiment 70. According to family accounts, Schiller had little enthusiasm for the Nazi cause and was highly critical of National Socialist ideology and party leadership, referring to Hitler privately as "the criminal." He did, however, remain loyal to Germany and signed the Nazi oath of allegiance, as required by his position. As Nicholas Stargardt has pointed out, many Germans who had little political involvement with the Nazi Party or love of Nazi ideology still fought for, and therefore supported, the Third Reich.[14]

Schiller's military service during World War II proved highly competent. He served in Artillery Regiment 556 during the German offensive into France in May and June 1940. Schiller received the Iron Cross, Second Class, for bravery on the battlefield in June 1940, followed in July 1940 by the Iron Cross, First Class. While Second-Class awards were quite common, First-Class awards were more rare and required the recipient to have already won the Second-Class distinction. He was promoted to first lieutenant in September 1940 and through the war was promoted through the ranks—captain, major, lieutenant colonel, and finally colonel. Within the structure of the Wehrmacht, this is evidence that they saw him as a valuable asset. After service on the Western Front, Schiller was transferred to the Eastern Front in 1942, serving in Russia and Poland. As the Eastern Front deteriorated for the Germans, he found himself in East Prussia in Loetzen by the end of 1944.

According to the family, Schiller's mental state, as well as his physical condition, became somewhat brittle as the war progressed. Characterized as easygoing and sociable before the war, according to his daughters' accounts, he was increasingly angry when home on

13. For developments in the Weimar and, later, Nazi police force, see Edward B. Westermann, *Hitler's Police Battalions: Enforcing Racial War in the East* (Lawrence: University Press of Kansas, 2005), ch. 1 passim.

14. See the introduction to Nicholar Stargardt, *The German War: A Nation under Arms, 1939–1945* (New York: Basic Books, 2015), for a discussion of "ordinary Germans" and fighting for the Nazi state.

leave and apparently quick to anger on the job, even to the point of throwing chairs at soldiers under his command. Regardless of these issues, his final promotion to full colonel came in late 1944. According to the family, in late December, he received a summons to appear as a defendant in court on January 2nd, 1945. The implications for Schiller were apparently dire. On New Year's Day 1945, Hans Schiller walked into the forest near Loetzen and killed himself with his sidearm. The German War Graves Commission lists his death on that date in Field Hospital 260 and his final resting place at Gizycko, Poland, in a mass grave after several relocations of German soldiers' remains at the behest of Polish authorities.

Schiller's death occurred at a time when the German officer corps was under extreme pressure from the Nazi Party. During the war, arrests and executions within the German military were frighteningly common as tools of discipline and control, especially after Operation Valkyrie, the well-known failed assassination attempt on Hitler in July 1944.[15] A heightened state of suspicion prevailed, along with renewed requirements for loyalty oaths and other symbols of obedience. Schiller could easily have been reported for anything he was overheard saying in this atmosphere. In the end, Schiller's suicide was also part of a pattern. In the last months of the war, a number of Germans—Nazi Party members, high-ranking soldiers, and even ordinary civilians—committed suicide.[16] The family stories about Hans Schiller's life, especially his post-1928 experiences, are not surprisingly colored by the Nazi era. According to his granddaughter Karin, an aura of mystery surrounded the family's experiences:

> The war was generally a topic off limits in my home. I grew up not knowing much about my parents' experiences during the war. My personal feeling is that they suffered from too much PTSD to discuss. And also during my growing up years I actually didn't want to know about it. There was a portrait of Hans Schiller in the house and I didn't want any of my friends to see it because

15. For more on the overall context, see Ben H. Shepard, *Hitler's Soldiers: The German Army in the Third Reich* (New Haven, CT: Yale University Press, 2016).

16. On the increasing rates of suicide, see Ian Kershaw, *The End: The Defiance and Destruction of Hitler's Germany, 1944–1945* (New York: Penguin Press, 2011), 355–56.

> I thought he was a Nazi and didn't want any association. It was actually embarrassing in my mind.[17]

It is worth noting that when her family finally did speak about Hans Schiller to Karin, they claimed that he was hostile to the Nazi Party, disliked Hitler, and that his suicide was directly linked to his being called to account for stating his hostility toward the regime in the last months of his life. It will require additional research to determine, if possible, the validity of such stories, however much they fit into documented patterns.

As for the Schiller family, after Schiller's death in January 1945 and the family home having been bombed out, it was clear how the war would end. Fearing the Russian advance, Schiller's family collected what belongings they could and moved to a town near Munich in what would become West Germany, travelling by night for three weeks to avoid the Russians. They were able to move in with relatives who had a house there. It was during this move that the original diaries on which the memoir is based were lost. They did, however, preserve the memoir itself and a number of pictures and portraits, including a photo album of Schiller's military service assembled by the family in 1941. These have supplied the illustrations for the current publication.

The situation in Munich was untenable, however, with little prospect for employment or housing. The family members sought visas to several countries, including Australia, England, and the United States. While they did obtain visas to South Africa, the family chose not to move there. Gisela Schiller married Friedrich Nuernberg, a chess champion and mathematician. After the war, he was part of the German exodus of intellectuals working for American defense interests, in his case Lockheed in Burbank, California. They were able to emigrate in 1953.

Meanwhile, Ingrid had married Karl Kochmann, an engineer, in 1949. Karin was born in Munich in December 1953 and brother Thomas in July 1956. They finally succeeded in immigrating to Kellogg, Idaho, in 1956, where Karl found work as an engineer for a silver mine. Ingrid's family eventually settled in the San Francisco

17. Email from Karin Wagner to Greg Loving and Frederic Krome, August 14, 2023.

Bay Area, where Karl worked in the steel industry. Schiller's widow Margarete died during a visit to the United States in 1967. Hans Schiller's handwritten manuscript was carried to the United States by Ingrid's family, where Karin rediscovered it.

Several comments on the translation itself are in order. We have largely remained true to the manuscript's sentence breaks and chapter divisions. As paragraphs tended to the longer side, however, we have added paragraph breaks for readability. Schiller was inconsistent in his use of written versus Arabic numbers, and here we have stayed consistent with *Chicago Manual of Style* usage. Military ranks are translated to align generally with the British army.

Geographically, many borders and place names have changed since the war, sometimes multiple times, especially in the east. We have indicated modern equivalents where it seemed necessary to track the action and give geographical context but have tried to keep this to a minimum so as not to distract the reader. We have included explanatory footnotes where cultural practices or idioms are involved, or where events bear upon major points of scholarship regarding the war. We have also tried to note the wider situation of the war in which Schiller's service took place.

What comes through most strongly in the narrative is Schiller's humanity. He has sympathy for civilians and soldiers, animals, and even the land itself as he sees everything chewed up by war. He is unsurprisingly biased in praising German culture and practice, sometimes stereotyping other cultures, but he points out what he sees as strengths and flaws on all sides of the conflict. He is patriotic, but not unthinkingly so, and sees hypocrisy around him with both seriousness and humor. He has disdain for incompetence and arrogance from anyone, including his own military leadership. Throughout, we see a thinking and feeling human being trying to deal honestly with the frustrations and horrors around him. The discovery of any document such as this is of historical significance, but the engaging nature of the narrative opens its appeal to audiences far beyond the academic interests of the historian. Schiller wrote at the outset that he was eager to be a "witness to world history." We are fortunate to now share in what he saw.

1

Declaration of War and Recruitment

We begin this story in the year 1914. The hot July sun lay over the Riesengebirge.[1] With my well-stocked backpack I slowly climbed the still snow-covered slope. The higher I ventured it seemed that the air became evermore fresh and clear, and I could see of the vista of mountains and valleys of Schlesien stretched below me. With every step I felt more the young Gymnasium student who for the first time was able to undertake a longer vacation adventure without being accompanied by his parents.[2]

I had hoped without stopping to rest to reach the top of the sixteen-hundred-meter peak, but I soon saw that I was not an experienced mountain climber but rather just a day tourist.[3] From the unaccustomed strenuous ascent I was breathing hard and my heart was pounding. I sat on a boulder that seemed to beckon me as if I had called for it, took a bottle of lemonade from my pack, and quenched an incredible thirst.

A group of laughing climbers descended from the mountain's peak. We greeted each other with a friendly "heil," and I asked how long it would take to reach the chalet at the top.[4] An older gentleman

1. Literally "Giant Mountain." Part of the Czech Republic today, along the border with Poland. In 1914, these mountains formed the border between Imperial Germany and the Hapsburg empire.

2. Gymnasium in the German schools is a secondary school for academically oriented pupils preparing to enter the university system.

3. Schiller was inconsistent in using numerals versus spelling out numbers. We have translated according to *Chicago Manual of Style* usage.

4. Before its association with Nazism, "heil" was a common formal greeting. With connotations of wishing someone well, the word would literally translate as "hail." A close approximation in commonly used English might be "How do you do?" Just a simple "hello" would be too informal.

guessed it would be in a half hour or so comfortably with my young legs. "We old folks needed at least an hour to reach the top," he continued. Then he added, almost as an afterthought, that did I know that today Austria had declared war upon Serbia?[5] No, I did not, but before I could ask another question he had already hurried down to reach his party that had gone ahead. I was completely taken aback by this information. Could it be possible that war would again be upon Europe after just so recently we had suffered through two Balkan wars?[6] For the last week I had not been near a newspaper. I wanted nothing more to do than have a carefree and unencumbered mountain trek and admire the rich nature I encountered with each and every step. However, now my thoughts became preoccupied with the state of the world over the last two months. I remembered the murders at Sarajevo. I believed that the murderers were bought and paid for by Serbians. I knew that this deed had been discussed through various communications between Austria and Serbia and that Austria made it clear there would be strict repercussions to this act. But I never seriously believed that this would lead to another war. However, it had nonetheless now occurred.[7]

By and by I grabbed my walking stick and took newly energized steps, climbing the mountain slope with a greater pace toward my goal. I actually arrived at my destination earlier than anticipated. After I took in the wonders of my surroundings, my stomach signaled that it was time to eat, and I eagerly sought out the chalet where I could dine surrounded by the gorgeous Austrian countryside. As I stepped into the chalet I was accosted by a cacophony of sights and sounds. Tourists in beautiful custom-tailored clothing and wealthy hikers had assembled here. One could hear many different languages

5. The traveler must be referring to Austria's ultimatum to Serbia on July 23, 1914, not the official declaration of war five days later, for reasons that will soon become apparent.

6. Two brief wars in 1912 to 1913, which stripped the Ottoman Empire of most of its remaining European territory.

7. Recent research has demonstrated the reliability of Schiller's memory of the summer of 1914. Few outside the corridors of power believed that the murder of Archduke Franz Ferdinand in Sarajevo on June 28, 1914, would lead to global war. Many common Europeans and even some heads of state went on vacation in July 1914. See Michael S. Neiberg, *Dance of the Furies: Europe and the Outbreak of World War I* (Cambridge, MA: Harvard University Press, 2011).

spoken, although it appeared that German was the primary language. It was so noisy with so many people speaking in so many languages you could hardly hear your own thoughts. However, if you listened carefully enough you could discern that even though people were talking in different languages, all were speaking of the impending war, as this news had arrived at the chalet by telegram merely an hour earlier.

I sat down at a table that was already occupied by an Austrian travel party. It was easy to ascertain that from the very loud talking and gesticulating and fists banging on the table that this noise was most likely due to the sizeable row of empty wine bottles on display. One of the men stood up, asked for silence, and with slightly slurred speech decided to address the entire restaurant. He scolded those that made backroom deals, swore revenge on the Serbs, and toasted to Austria and Germany that all would be made right and Germany would not leave Austria hanging.[8] Most of the people agreed with his view and clapped and applauded. Only in one corner where a number of Czechs sat was there complete silence. Thereafter the conversation turned to victory speeches against the Serbs. From table to table the conversation went back and forth, usually saying it wouldn't take but two weeks to bring the enemy to its knees. How could it be otherwise since it was a clear-cut fight between a dwarf and a giant? A few people, however, shyly proposed that the outcome could be quite the opposite because the Serb was well thought of as a soldier. However, these people were outnumbered, shouted at, and eventually stopped speaking.

I did not have the patience to listen to any of these rants for much longer, as it appeared to be an exercise in futility. I paid my bill, got up, and quickly departed into the Bohemian valley below. My next and last stop was Trautenau. As a history buff, I wanted to tour the battlefield of 1866.[9] On my solitary travels I had the leisure to ponder the

8. Just days after the assassination, on July 5, Kaiser Wilhelm II pledged unconditional support to Austria in whatever it chose to do, the so-called blank check. Such unqualified support propelled what could have remained a localized conflict into a global side-choosing that would lead to worldwide war.

9. The Battle of Trautenau was an engagement during the Austro-Prussian War. Despite winning the battle, the Hapsburgs suffered heavy casualties. See Geoffrey Wawro, *The Austro-Prussian War: Austria's War with Prussia and Italy in 1866* (Cambridge: Cambridge University Press, 1996), 145–51.

state of an ever-changing relationship between Austria and Prussian Germany. At that time they were fast enemies. The chasm seemed too large to ever mend, even at some future point in time. Today, however, the same Austria now looked toward its arch enemy Germany as the great savior, although until quite recently Austria had wanted nothing more than, with pure hatred, to decimate all of Germany.

The small villages that I passed through still were very peaceful, and the farmers and country people were completely occupied with producing the harvest. In my naive thoughts I had envisioned that the outbreak of a major war would be quite different. I had believed that with the announcement of war, suddenly and dramatically everything would change in an instant, with soldiers, cannons, and all of the parties involved in full combat mode. That all the major streets would be filled with troops marching. However, none of this was evident, and people went about their day-to-day business. Even though this war would involve these people first, I did not hear any military or nationalistic songs. It appeared that they were unconcerned about the events that had been announced and went about their business as though nothing had happened.

After two days I arrived at Trautenau. It was the first large city that I came to. In the first few streets I encountered I saw a few soldiers, and then a troop came marching through. I saw many others in the town in full uniform mingling with the locals. However, it didn't appear organized or in full force. The city had its own military installation, so it might have been that these soldiers were stationed here from that unit. I did not see any enlisted men nor any wagons or horses that had been put into war service, and so I asked an officer who happened to sit next to me in a café at lunch and with whom I quickly started a conversation about how peaceful the situation seemed. He told me that for the time being only a few troops would be sent to the Serbian border, and he didn't foresee any large mustering of the troops, as the whole affair would be over shortly. The officer also confided to me that his major had just conveyed this information. My tablemate assured me that to overthrow Serbia would be a matter of just two weeks, and any defense from the Serbs would not be forthcoming.[10] He himself would like to partake in battle because he was a German.

10. Schiller's recollection that people expected a short war jibes with what historians call the "short war illusion." Even though many military experts expected

Other than that, the fascination with war was not high here because this region was overrun by Czechs who didn't care for the Austrians and would only wear their uniforms if forced to do so. They wished that Austria would fall and that then Germany would rise and regain the independent kingdom of Bohemia. I listened with great interest to this corporal whose name I did not know. It was a complete revelation to me that Austria also had its own internal battles with the Czechs in the same war in which we Germans had to deal with the Polish in the provinces of Posen and Westphalia in the like manner. With a feeling that perhaps he had thought of too much doom and gloom, I took my leave.

We had chatted for far longer than I had anticipated, and now I needed to hurry because I still wanted to watch the orchestra perform on the battlefield before my train departed. I managed to find the little church in front of which a small marble tablet proclaimed that a large bloody battle had taken place, but of course there were no reminders of that. Now only the crumbling remains of a cemetery attested to the fact that the battle had taken its many victims. It was very difficult even to make out the individual names of these casualties. I did not enjoy walking through this destroyed graveyard. As it was, I needed to make my way back to the train station. So therefore I left this particular place posthaste without any good memories to accompany me.

It was amazing how many people were scrambling around the train. I asked if the traffic around here was always so packed. I was informed it was only this busy because it would probably be one of the last occasions that civilians would likely be able to travel freely back to Germany. Very slowly, the little train crept into the station, and before it even came to a complete stop people were pushing and shoving to get onto the train. Even though I was lucky enough to get a seat, I soon had to give it up to a portly and very talkative woman. As we traveled, it soon become apparent that the lady was a women's rights activist who also complained relentlessly about servants and the price of meat. Her high-pitched voice really began to get on my nerves along with the extreme summer heat that made the inside of

---

the war to be bloody, few anticipated that modern states could sustain modern war for long. On the early clashes in Serbia, see Hew Strachan, *The First World War* (New York: Viking, 2004), ch. 1.

the train feel like a hot oven. I felt rivulets of sweat constantly pouring down my face. At every station stop I left the train to get water from the nearby fountain, and each time I jumped off, at the request of the large-sized lady, I also procured a cup of what she called "goose wine" for her. "Why are you reviving this fatass just so she can continue to pester us with her endless chatter?" whispered a fellow traveler to me.

But luckily even this voyage had to meet its end. I departed in Breslau. Suddenly I felt the mood here much lightened. You could even buy the special newspaper supplement, which explained all the goings on in Austria, how they were mobilizing for the oncoming war, and described the minor skirmishes already occurring at the border. It was also expected that Russia would shortly join the war. If that happened then Germany would be pulled in, as well as France, and then all of Europe would burn as one.

A sort of pleasant shock went through me. If this would indeed occur, perhaps I could also enlist. One of the many Bromberger regiments would probably accept me.[11] Then I wouldn't need to complete my schooling, which was suddenly very important to me, and this war would well be worth the effort.

Early the next morning I continued my journey home to Bromberg. It was the 28th of July.[12] The majority of my fellow travelers were military reservists who had already received their orders. They argued loudly over military maneuvers and bragged of their own area of military expertise and that of their regiments. A sergeant, who was a machine gunner, explained confidently that no Russian or Frenchman could match his weapon. Recently, some innovations had been made so that one gun could almost take the place of an entire company of gunners. We couldn't believe all that was being said, but it certainly made me feel secure in the power of the German military.

Late at night I arrived in Bromberg and saw that the train station was occupied by the military. But otherwise in the streets I didn't

11. Bromberg, Schiller's hometown, is now the Polish city of Bydgoszcz. In 1914, the German army reflected the federal nature of the Kasierreich, where military units were associated with specific regions, and the four major kingdoms—Prussia, Bavaria, Saxony, Württemberg—ran separate military establishments. So, Bromberger Regiments refers to units raised in Schiller's home region.

12. 1914, the day of the official Austro-Hungarian declaration of war on Serbia following the July 23 ultimatum.

see many in uniforms. However, a lot of motor vehicles with officers were whizzing through the streets along with reservists marching along. The blue peacetime uniforms were being replaced more and more. They were exchanged with the practical and beautiful field grays. These days passed as if in a dream. And always stronger was the wish: if only I could go to war! To be able to serve as a volunteer. You would then experience something that would stay with you for the rest of your life. You would be a witness to world history. For a seventeen-year-old, that was a marvelous prospect. At the possibility that I myself could die, I never even gave a thought, nor even to the tremendous toll of blood and country. I just wished in my youthful naivete for war, as it had always seemed so dramatic and nationalistic as portrayed in schoolbooks. And so, entirely from this perspective, I experienced the entrance of my fatherland into the world war. But for now, it hadn't yet come to that. I only went home to eat and sleep, but otherwise I stood in front of the newspaper offices where the latest headlines were always posted outside. I was not the only one that did that.

Hundreds of people swarmed around these offices, including many of my school colleagues as well as the younger teachers. There no longer was any sort of divide between the students and the younger teachers. With every new telegram everyone started another discussion about its meaning. Now even my opinion was deemed as important, and people were listening to me as well; it was the first time in my life that I felt a sense of pride and equality. Everywhere there was chaos. The whole town was vibrating. Anyone who looked a foreigner was immediately suspected of being a spy and arrested. You could say we were suffering from a spy psychosis even though it appeared that it usually struck only the most innocent victims.

Everything was about patriotism, and it felt good voicing one's nationalist feelings. At every public function one would hear the patriotic songs of "Wacht am Rhein" or "Deutschland Über Alles."[13] Everyone was playing these songs, including the local organ grinder.

13. While recent research has revised our traditional picture of a general war enthusiasm, Schiller's account accurately reflects that among his generation, there was a high level of patriotic fervor, in particular among high school students, university students, and faculty. See Jeffrey Verhey, *The Spirit of 1914: Militarism, Myth and Mobilization in Germany* (Cambridge: Cambridge University Press, 2000).

Now all were united, poised for war and excited at the prospect, as I had always envisioned it might be. And all of this was happening before war had even officially been declared. Very important and strategic were those that had fought in the war of 1871, and these individuals were now thought of as experts in fighting.[14] The old veterans dressed in their uniforms and pinned on every medal they had and then strutted up and down the streets and held forth on their past experiences and gave everyone advice on how to wage this coming war. They were suddenly looked upon by the youth of today with extraordinary respect and reverence since they had already stood in the line of fire, even though it was during an era where there had been no machine guns or other quick-firing weapons. This frenetic anticipation for war that everyone felt deep in their bones was completely overwhelming and was all one could obsessively think of.

Finally, late on the evening of July 31st, the announcement finally came that war had been declared. I hurried to the street, met up with friends and acquaintances, and asked them if it was true, and they confirmed this news. I ran over to the *East German Daily News*, which was surrounded by people. There hung the telegram: "Sunday, August 2, first mobilization day." Such an important announcement was delivered in just the briefest of statements. The decision had been made. This night found me completely sleepless. The city was awake with sounds I had never before heard. From time to time one could even hear parts of the "Deutschland" song. Everyone was in the same state of mind. In spite of varying partisan interests and all of the criticisms leveled from one to the other, now we were the old Germany again, standing together in arms that could never be defeated if we stood together. So much was happening, one thing after the other, and all in very quick succession.

About twenty-four hours after the mobilization announcement, the news arrived that Germany had declared war against Russia and then shortly afterward also against France.[15] Now total jubilation with no limits set in. It was likely the rejoicing of the youth and others who would never see battle that were the loudest, celebrating in

14. The Franco–Prussian War of 1870 to 1871, at the end of which Germany annexed Alsace and half of Lorraine, resulted in the unification of the German empire.

15. August 1 and August 3, respectively.

streets, cafés, and bars. In some homes, of course, relatives were anxious about their loved ones going off to war. I did not notice any of that. My wish had been fulfilled; the die had been cast. Everything else left me cold. Soon the active military were departing, accompanied by music, and they were sent away with people waving flags, throwing a sea of flowers and notes of goodwill toward them. They were marching toward the west. The newly formed reserve troops were heading toward the east. It was difficult to know where the thousands of gray uniforms were coming from because so many had already left. It appeared Germany was rich in unending population reserves. Around the general vicinity as if overnight it appeared a giant mustering base had formed. Because of this show of might one could look without any reservations into a bright future. On August 8th the Germans captured the famous fort at Luettich and immediately the city changed into a gigantic sea of flags.[16] We didn't care that in the interim, England had also entered the war but on the side of our enemies. Tirpitz had assembled a naval fleet that now appeared to have the same strength as the British.[17] It wasn't about numbers but about the confidence found on the German side.

There was an incredible rush by volunteer civilians to muster to arms from every region and walk of life. However, the most willing of all appeared to be intellectuals. The universities and upper school classes were practically empty. Everywhere emergency board exams and finals were held so that the young volunteers could finish their degrees and then go off to war. By coincidence I heard that there was also an exam for "Einjaehrige" in one of the government buildings.[18] However, the time was not given. I went there anyway to find out if I could participate. To my astonishment, I was told by a government official that the exam had just started and asked if I had brought with me the necessary paper to take this exam. Naturally not, I said. Then I should rush over to the nearest stationer's store as fast as I could.

16. The Battle of Liège in Belgium was the opening battle of the war in the west.

17. Admiral Alfred von Tirpitz (1849–1930), secretary of state of the German Imperial Naval Office and architect of the pre-1914 German Fleet.

18. This exam would allow Schiller to be an "Einjährig-Freiwilliger," or "one-year volunteer," reserved mainly for those of high enough social class to be considered future officer material. They normally paid for their own expenses and equipment during their training.

Not even five minutes later I stood in front of the official, and we went to the exam hall where at a long table sixteen examinees already sat and were furiously writing. Not a one was known to me. They looked at me reproachfully, wondering what I was doing here at this late hour. "There are three essays from which to choose, but you must hurry because in one hour this section must be completed," said the testing official. I wasn't in a panic because writing German essays was one of my strongest suits, and no one at school had ever bested me. I chose the theme "How does the present situation remind one of the former German emancipation?" This theme was very near and dear to me since it was occupying my daily thoughts in entirety at the time. Therefore, I easily finished the essay in the time allotted. I even managed to deliver an essay that was graded as one of the best with a "Sehr Gut" as I was told the next day by Professor Jacobs, who was the examiner. Next, I needed to write a translation of Latin, which I believed I did well enough, and finally mathematics and French. The latter was more difficult for me, especially because my neighbors were no better than I. Then we were dismissed for that day.

The next day the oral examination was to take place. At eight in the morning in the same examination hall sat seventeen pale and stressed-out students who were quite insecure about their prospects. The following individuals then entered the room: one senior official, one official, and three military majors and four professors. The next five hours were not the most pleasant of my life, but finally it was over. Then after a short discussion we were informed by the head official that we had all passed the examination. We were so overjoyed! And it had happened so unexpectedly that I could hardly believe that I had just graduated. I still remember how I hurried home and burst into my father's bedroom where he had just laid down for an afternoon nap and announced: "Einjaehriger volunteer Schiller at your service." I can still feel the fifty-mark bill that my father pressed into my hand. Then I invited all of my school chums over to the house who hadn't known anything about this exam and therefore their congratulations to me did ring a bit flat. Why did I have such luck and they didn't?

With double the energy I tried to get into one of the regiments. "Everything taken" was the answer I usually received. What to do? I was actually ashamed to run about in my civilian garb. Then I heard that the Red Cross was still looking for volunteers. A few of my fellow students were already engaged there. I was accepted and received my white armband with the red cross. For me, this armband was now of utmost importance. But the work was not fulfilling, as it involved taking hospital linens in and out of supply trucks. Only on a rare occasion was I allowed to help carry a stretcher with a patient. In my mind, this type of occupation had nothing to do with being a soldier, and after a few days I had already had enough of it.

But then I learned by luck that Field Artillery Number Fifty-Three was accepting volunteers. Like a bolt of lightning I sped over to enlist. A hundred or more already stood in front of the barracks. After standing there until our legs were numb, they finally let us in. In the large military men's quarters we were first undressed. Then a doctor came and examined us. The young man standing just in front of me was immediately sent home. I thought perhaps I would suffer the same fate. But the younger doctor cleared me for field duty, and suddenly I was a soldier. This took place on the twentieth of August. On that very same day I received my uniform: jacket, riding pants, and riding boots. Those who had not graduated were given the simple field battle uniform, which they didn't much like, as those in the cavalry looked more distinguished. We received the blue peacetime uniforms that had just been returned by those going out to battle. Uncleaned, full of sweat and grease, they were pressed into our hands. At any other time we would have been revolted by the sight, but now we looked upon these uniforms full of reverence, as if they were our salvation because they lifted us beyond that of the common folk. Proud in these new clothes, I made my way home. The shock my parents experienced one could well imagine, as they suddenly saw a soldier enter their home who upon further inspection turned out to be their own son. Even so, their joy was great because every family that had even an ounce of nationalism held it as a duty that at least one family member should serve.

The next morning at six a.m. my service started, but even long before the mandatory call time many of us were already gathered at the barracks, full of anticipation at what was to come. Suddenly a number of corporals came out and divided us into two groups. One of them was classified as the graduated students. Both divisions were about equal in number. As soon as that business was completed our future sergeant was introduced to us, a slender man with sharp features and a very businesslike comportment. His voice was clipped and short. He would not tolerate any back talk and we realized that our carefree ways had abruptly come to an end and now we were to become rough soldiers with rough habits and rough talk. With a critical eye he looked us up and down and strutted straight to the middle of the line. He then said: "You are now soldiers. I am happy that you are serving your fatherland. Right after basic training you will be sent to the front. If you do your duty, then that is good. If you slack off, you can go to the devil and then afterwards I will also have a little word with you." After that he called his corporals and lance corporals together, and then we were divided into fifteen men for each company.

I was assigned to a company headed by reserve volunteer Mueller, who in his civilian life had been a beer wagon driver. His nose glowed like a one-hundred-watt bulb. Within short order we realized his nose was a consequence of his profession, although he maintained his red nose was a result of frostbite. Other than that, he was a very personable fellow who treated us well and was happy whenever he had a full glass in front of him. This pleasure we managed to give him quite often. Unfortunately, when it came to teaching us artillery maneuvers, he fell quite short as he didn't know much himself. He was a peaceful sort, but most of the other junior officers could be made out far and wide by their constant yelling. The less educated, the worse they were. It was as if they tried to cover their ignorance through anger and then became even more enraged because they couldn't succeed. The higher-ranked officers were old fogies that had been resurrected from somewhere and were mostly out of sight. However, if we had a question or a need, they tried their best to fulfill it. We were satisfied with them.

Only the commander, a half-crazy attorney, screamed at us publicly in such a fashion that no one would ever believe it. We tried to avoid him as much as possible. Never again in my entire military career experience did I come across such a hideous person as this Captain Laengsfeld. Within a few days of enlisting, I experienced a little surprise. I received the official acknowledgment from the school attesting to the fact that I was released for military duty. In the meantime, a government order had been proclaimed that all graduated students that volunteered to serve would be inducted at one level higher than a regular volunteer. However, they had to have had at least an average grade-point average. I was now slightly irritated because I actually hadn't needed to take the exam because this would have automatically made me eligible, and now I felt as though I was a double graduate.

Weeks and months passed. The autumn came and with it the first snow. Initially on the battlefield our troops had experienced victory after victory, but then the front stopped moving and there were fierce battles.[19] However, we still sat in our garrison and could only shout "Hurrah" when our comrades had achieved another victory. We became well educated in all facets of military equipment. At least we believed we were competent. Now we wanted out. In the meantime, I received my first promotion, even though it was not visible from the outside. Our sergeant Goetzke demoted our barracks monitor because he had not kept it in good enough order and promoted me even though I was one of the youngest. This distinction gave me great satisfaction because now I was in charge of twenty-eight older comrades. It wasn't always easy because one had to serve as supervisor and comrade at the same time, but even so I was able to carry out my duty successfully until we left for the front. I received a number of compliments about how clean our living quarters were and through this I received my first taste of giving orders, which later came to serve me well.

Despite the rough nature of Sergeant Goetzke, I remembered how well he thought of me, so that in comparison to many others I made sure that every order he gave and every duty assigned was completed without any complaint and with good nature, and I tried my hardest to keep my superiors happy. However, even with all of this my wish to depart to the front grew stronger with each and every passing day. The military exercises in camp were almost too much to bear, and it was said that it was actually easier to be at the front. A few comrades had departed for the front already, and they wrote accounts that made us envious of their position; why were we graduates held back? We complained. Then we found out why: because they wanted to train us down to the smallest detail. We were designated to be future leaders, and we wouldn't have been able to sufficiently carry

19. The initial Russian advance into East Prussia, which nearly reached Schiller's hometown of Bromberg, had been turned back beginning with the decisive Battle of Tannenberg in late August 1914. Russian forces were driven from East Prussia by the end of September. The German advance into Russian territory stalled at the Battle of Warsaw in late October, setting up a winter stalemate. Schiller will join the action in January 1915 as part of the slogging German advance against the Russians through the spring.

out our duties without the most comprehensive training. Those who didn't want to become officers could immediately depart within the next few days. However, none of us wanted that. So therefore we all stayed. We practiced more parade marching and saluting. We continued to drag the field guns through deep sand, we groomed the horses and cleaned the munitions wagons, and we also sewed missing buttons on our uniforms.[20] We consoled ourselves that this war would not be over soon and that our time would still come. My time to finally deploy occurred just as the New Year rang in.

20. Schiller uses the generic "Kanonen" here. From later references Schiller makes, and photographic evidence from family archives, this would have been the basic Krupp 7.7 centimeter field cannon, maneuvered in the field by horsepower or manpower.

2

Battles in Russia and Poland

January 1915! Slowly the military train neared the Russian border. The heavy cold raindrops poured relentlessly against the windows and blocked the view. As we passed, the scenery appeared silent and one-dimensional.

I sat hunched over in a corner of the compartment and covered my body that was stiff from the cold with my overcoat and tent cover and lit a cigarette. While I followed the steam clouds from the train and watched them disappear, I had the peace of mind to reflect upon the past few days. What had they all brought forth! Even the difficult training period I had just completed I reflected upon. Thanks to God it was now completed. That was now all behind me. I saw the riding arena and the nag that always bucked me off when we were supposed to jump a hurdle. And I saw the barn that I was allowed to clean on Sunday afternoons while the other comrades dressed in their finest uniforms and went to town! I remembered how I had polished the boots of an enlisted man who had no idea that I was a graduate and a rank above him, and I had to do it twice because apparently I had left a speck of dust somewhere. Later on he apologized, and it didn't affect me one way or the other.

I thought about the times we laid in bed without any lights and sang patriotic songs. It seemed almost festive with the lights off. I even thought about the sixth of January as I was walking about the camp and met our newest leader, and promptly Sergeant Kudweg asked me if I wanted to go to the front and if so I would be promoted at the same time. "I would like that very much," I answered. "Alright, then I will recommend you to the captain," he answered. I should, however, prepare and pack my bags immediately. What wouldn't I have rather done! It was the best order I had ever received thus far. That evening I was called to the office where I was told that they had received the papers to promote me to "Gefreiter," which at that time I thought the most important rank ever.[1] I also immediately received my corporal's buttons and was congratulated by all. It was the first time that a volunteer from our division had ever been promoted. That made me very proud, and therefore I hastened to pin my new-found status on my collar and quickly ran over to the junior officers' quarters and bought one round after another.

That evening the heretofore mentioned Mueller really made out in terms of his drinking, but it was all on my dime.

Then I hurried back home in order to notify my parents of the news. In order not to have a long, drawn-out, and painful goodbye, I merely told my parents that I was to be assigned elsewhere for quite awhile. Therefore, I was able to bid my farewell without any tears and commotion. In the early morning of the next day, I took my fourteen men and marched through the sleeping town to the railroad station in order to travel to Kolberg where the Artillery Regiment Number Two was stationed and to which we were assigned.[2] Here in this beautiful Baltic Sea town I spent some very enjoyable and relaxing days. I also received my gray field uniform and then was assigned as the leader of a sixty-man reserve troop and sent to the front. It was very unusual for such a large group of men that a regular officer or noncommissioned officer would not have been selected as the leader. Without even being given the proper marching papers, we were sent off. The only thing that the adjutant told me was: "The regiment is encamped at Ranska near Bartoschowka. You will travel by train to the last stop. From there on you will try to march on foot to reach the other troops." So then we were sent off on nothing but a song and a prayer. And now I sat here and let all these thoughts go through my head as the train passed Ostrowo, straining and puffing as it rolled over the border and into Russia.[3]

What a pleasant surprise when we were told that we would go to the Eastern Front. In France the easy victories had come to a halt, and no one thought it would be easy again. The standoff had made fighting come to a complete stop and therefore sitting in the same

1. Gefreiter is a rank equivalent to Lance Corporal and the first rank to which an enlisted soldier could be promoted.

2. Kolberg was then part of Western Pomerania and is now part of Poland.

3. Ostrowo was the administrative center of the Posen district of Germany, now Ostrow Wielkopolski in Poland.

trenches day in and day out seemed very boring. However, here in the east the mighty shadow of Hindenburg was rising; Ludendorff's genius was evident in more and more battles in which he drove the enemy back.[4] All of Germany was watching the east, and here the decisive battles would take place. We realized that we had the prospect of participating in these expected victories. Soon we would march into Moscow, and then the war would end. The misfortunes of Napoleon would not befall us. That's how we thought, and that's how we spoke, and all the time we never knew how ridiculous we actually were. Dusk began to fall.

With a shrill whistle the locomotive came to a stop. A larger train station became visible, and we saw the first signs of war. Half of the station had been burned down, and many of the houses only had their foundations left. A sign that had been pockmarked by bullet holes indicated in the Russian alphabet the name of the town. It was Kalisch.[5] On the platform and between the tracks, a lot of Jews were swarming about. They were wearing dirty long robes that fluttered around their skinny limbs. They aggressively pressed themselves up the steps to the train and tried to sell us overpriced sugary sweets that had already been soaked through with the rain. Even so, they found many good customers at hand, because it seemed even though we were now in the enemy's lands, the troops wanted to buy a foreign souvenir or memento.[6]

I advised the chief of the railroad station, who was an older lieutenant and had set up his quarters in a rickety shack, that I had arrived with my troops. When he heard that we were all volunteers he became quite chatty and showed us all the damage that the artillery fire had done. With glowing eyes, we looked upon the pile of destruction that remained, which had previously been a town. He also lectured us about the latest battles that had ensued. After that, the

4. By 1915, Paul von Hindenburg's status as a military leader was already being touted by German propaganda. He and his quartermaster, General Erich Ludendorff, were popular icons for having beaten back a Russian attack on East Prussia in the early months of the war. See Anna von Der Goltz, *Hindenburg: Power, Myth, and the Rise of the Nazis* (Oxford: Oxford University Press, 2009), ch. 1 passim.

5. Once part of Eastern Prussia, Kalisch was briefly on the front lines between the German and Russian armies. Now Kalisz is in Poland.

6. Though this could be merely descriptive and not necessarily derogatory, Schiller's impressions here do align with the stereotypical image that many Germans had of Jews. This is the only mention of Jews in the memoir.

march forward had come to a halt because the Russians had sent reinforcements from Siberia. Now we were both firmly encamped on either side and were just awaiting the spring. In the meantime, we would be able to reinforce our troops and then commence an attack on the entire front line. After that, a few nurses from the Red Cross appeared and dispensed coffee and buttered bread, and then the train continued its journey.

We continued to travel through the main part of the town, and we were able to see the utter and complete destruction. Everything was destroyed, and between the craters you could see people digging through the ruins to see if they could still find anything useful. How glorious a sight would it be if your battery was the one that would blow the enemy's entire town to smithereens, and how glorious a sight to behold if you were the one responsible for blowing up entire buildings and could witness the red flames shooting up into the sky, the walls collapsing and burying all those beneath it. And then the powerful flames would turn the very night into day. Yet even while I was dreaming of glory, I felt a sort of sadness come over me for all the suffering that had occurred and of the destruction and agony that would remain after the victors had had their way.

Further and further the train rolled, always toward the east. With every hour the scenery became ever more one-dimensional. Soon one could see nothing but fields of snow and occasionally a small patch of spindly trees. Very seldom the remains of a house and sometimes another destroyed village would come into sight, and we had to look twice to even believe we had actually seen it. Many times, we would stop at little train stations or even larger ones, and we would observe people wrapped in heavy clothing like mummies with guns slung over their shoulders and a burning pipe in their mouths. They looked more like night watchmen than soldiers and didn't give you any sense of security. It was now pitch black, and the rain had turned to snow that found its way through the drafty windows and into the compartment. We thought it best to go to sleep. Two men laid on the benches, another two on the floor, and two in the luggage nets, and the seventh slept in a tent that had been fastened to the ceiling. Therefore, each had his own spot. It was astounding how at that time we thought we had already gathered so much military experience, and we felt as though we were accomplished old soldiers.

As we woke the next morning, we found we were covered with a thin coat of snow. A window had opened during the night without us knowing about it. It had become very cold. The thermometer showed it was fifteen degrees.[7] We sought out body warmers and wool hats and put on double socks. Every time the train slowed or stopped we would run alongside of it just to try and keep warm. We also liked to see if we could keep up with the locomotive, and to the chagrin of the engineer we always won because he could not go any faster on the tracks, which had only been provisionally repaired by our men after we had destroyed the area. Only one time, full of anger, he went forth full steam ahead against our triumphant looks and teasing remarks. Then the faces of the runners fell and turned glum, and they had to hustle just to catch up with us at the next station. After this, the sport was over, and the engineer had had the last laugh.

Sometimes we saw some mounds of earth with a simple wooden cross made of two sticks that were bound together with twine. We usually found the helmets of the dead on the mounds as this was the most characteristic symbol of a soldier's grave and remained so until the end of the war. They had been buried just a scant three weeks ago, and yet no one seemed to care about them. How long would it be before wind, rain, and snow would totally cover any trace of them? Year in and year out they would lie, forgotten, their bodies moldering until they turned to ash. I found it depressing and thought that perhaps I could suffer the same fate. However, at this time I didn't want to dwell on death as I was still young, fresh, and full of ambition. In order just to suffer this poor fate, I wouldn't have volunteered so quickly, or so I thought.

We didn't make much progress this day. Every other minute we stopped. The cold increased. However, the next morning the surrounding vicinity was more lively. On deeply covered snow paths you could see supply and munitions wagons in ever increasing numbers pass by. The villages grew in number, the houses were kept up better, and people dressed in a more urban manner. Everything indicated that we were nearing a larger town. And soon we reached it. It was Thomacrow, the last train station before the front, and it was the main garrison of the German troops. We had arrived at our destination, although it was not our final destination.

7. Though Germany officially adopted the metric system in 1872, Schiller must be using Fahrenheit here. Fifteen degrees Celsius (59 degrees Fahrenheit) would be too warm for the context.

The extensive station was bustling with life. In front of a large wooden shack that served as a commissary, many trucks stopped and were filled with provisions. A horse transport that had just arrived was unloaded on a ramp. Numerous officers from various regiments stood there and argued about who would get the best horses. In front of the mighty government building, part of which was still habitable, a hospital train stopped, into which those seriously wounded on stretchers were moved quickly and quietly. It did not appear at this point there were any nurses here. In the distance, I could faintly make out the sound of artillery fire and cannons. I went to the main office after my men had left the train and to the train station's command center to advise them that we had arrived. I was told that I needed to wait with the replacements outside until I received further orders as to what we were to do next. I asked for a room in which we could stay and made the argument that we had been sitting in an unheated train for four days and had not even had a warm meal or drink except for a cup of coffee in Kalisch and that it was fifteen degrees outside. We were told that we needed to get used to this because we were no longer in our garrison. Every single tiny spot was already taken and we could even check it out ourselves. Or did we think that because we suddenly appeared that miraculously all the salons of the city would be emptied especially just for our use? It appeared that everyone here was quite on edge. Our train had departed in the meantime and with it went the last vestiges of our homeland.

We sat down in a ditch and pulled up our coat collars and covered our legs with the tent covers and let our stomachs continue to growl and then complained for the first time about the war. Nobody cared about us nor had any pity for our situation. For about two hours we sat there. All of a sudden, I mustered my courage and returned to the command center and became very forceful. Either they help us or I will take my troops into town and get help myself. This threat was risky because it bordered on insubordination, but I was boiling with rage and felt responsible for my men. That helped! The commander appeared and gave us a pile of wood with which we could light a fire, and I also received three large bags of provisions that were filled with canned peas and meat. Then the troops came back to life. Soon the meal was cooking, although it was very plain. Because there were no plates we scooped the meal out with our cups. However, it was something warm after so long a time, and the warmth of the fire did us all good. We could now move our stiff limbs and we felt re-energized. As soon as we were given a few cartons of cigarettes, all of our bitterness was forgotten; we threw one log after another into the fire and found the situation amenable and soon sang the homeland song. And as quickly as that the mood of a field soldier could change. Later on, I discovered this would happen quite often.

Near the evening hour we needed to appear in front of the military command offices. We had to carry our backpacks and provisions ourselves. That was an unreasonable request that we could not allow. Why were we even in the enemy's lands? Very quickly a few sleds were procured, and with these sleds we moved our equipment and ourselves into town. We were assigned a schoolhouse as our quarters that was not soon forgotten by some of our comrades, as this was their first experience with a lice infestation. [8]

A long rest here was not possible because early the next morning I was summoned back to the command offices to receive further orders. The captain advised me that my regiment was still encamped near Bartoschowka. We should depart at once as it was about forty kilometers away. The comrades assembled our backpacks, strapped them to our backs, and started the march, but without the sleds because we couldn't find any that had not already been taken. Because I didn't possess a map of the area, I wrote the names of the villages that we needed to pass through on a piece of paper. At first we able to use a well-paved road, but then it turned into a miserable path. By noon we hadn't even made it a third of the way as we entered a small village to cook our lunch. Even here each house was occupied by the military, and so we had to stay outside once again.

I went into one of these houses and was blown backward in great shock due to the incredibly foul stench that accosted me. An old Landsturmmann in shirt sleeves sat at a table and was playing cards with a number of comrades, and he called to me, laughing, "Come on into the salon . . . we won't bite!"[9] I could not refuse this friendly invitation and so I entered and looked more carefully about

8. A recurring theme. Fear of lice and lice-borne diseases was a common theme among German soldiers and officials. German officials spent a great deal of time and resources on containing the threat from lice. See Paul Julian Weindling, *Epidemics and Genocide in Eastern Europe, 1890–1945* (New York: Oxford University Press, 2000), ch. 4 passim.

9. A Landsturmmann is a member of the Prussian Military Reserve.

the room. Now I was able to make out in the half-darkness wherefrom this terrible smell emitted, as half the room was dedicated to a sow with piglets, a goat, and a number of other animals. Only a low wooden board separated the room. In the front, about six or seven old and young men and women in dirty torn rags were eating their lunch, which consisted of boiled potatoes and salt. They didn't have forks or knives, nor did they have any plates. They ate out of a huge wooden trough that was placed between them and pulled out a potato now and then onto their laps and threw the peels on the floor. Next to this group sat a woman who was breastfeeding her baby and at the same time was energetically eating from the trough. In one corner sat about half a dozen children who were fighting over a bit of hardtack that had been given to them by the card players. I asked them how they could stand it in here and received the answer that one could get used to it. And additionally, these types of conditions were common in all of Poland–Russia and that I would soon think nothing of this lifestyle. Oh was that ever a glorious prospect!

I quickly bid my farewell and retreated back into the open, but hours later I was still thinking about this house that was but half a house and half a stall and of the horrible stench that still wafted about me. I had always heard about the primitive conditions here, and even in school we learned about it, but I never thought it would be this uncivilized. I didn't even see any beds. These people who cohabited with their animals seemed more like animals themselves. However, it was not poverty that forced them into this lifestyle but born intransigence and ignorance. That I soon discovered. I felt sorry for the poor comrades who had to stay here and yet had no idea that in a few months' time I would have been overjoyed if I had been assigned such quarters.

Right after lunch we continued our difficult march. The extra weight of our backpacks that we were not used to was evident and strained our backs. As it turned dark and the path was no longer visible, we stopped and spent the night in a half-destroyed shack through which the snow blew. We couldn't see any villages in the distance. On the straw and hay we placed our tents and slept on top of those. We were so tired and exhausted that we didn't even feel the cold hard ground and immediately fell asleep.

We departed half frozen the next morning. Now besides having to carry our gear we also had to carry some footsore comrades because we didn't want to leave them behind. It was an extraordinary effort, and a lot of swearing ensued. However, the ever-nearing sound of cannon fire made us realize that we were not too far from our destination. That same afternoon we neared a village that could be Bartoschowka. A solider we passed dressed in a gray field uniform confirmed this fact.

About half an hour later we arrived at our destination, exhausted. We were curiously observed by the old guard, who peered at us through the windows. I immediately reported to the commander of the First Division, whose name was Captain Russelt. He sat with his officers in a primitive wood shack with only a small stall-like window that allowed in a bit of light. He was happy with our punctual arrival and gave me his hand and hoped that we would be comfortable. Then we were divided among ourselves to man the front lines. I was assigned along with a few other comrades to a light munitions company that was embedded in a neighboring village. We asked the old reservist who showed us the way to the village why there was presently no cannon fire to be heard. This was happening more regularly because both sides were suffering from exhaustion and only very seldom were there any serious battles. The losses seemed to be bearable.

The village in which we were stationed was even more primitive than anything I had seen thus far. The entire village consisted of only nine houses. In one of these I was sent and told it was now my living quarters for the immediate future. In the one room I immediately found at least a dozen other comrades who laid on straw and slept, along with others who were playing cards, and around the fireplace sat a number of Russian peasants, which at the moment I couldn't even count. Men, women, and children. You couldn't even distinguish one from another, and it appeared as though they were one large mass. As I politely wished them a "good evening" only two voices answered back; the others only found their voices after I had announced myself to the comrade in charge and told him that I was now in the group.

Then they got angry and claimed that too many people were already assigned to this house, and why wasn't I somewhere else. To my retort that I certainly had not chosen this assignment, I only heard angry growls. Even so, I tried to start a dialogue, but it didn't do any good because this group came from Pomerania. And these fellows only spoke the dialect of Pommern, which at that time I didn't understand. When they realized that I didn't come from their beloved

Pomerania, they treated me like an interloper and shut me out. To add insult to injury, I was a lance corporal, and that was a rank above them, thus making me their superior. That we had been promoted before even leaving for the front while they were still simple enlisted men was simply a scandal. I could sympathize with their side of the argument, but from my perspective it wasn't my fault that I had been promoted above them. That was the reception I received from the field garrison. I was really devastated and unhappy about my relationship with these people with whom in the future I should share happiness and sorrow, loyalty, and even death. However, I tried to pull myself together and show them that even though I had just arrived I would be equal to the challenge and duty.

At that time there was no military training on the front lines. When there was not a munitions truck to be driven to the front line, one had nothing else to do but lie around. This type of lifestyle did not sit well with me, and it robbed me to a great extent of my fascination with war. Two weeks I had already been here, and in all this time on only three occasions was I allowed to drive a truck behind the front line and unload a few baskets of munitions that were then carried to the front lines by the members of the battery. [10] You couldn't hear a shot being fired anywhere, and everything seemed so peaceful that you could almost think you were still at home. Only the commissary and the good beds were missing. Even so, my comrades drove like maniacs back to the village as if they were to be blown up into pieces at any moment. I felt like an old fighter because by this time I was infested with lice for the first time. Four weeks later they had almost eaten me up. One evening the solider in charge returned and informed me that I was now reassigned to the Second Artillery Battery. I needed to report the next evening. This news was the only bit of joy that I ever experienced in these quarters and with this assignment.

Along with another comrade I stomped through the thigh-high snow a scant twenty-four hours later. When we reached the front line, I was taken aback because it appeared to be very different from what I had always envisioned. The six field guns were placed fifteen steps apart and quite unevenly and had been buried almost entirely

10. Wicker containers were used to transport ammunition to the guns and held three shells each.

in the hard ground.[11] Around them was a high wall of dirt that was supposed to shield the soldiers. A few yards behind the field guns the munitions lay covered with a tent cloth. Next to each gun there were foxholes for the soldiers manning the guns. The battery was placed on an open field. In front of them there was a small slope that shielded them from the view of the enemy. I came to the sixth gun that flanked the left side. Through a very small opening that was covered to keep out the cold by a blanket, I crawled into this hole that was to be my home for the foreseen future. I pulled my satchel of belongings in behind me. The room was about two meters wide and long. On a box was a kerosene candle. I was able to make out five or six unshaven faces.

After I made myself known to Corporal Radmer, and after the initial greetings were completed, I sat on a hay bale and made myself comfortable and suspiciously looked about the surroundings. But I was quickly done with my inspection because aside from the box and candle and the equipment of the soldiers, there was nothing else to see. You couldn't even sit upright, and if you tried you hit your head on the ceiling that was made of wood beams and sand. I allowed myself to ask the question as to why this "palace" had been built so low to the ground. Because it was warmer this way and also safer against artillery fire. The realization struck me that of course that was precisely the reason, and I was embarrassed about my stupid question.

The first thing I was asked was of the news from home, and after I was finished with that I was asked about my personal situation. Even here I was met with stony silence when they realized I was not a simple reservist, and their surprised reaction as to why I was already promoted made me realize that the same difficulties I had experienced at the artillery unit were possibility awaiting me here. However, within a moment I found that these fellows were much more amenable and friendly than the old-timers that I had just left. I suddenly realized the march to this place with a heavy pack had so exhausted me that I was no longer interested in further speculations. And then the reservist in charge put out the light. Then I turned on my side and slept for the first time in a real foxhole.

That very first night I had my first brush with a serious war

11. Schiller now starts using the more specific "Geschütz" in reference to the cannons involved.

experience, and this is how it played out. In the middle of a deep and satisfying snore one of my colleagues pushed me in my side. I woke up and noticed, still half asleep, how the gunner was trying to strike a match and yelled, "Alarm" and "To the guns." At the same time, I heard heavy artillery fire and explosions around me, though initially I did not know what was going on. But the others were already outside; I realized that and followed them. I got up so quickly that I immediately hit my head on the low ceiling beam because I had completely forgotten that my living quarters were now the height of a dog house. I heard the high commanding voice of an officer that seemed to rise above all the noise and confusion. Shortly thereafter I felt the strong vibrations of our own guns firing.

By now I had recovered from hitting my head and sprang quickly outside. With only two strides I was in the cannon pit. It was ordered that we fire quickly with shrapnel shot. The crew was ducked over in the firing pit. The air was filled with explosions and whistles and afterward a thunderous explosion with an impact that forced everyone to fall flat on the ground because now pieces of the exploding shells were whizzing through the air. With every hit the whole vicinity was bathed for several seconds in red fire. We used the light from the fire to check if our guns were pointed in the right direction. The munitions in our gun emplacement were now empty. I was tasked to find more. I sprang to the ammunition pile and grabbed the nearest basket and ran back as quickly as I could. I thought about how dangerous it actually was to leave all these munitions just lying about in the open. If just one direct hit had reached the munitions supply the entire battery would have gone up in flames.

As I was thinking this thought I was suddenly blinded and found myself flat on the ground. I had no idea how I fell on the ground because I did not trip over anything. However, at the same time the battle was suddenly over. Five meters from me a shell had exploded, and the force of it had blown me over. The corporal explained this to me while laughing as I appeared back at the cannon with my munitions. Why would he think that this was the least bit funny while we were all at death's door? However, just a scant month later I found myself laughing at the same situation.

All of a sudden there was a series of six loud explosions almost at the same time. The enemy was shooting simultaneously at several of our positions. We heard the call for an orderly from the neighboring position. We didn't even react and just kept shooting. The thought occurred to me that someone must have been hurt. Very cool and collected, I heard another commanding voice, and I saw how everything just continued to operate. Only when the explosions came did everyone duck, but otherwise it was just like the exercises we had practiced. And I felt how the peace and steadiness came over me as well, and I felt as though we were all acting in the same manner. After twenty minutes, the enemy ceased its fire and so did we, and it was as though I had been there alongside all the rest of them for six months.

And then all of a sudden everything was still and quiet as though nothing had happened. Only at the very front the infantry fire was still to be heard, but it didn't bother us. At our neighboring station there were injuries to two of the artillery operators; one was wounded in the arm and the other in the leg. An ambulance had just arrived to take them away. "Greet our homeland" everyone called to them as they departed. One answered with "We will be coming back soon." Three years later he wouldn't have said that. Then the commanding officer advised us that the charge the Russians made against us was successfully defended. The Russians were not able to penetrate even one of our positions. As we crawled back to our "villa of protection" the sergeant said to me, "You have now been baptized by fire. It was quite a proper attack, but this experience shouldn't damage you."[12] I had to believe that.

Three more weeks we were encamped here, and nothing extraordinary occurred. Only when it was necessary did we ever leave our foxholes. The enemy shot in our direction now and again, but we didn't care about it because there were only intermittent shots. However, a messenger did sustain shrapnel to the back of his head. Every evening we sent a few groups over just to show them that we were still here. After we did this we had another twenty-four hours of peace. This free time I used to write numerous letters to my friends and relatives. I had quickly found out that writing letters was very advantageous to me as then I received many care packages from all sides, but the most came from my own parents. I was so overwhelmed with delicacies and sweets that I gave the extra to my comrades, who had

12. Here "villa of protection" is literally "Villa Minna." "Minna" is a female name deriving from Old German, which can mean "love" or sometimes "strength." We opted for the latter sense as best fitting the situation.

hardly received anything. No wonder that the entire battalion was suddenly interested in whatever post came to me. However, this also seemed to bring us closer together.

During this time a dramatic change in weather conditions occurred. The snow melted and it started to rain. We then had lots of work as many of the foxholes became flooded. And if we didn't want to start swimming, we needed to bail the foxholes out with our cups and kettles. The whole camp became almost unbearable, and we wished we could leave.

And then in mid-February a new regiment relieved us. We then proceeded on dirt roads about fifty kilometers to the next train station. Every few minutes a piece of equipment was stuck in the mud, and then it was it was commanded: "Artillerymen come here," then we reached into the spokes and pulled and lifted until the wheels could start turning again. That sometimes took a half hour or even longer. The rest of the battery was already out of sight. Then we had to run to catch up again. The sweat just poured out of us, and then it dried again. Such marches were not wished for, but still they were necessary, as we all knew. Very quickly we loaded ourselves onto the train. Where were we going? Not to the west, because the train was traveling northward. The next morning, we found ourselves on the border of East Prussia, and then we drove a bit through German territory and were soon back on Russian ground. This region seemed to have been spared by war because the houses still stood untouched. There were even estates with large homes, and that was a very unusual sight. In the barnyards it seemed very neat and tidy; everywhere you could see small gardens and fruit trees that gave a well-kept and friendly appearance. We took this as a positive sign that the war here would be an easier experience for us.

We asked a few comrades that were on the opposite track on an ambulance train of the news. They spoke of a major offensive that was to take place in the next few days. Nobody knew any of the details. However, just lately, more and more ambulance stations had been established, and that pointed to the fact that numerous casualties were to be expected. It was clear to us that we would soon be drawn into this ensuing battle, and we were absolutely right.

3

Kurland

Suddenly in the middle of the night we were told "prepare to exit." We had landed in Mlawa.[1] A long temporary ramp extended from the train and was illuminated by two small kerosene lamps. Because the windows appeared as though they had not been cleaned for years, we needed to rely on our senses to get down the ramp. In addition, this poor light did nothing to illuminate the night. Only a few flashlights were to be seen. On the very spot that our drivers were occupied by unloading the vehicles there was a lot of noise and commotion. A horse had slipped from the bridge in the darkness and broken a foreleg. We heard Captain Geitner swear like the devil as he came at us with waving arms, so we quickly hid behind the cannons because we knew that when he was in such a mood he would assault anyone within striking distance.

Finally at about seven a.m. we finished with unloading so the officers could report that the job was done and the train could again depart. Immediately we got into position and marched into the town. The town made a good impression on us and distinguished itself from the small East Prussian cities we had just passed and identified itself by the onion-shaped domes of the churches. From one of these cupolas we saw a huge flag that could be seen near and far, which identified the town as a neutral town attending to war casualties. From the distance we heard the sound of cannon fire, and since the wind was coming in our direction we estimated it to be about twenty-five kilometers away. As we came to the central market, we saw the vehicles of the commanding officers. The individual battery leaders were sitting on their horses and waiting on orders from

1. Now in north central Poland, Mlawa was then on the border between Russian and German territory.

the commander. It appeared that this meeting had ended. The officers saluted and immediately dispersed in all directions. As one of them rode off I heard him say to our lieutenant, "Today we will be very busy, Pauli. Whenever someone isn't up to the task, then we are called." Therefore, I realized that the situation was quite serious and the attack had already begun.

As soon as we marched past the last houses and left the pavement, we received the order "To your guns immediately." And now we marched toward the front without any rest for several hours. We tried to eat while we were driving. It was not possible because we were sliding back and forth and up and down on the iron seats, and we needed our hands to secure ourselves in order not to be pinned under the wheels. Every bite we took came back up again. After that we gave up. Very long munitions lines were coming toward us. We learned from them that ahead of us a battle had already been underway for several hours, however with very little success. Four infantry divisions and two cavalry brigades had been engaged, but the enemy was a lot stronger. The enemy had an excellent position established in the city of Pracznicz that they had built up earlier in anticipation of a battle in this strategic area. The fate of the whole day revolves around this place.

We had to stop in front of a narrow alley that was surrounded by high walls on either side because a broken-down supply wagon was blocking our way. We needed to clear the path first. In the forest lay the remaining parts of Infantry Regiment Number Thirty-Four, which had attacked in the first gray morning light and was now mostly demolished. Now they had assembled here and were cooking their meal. I saw how they had tried to dig a few graves with picks and spades in the hard and frozen ground for their dead. They had put a tent cover over the bodies of their fallen comrades. I picked up the edge of the cover and saw under it a first lieutenant with the entire back of his head missing. His field gray uniform was completely spattered with blood and was difficult even to recognize. His eyes, which were encrusted with blood, were wide open, and his stare looked as though he were still seeing something terrible in front of him. I became scared of this apparition and quickly threw the tent cover back over him. I ran back over to my battery and at the same time thought that just a few scant hours ago this had been a human being just like us. However, now there was something strange and distant between the living and the dead that I couldn't properly process.

In the meantime, the sounds of battle were becoming more distinct. It seemed as if it had become closer. The Russians had started firing continuously with heavy artillery into the forest. The Russians probably thought the reserves had arrived and were encamped in the forest. Some of the shells that landed exploded between the trees and ripped them out of the ground by their roots. This would become my first major battle. I did not have any fear, but within me I felt a sort of excitement building.

Finally we could move forward. Not far away behind some bushes and small slopes we hid our ammunition and guns and fired back. From further away one could hear the steady tac-tac-tac sound of the machine guns and infantry. On the horizon there suddenly appeared a huge black smoke plume over the city of Pracznicz that we had not been able to capture and was now reduced to flames. The road soon became impassable because it was littered with craters made from fresh artillery strikes in which our vehicles became trapped. As soon as we swerved into an open field, suddenly four shells exploded next to the last munitions wagon. A dead rider and a horse with its belly ripped open were the result. We tried to get away as quickly as possible. From now on we zigzagged across the fields that were littered with rocks and branches.

We stopped at a large farmhouse. To the right near a small hill we noticed a signal air balloon rising. This was a sign that indicated to us that the division leaders were quartered there. A number of higher-ranking officers were standing around a table that appeared to hold maps. I immediately recognized Lieutenant General Freiherr von Holland, a fellow citizen from Bromberg. I had sat with his sons on the same school bench. He was the heaviest soldier of the army and weighed almost three hundred pounds. The reason he hadn't been pensioned long ago was because it was said he held a fast friendship with the Kaiser. Now he was heavily engaged as he was constantly barraged with aides who brought messages back and forth and immediately departed as though they themselves were chased by Satan. It was very amusing to watch the goings-on.

Then a bugler brought us our marching orders. In a nearby trench, we positioned ourselves to fight the enemy. Everything went according to plan. The barriers were erected, the munitions wagons were placed beside the guns, and the horses were taken back and withdrawn from danger. Meanwhile, the captain had run up the hill in front of us with his immediate staff, the binocular telescope, the aiming device, and the portable telephones, had chosen an observation post, and had telephones run to us from there. That job was completed in a matter of minutes, and soon we received the orders through the telephone: "Entire battery take aim setting one, twenty-two hundred meters." It was just like at the barracks. For a moment you heard the turning of the machinery, and then came the order "Fire," and instantaneously six guns fired in unison, flames shooting out. "Reduce by two hundred meters." Now came the second firing of artillery, and this continued for some time. The entire operation proceeded in an orderly fashion and wasn't anything to get excited about.

But eventually the Russians seemed to have had enough of us. Far in the distance we saw the Russians overshot our target, and then we saw the explosions behind us. They apparently thought that we were firing from that position. We were hoping they would continue to fire in that direction. But we were soon to be proven wrong, and then we saw with misgivings how their firing was coming nearer and nearer to our position. We saw as they were getting closer, and that after the sixth or seventh volley they would have reached our position. But thank God we soon received the order to evacuate. It was astonishing how quickly we were able to move out. No other orders were necessary. Everyone knew exactly what to do, and everyone worked as quickly as possible. The captain came running over, said something to his lieutenants, hoisted himself on his horse, and sped off. Then we quickly followed. As we drove we heard that our first line of assault had entered Pracznicz. Our battalion was to follow immediately to protect the infantry in order to engage directly with the enemy.

Immediately we proceeded cross-country, passing firing batteries, reserve troops, and munitions wagons pushing forward. The heavily wounded were carried behind the lines; the lightly wounded were leaning on each other and dragged themselves back to the field hospital stations. Their road was still long. Would they arrive safely? I had no time to reflect on this as we were suddenly in the line of gunfire. Still, it appeared we had not been detected yet, and we continued on without any casualties. We had left the first enemy trenches behind us that had been stormed by our own infantry. A quick glance showed that as they retreated they left guns, backpacks, munitions crates, and all sorts of other items strewn here and there. A few dead enemy soldiers were crouching behind their barricades still with their guns clutched in their arms exactly as death had caught them. There were even some dead German soldiers among them.

Now we had reached the outskirts of the city and entered a street that had been blocked by a barricade that had just been recently removed. Within the city Russian soldiers had locked themselves in several blocks of houses and were firing through cellar windows. The infantry was dealing with the situation, giving free rein to drive through. Step by step we moved forward; oftentimes we needed to stop. The prisoners were collected in an open square and estimated at a few hundred. All of them appeared to be tall men and dressed in new uniforms. We asked one of them who spoke some broken German to what troop he belonged. He named one of the Petersburg Guard regiments and said we had the entire Russian Guard in front of us. His commander had just recently read to them an order that had stated that this town needed to be protected at all costs.

It didn't matter what it cost in lost lives. The soldiers had known that our plan was to storm the town, so they should have been well prepared. Angrily hollering, an assistant wedged himself through the crowd and cried for our battery chief. We needed to exit the town immediately and get into position and he would guide us. In the next narrow alleyway, we already were blocked. The entire street was hemmed in by numerous supply wagons that made it impossible to proceed forward. I heard the captain threaten that he would level the entire line to the ground if they didn't move over immediately. However, that didn't help either because they were as tightly crammed in as we were. A very depressing situation when you thought that we were locked in here while our comrades not far from us were counting the seconds until we would arrive. The sound and echoes of the heavy artillery explosions were difficult to bear in these narrow streets.

Very close to us, numerous houses were burning, and the heat of the fire made us think we were in an oven. The horses became frantic with the closeness of the fire and started prancing wildly. We would not be able to control them much longer. As we tried to settle them one of the officers was kicked and shattered his knee. Finally, we were able to proceed. My neighbor, who was seated next to me on the gun carriage, poked me and said: "You best eat the rest of your chocolate now because who knows if by evening you will ever eat again." At the end of the alley, where we saw the open fields, it seemed as though we had traveled into hell. There was a lot of action, loud explosions, and the dirt was shooting upward from the impact. In the air, pieces of shrapnel were flying and shells were exploding below. Thousands of rounds of gunfire were flying toward us. In this gunpowder haze we saw the dead and badly wounded, dead horses, and upturned wagons. We saw men spring up and then fall right back down again. It was all too much for the eye to take in at once; it was all too surreal.

I can only remember a few details over the next few hours. I remember when we got into an open area that there were two of our batteries in front of us. They were immediately covered with gunfire and shellfire. Only a few field guns could even get into position to shoot back. The rest of the guns were silent as the gunners lay dead next to them. I also remember that a volley of shrapnel came toward us, hit the horses, and resulted in the overturning of three of our guns simultaneously as they fell from the carriages. My cannon was quickly positioned. In a full gallop the horses were chased backward, and then we started shooting against the enemy.

At the same time the enemy started fighting aggressively toward us. I don't know how far they came toward us; I didn't know what was coming from the left or from the right. All I knew is that we were furiously shooting and reloading and shooting and reloading again. We couldn't even gather our thoughts, and it seemed like everything around us was sinking away. After a long time, the lieutenant appeared and ordered us to fire more slowly because we had no additional ammunition. This push has been stopped. The first push resulted in two dead and five wounded, but while he was still speaking, the enemy decided to change aim and fire directly upon us. Behind us, in front of us, left and right, the air crackled and whizzed with fire. Sand and shrapnel flew around us and landed on our fortresses. Our gunner gripped his chest and then fell on his seat as though he had been folded like a pocket knife. Explosion! Another comrade fell over the end of the cannon as if he had tripped. Gut shot! By the neighboring gun the commander lay dead. One of the munitions carriers was wounded.

And without any respite the air cracked and whistled with deadly force all around us. Then I remembered when I was shot at in Bartoschowka and my helmet flew off and I thought I was in the midst of battle, but it had been nothing in comparison to this! This was a new modern battle with all the trappings that men had invented to murder each other. If only our infantry could hold out. It appeared that we didn't even have that many men left. We would do our duty if we could. A sudden and huge explosion, bigger than anything we had heard thus far, made us stop and listen. The munitions wagon of the second gun had sustained a direct hit and flew into the air, ripping apart those soldiers servicing it. We hardly took any notice of it; the next moment perhaps it was our turn. Where had my enthusiasm for war gone in this situation? Now I just needed to get out of this hell, and that was the only thought that occupied my mind.

Wasn't it surely a miracle that I was still alive and not even injured? Was it just coincidence that I wasn't part of the other crew which had just departed for the afterlife? That's when I came to the conclusion that life is more or less fated. If it was meant to be, I would escape out of this with relative ease, and if not, I could just as easily think I was in safety and then be randomly shot from an overpassing fighter plane. My fate had already been sealed, and I was helpless to change it. That gave me a sense of peace. I was so calm now that I was able without any fear to survey the area to determine how we were positioned.

Two hundred meters in front of us lay our infantry trenches, but they were covered in smoke and haze. At a few places where you could still see, I noticed the enemy. The distance between us could be no more than four hundred meters. Between explosions I saw the other two batteries. They were covered in fire just like us and did not shoot much. I wondered how it was going for them? As dusk fell, the Russians started a new push. We felt it because their gunfire stopped and their artillery started firing. We fired a barrage of weapons in front of our line and their push was thwarted. Now they might have had enough of us, we thought, and didn't know that our own fate this day had already been decided, because in the meantime the enemy had assembled a huge new corps that had been standing in reserve and then made a surprise attack into our left lines. The tiny remnants left of Regiment Thirty-Four that had just been embedded there were swept away, and even another infantry regiment was not able to make the impossible possible and counter an attack of twenty to one. Slowly but surely, we defended ourselves while moving backward. If the commanding officer had had a fresh division to put at our disposal we would have won the battle. But this missing division was the deciding factor and the day was lost for the German troops. So with heavy hearts the commanding officers gave the order to retreat.

The command sounded like a salvation: "Pull back guns and fire alternately." And even though we were retreating, now the most dangerous part was upon us. Until now, the cannon shields had protected us from the artillery firing. But now we were ordered to grip right and left into the spokes of the carriage wheels to retreat, and therefore we had no protection at all. With unrelenting strength the enemy fired at us. I threw a backward glance to the first houses where we had pulled our cannons initially. Oh God!!! How terribly far could two hundred meters be that had to be covered? And since the enemy had discovered that we were retreating, they unleashed a furious display of firepower so that you couldn't even distinguish individual hits, and it felt as though you were in the middle of an exploding volcano.

Step by step we were able to get further away. But with what sorts of casualties! Our lieutenant fell as he received a direct hit in his shoulder, and by our neighboring cannon, two men lay with shrapnel wounds in the stomach. The other artillery groups were no better off. And finally we reached the buildings that for us symbolized the Promised Land. Very quickly they shot whatever they still had left at us, and then we got back on our seats and retreated through the burning town. Under the protection of heavy artillery firing, the infantry was also able to retreat because the enemy was too exhausted from battle to follow. Later we discovered that the way our commanding officer gave the order to retreat was a masterpiece in the art of war. Very few cannons and machine guns that were left behind were still usable, and as for prisoners, the Russians only had severely wounded men who couldn't have been transported anyway because that would have meant their sure death.

But one of the ego-driven commanding generals still didn't want us to get away so easily. So he sent his entire cavalry after us, including a mounted artillery unit, to hold back our retreat. We had no knowledge of this occurring. It had become pitch black. We were still shattered by what had transpired today, overly exerted, overly tired, and overly hungry. We crawled next to our gun carriages, which were packed full of wounded from all the different units. We were told that we would march throughout the night. No one had any desire to speak; everyone was occupied by his own thoughts. With great effort we just put one foot in front of the other, and our only blessed thought was that we were at least one step further away from the enemy. The mood was that depressed. Before and behind us, a large number of infantry units were slowly trudging along, carrying their wounded with them. They were as silent and quiet as we were. They had lost half of their men. The rattling of the wagons was now louder than the disappearing sounds of the battle behind us, and now we seldom heard anything, and only from very far away.

Suddenly we detected a few shots right in front of us. We listened attentively. Shortly thereafter we heard the crack of continuous firing. More firing! It couldn't be happening very far from us. A few shots whizzed over our heads. It then appeared that in the darkness our own troops had misdirected their aiming scopes. What on earth was this firing about? Our march colonnade stopped. A few of the cavalry galloped by us. We started firing defensively. The infantry received some sort of order and started moving. We stayed where we were. The captain was called to the commanding officer; we saw him in full gallop, followed by a bugler, and in the dark of the night they disappeared. The gunfire became more pronounced, and we retreated behind our munitions wagons for protection. As the battery commander came back, we set up our positions. There was nothing to be seen. In the distance, we heard the sound of "Hurrah!" A wagon came upon us from the front, and we saw that it had wounded in it, and so we asked what was happening. Then we found that our scouts had been intercepted by surprise. They didn't know anything else because they had been told to immediately retreat.

After an hour all noises ceased and we moved further. We found out the next morning that our infantry had accomplished something extraordinary during the night. As soon as they were attacked, they figured out the position of the enemy by determining where the shots were coming from. They saw through the light the firing of the weapons gave off and approached with bayonets drawn. Without the need of any artillery covering them they were able to surprise-attack the enemy dismounted cavalry unit, and in the first surge of fire were able to defeat them, and even seized the artillery in the general confusion. They were able to capture more than one thousand Russians. They were able to take nineteen field guns and thirty machine guns. This success gave us more optimism and took away the enemy's desire to chase us. But even our losses were very heavy on that night in Pracznicz. We found this out some days later. We lost a total of over thirteen hundred men, and it was mostly our active fighting soldiers. But the enemy that was three times stronger than us must have lost at least twice as many in this bloody battle. We couldn't prove it, but it looked as though that could be right.

We only retreated thirty kilometers, and by the first light of dawn we had already established our new positions. But for days after this battle, which was one of the bloodiest in the east, we still noticed the great moral effect on our enemy. It didn't strike back in full force but followed more meekly and frightened, thinking that our new position might be a trap into which it could fall. This break in fighting was very agreeable to us. We received new reserve troops and resupplied ourselves and our ammunition. Our unit had sustained eight dead and eighteen wounded. They were forgotten in an instant, and no one spoke of them or the battle because it had been so traumatic that one just wanted to move beyond it.

Soon we discovered that new divisions had arrived, and a new assault on Pracznicz was planned. We didn't want to believe it. This is because the village near Chorzele was a decent place to camp. My regiment was excluded from taking part in the assault on Pracznicz. One day we were relieved, loaded our provisions, and moved even further to the north. They had planned for us to take part in the now famous battle into Kurland.[2] It was a complete surprise when we moved in on the Russians and they were only able to weakly defend themselves. But soon they had recovered from their shock, and then our quickly moving assault was over. By the friendly little town of Rossinie, a decisive battle would take place. After a three-day artillery battle, we were able to pierce the enemy's position. So we broke through the wings, captured many soldiers, and the majority of their hardware. Under daily assaults we drove through eastward. We only stopped at the Dubysa [river] where fortified positions that had already been built before the war were very strong.

The stalemate had begun. Until now I had actually enjoyed myself. Every day found a different adventure. Sometimes in one day alone we dismounted up to three times in one hour, fired at a few positions, and then continued further. It was almost a sprint with the enemy. Only at Schirwindt right at the beginning were we attacked by an enemy battery. At that time my artillery captain sustained a shrapnel wound in his stomach that was no larger than a hazelnut. It was still big enough that we had to dig a grave for him. And later on, we only detected the Russians again near Rossinie, where they were relentlessly firing on a bridge that we urgently needed to cross. At

2. Part of Russian territory at the time, Kurland (Courland) is a province of current-day Latvia on the Baltic Sea. The action in the narrative immediately following takes place in what is now Lithuania.

that time two gunners were wounded who had arrived with the latest replacements. We didn't need them or miss them and they were only too happy, after so short a guest stint, to head back to the garrison.

Now we lay here and waited to see what the Gods and General Ludendorff had in mind for us. A lot of news came our way. Some was believable, some was even true, and some was just outright gossip. What was true was that Pracznicz had actually fallen into our hands, that entire units of Russians were deserting, that officers had been shot by the soldiers, and that Czar Nicolas fled. These were things that one could hardly believe. Before we could even realize it, spring [1915] had arrived and helped raise our spirits immensely. The sun that was shining more warmly with each day had helped to melt the snow and ice, the trees showed their first signs of new green growth, and with that the entire landscape had been transformed.

Now it became quite evident how vastly different it was between Russian Poland and this territory. Here you could find well-tended fields, massive houses, separate barn areas, and people dressed in clean although simple clothing. Over there, dirt and rags and misery. The lieutenant gave us a lecture about the high cultural standing of Kurland. German farmers immigrated here in the Middle Ages, settled, and civilized the area. German businessmen soon followed. They founded towns and small villages, and therefore commerce and orderliness was established. Even through the passing of hundreds of years speech and customs changed remarkably, but because of the foundation set long ago, everyone profited. In the larger towns it was said that even today you could still find German schools and German churches. And, most of the larger land tracts were still in German hands. We could hardly believe this at first, but later on we saw for ourselves that it was true. A number of residents welcomed us and thought of us as emancipators from Russian terror. We thought after we won the war that this part of Kurland would become a part of Germany for sure. And some of the farmer's sons in our unit already decided where they would settle once the war was over. Here one could live! Even though trains, paved streets, and telephone wires were not installed and there was no industrialization, it wouldn't be long before the new Prussian leadership would have changed all that.[3]

3. Schiller's memory is correct; Germany's war aims in the east did include plans to annex Kurland to the Reich, and such information was passed on to

And while we were discussing all of this it was clear that it was a moral duty to Germany that we needed to take back what our forefathers, the Teutonic Knights, had first conquered.[4] We were already dividing the spoils of war and were pretending as if the war was already won and over. It was useless, we knew it, but we needed something to talk about.[5] Why couldn't one dream and fantasize a bit since life was already far too grim? I had discovered this in the last few weeks. I really felt I had undergone a transformation. I had long ago gotten used to the rough field conditions, was hardened against the weather and physical hardships, and found out that each man had to care for himself first and foremost. Schiller in his drama *Wallenstein* said: "No one else can step in for you, you must stand alone." [6] How this philosophy could be incorporated with the concept of comradeship had never been clear to me.

Because the fighting had died down, this would have been the best opportunity for us to restore ourselves. And that was really necessary. But despite this, we could not escape the commotion and the work we still had to do. So that we wouldn't show the Russians our weakness and tried to demonstrate our might, we were forced to change our location almost daily. So each time we had to build new trenches around our guns, we had to fortify the artillery, and dig new foxholes, as well as lay new telephone lines. For all of this we needed a firm foundation made of fascines because the ground was like a moor.[7] After much sweat and toil we were able to make the roadways

---

soldiers. See Vejas Gabriel Liulevicius, *War Land on the Eastern Front* (New York: Cambridge University Press, 2000), 33, 95.

4. Literally "German Order of Knights," more commonly "Teutonic Knights" in English, this order was established as part of the Crusades in the twelfth century. In addition to action in the Middle East, they took part in the conquest of the Baltic region, under pagan control at the time.

5. As contemporary German readers would have known, Kurland became part of Latvia upon Latvian independence in 1920.

6. Friedrich Schiller (1759–1805) wrote a trilogy of plays centering on the career of Albrecht von Wallenstein, a Hapsburg general during the Thirty Years War (1618–1648.)

7. A fascine is a rough bundle of brush or other material, in this case laid down to aid the passage of vehicles over marshy terrain. The roads in Russian territory were notoriously bad. This was actually an intentional Russian defense strategy, which backfired since it hampered their own movements as well.

a lot better in that they had been almost impassable for the heavy artillery. We had to establish reserve positions as well.

If only the area had not been so devoid of lumber. Every tree trunk had to be carried in from far away. The comrades who had it easiest were the ones who were sent out to obtain provisions. When they came back with their bounty they were greeted warmly with "Hallo" and then were evaluated on the quality of their provisions. For the most part this evaluation was positive, as most of the villages that they went to had not been completely plundered and there were still items to be gotten. The ones you really had to feel sorry for were the poor peasants who had to sacrifice what little they still had. They weren't exactly living the high life, and now we were taking the last little bit of what they had. Although I did eat of the goose and the pig that were laid in front of me (and it did taste good), I never went back to seek out those provisions. I remember one time how we went back to look for these provisions, having done it just one time, and remember how the family cried and pleaded that we were taking their cow, which was the very last animal still remaining.

Officially, orders from the high command forbade seeking provisions in this fashion, but at the front no one really paid any attention to that. Even the officers closed their eyes to this practice because they received the best parts of the meat and their tastes were even more refined than ours. Eventually this highway robbery—because that's exactly what it was—got completely out of hand. Every gun always had at least half a pig, several geese, and chickens hanging next to its dugout, and only the most desirable parts of those had been eaten. The rest was simply tossed away. It was a sin and a scandal, but everyone was happy to take part in this type of misconduct for as long as they possibly could. Never during the rest of the war would we ever see something like this again on the front.

The farmers were extremely frustrated with these practices and only wanted to supply us if we had vouchers to present to them, because they had discovered that they were only required to give up these provisions if they were presented with a stamped document or paid immediately. And even then, they also needed a receipt that the items had been delivered to the army. But since we couldn't obtain these documents, we needed to make our own forgeries, and it worked extremely well. You only took a three- or five-mark piece, with your own breath dampened the back that had the eagle, and then stamped it on a piece of paper and wrote a few words beneath the stamp, but it was nothing like a voucher. Then we took off with the swindled animal. If the farmers later traveled over to the command center to get reimbursed, they ultimately discovered they were holding nothing but a worthless piece of paper. It was a pity for them and for us an extremely lucky break that the inhabitants could not speak German. It was very funny what I once saw on one of those vouchers: "In exchange for this paper I am buying a pig: this paper is now yours and your pig is now mine." That's how we lived in Kurland.

For me one of the most unforgettable experiences was the celebration of Easter, the biggest and most holy celebration of the Russian [Orthodox] church. On this day one exchanges brotherly kisses and forgives all enemies. The evening before, a member of the Parliament had begged for a twenty-four-hour reprieve of all fighting. And this was granted. As soon as the sun rose, we all ran off with our binoculars to see what the Russians had in store for themselves. We saw all their trenches were bedecked with greenery, and all the men were wearing fur caps made of bear pelts. They stood there and waved in our direction with white cloths. Eventually, they became even more trusting. In very small groups they came almost directly in front of our line, brought us vodka, and wanted to have cigarettes in exchange, for it must have been hard to get them. We gave them cigarettes whether or not they had liquor, and they retreated very satisfied. Of course, they were more than prepared to kill us all the next day. In some instances, a few German soldiers wandered over to the Russians. Luckily almost all of them managed to return safely. However, one officer must have been captured because he never returned. So the good-natured and trusting German behaviors were put to the test and not rewarded, and perhaps that was the reason that in the later years of the war contact with the enemy was strictly forbidden.[8]

And thus the time moved slowly and monotonously forward. Then we were awakened from the daily tedium and indifference we felt. All of a sudden there was movement on the Russian line. A new commander had replaced the old one. Now he had to prove what he could do. In order to break through our line, he kept shelling us to

8. This is reminiscent of the famous "Christmas Truce" of 1914 on the Western Front. Similar but lesser-reported episodes did occur on the Eastern Front.

find our weakest position, so we had no rest. There wasn't even one night when we didn't have an alarm. We felt that the laziness was now behind us, and fighting had begun in earnest. So that we would also fight back and show our might, we decided to move forward over the Dubysa. Even our division took part in this. After we spent many hours shelling the enemies' position, our infantry, under the protection of fire, moved forward. They crawled down the steep embankment into the river and waded across, neck-high in water, and climbed up the other side. They were able to directly engage the enemy in fighting and pushed him back.

As the Muscovites wanted to launch a counterattack, our battery leader got an order to bring two guns over the river. It was probably only an order to attempt this, because how could two heavy guns be pushed down the embankment and through the river and up the other embankment again? It was already almost to the breaking point for one man to cross with his weight alone. But even so, we achieved the unbelievable. It took every man we had and heavy ropes to pull the artillery over the river. We let the gun carriages down first, pushed them through the water, and maneuvered them back up. In two hours, we had completed the task. Even before the guns could be positioned and dug in, the enemy had discovered us. Numerous shrapnel shells exploded only ten meters from us, so that we had to throw ourselves on the ground for cover. When we were able to stand up again, we heard two men who had been hit calling for help. Luckily, the enemy artillery fire was a little further away from us at this point. We were happy, because now our show-offs had more work to do; they had gotten rather loudmouthed of late, our task masters.[9] Even our own Wachtmeister Wendt, who hated all those who had finished their education and gotten a diploma, so full of his own importance, with his bulging fat belly, especially for him, such a little lesson might be helpful.[10] When we envisioned his frightened face it made us all laugh for a change.

9. Literally "Herrenfahrer," or "gentlemen drivers." Obviously tongue-in-cheek here, it was a term used for race car drivers at the time. In the twenties, it began to be used as a term for rich self-financed drivers, often of the self-indulgent and not necessarily overly skilled variety. The facetious meaning is clear but does not translate well.

10. Wachtmeister is an equivalent rank to sergeant major.

But the conquered battleground brought forth a horrible scene. For the first time, by the dozens, I saw the Russians entangled in their own barbed wire, a vision I will never forget. The counterattack that we had anticipated never materialized. The firing died down evermore, and on this day no one tried to push us back. This was the final major battle for us in this area.

Shortly before Whitsuntide we heard that we had become reserve army, and our barracks were to be staged far behind the front lines.[11] So we quickly packed our few belongings, hitched our artillery to the horses, and merrily bid our farewells to the front. We were glad that we had the fine fortune to be leaving this place so that we could enjoy the beautiful holiday without worrying about whether or not you would have to bid your own goodbyes to this life. Everyone started making plans for the future. Now we plotted on how we might obtain a few kegs of beer. Under blooming lilac trees, we wanted to celebrate and wanted to drink as never before. This was now our greatest wish. After a very strenuous day of marching, we neared a farm estate and we met up with other divisions.

When we awoke the next morning, we were greeted with some news: we formed into our batteries, and then the commander explained to us that each of us had to give up two guns, including all personnel associated with each, and that these guns needed to go back to Germany and be reassigned to a new unit. It looked like a total reorganization of our artillery, as previously each had consisted of six guns and now would consist of only four. Through this change, the units would be more mobile. I liked that idea. I was part of the groups that were assigned to return back home. I was certainly not unhappy over this, only the shared experiences of the last months had brought me closer to my comrades. Still, they weren't really enduring friendships but brought about by circumstances and necessity.

By noon we were already on our way, guided by young lieutenants, in order to reach the German border by foot. We had to sacrifice the Easter celebration, but in exchange we got to see our Fatherland. That was a much better deal. As we passed a village we found out from some of those stationed there that now Italy had joined in the war effort against us.[12] This news made little impact on us, because

11. Whitsuntide is also known as Pentecost; May 23 in 1915.
12. Italy declared war on Austria-Hungary on May 23, 1915.

even if we had more enemies, it didn't really matter. All of Europe was against us now anyway. Suddenly, we realized that maybe we were going home to new regiments only to be fighting against the Italians. This theory took hold of us, and we firmly believed that we were now going to Italy. We were happy that everyone was jealous of this. Yes, Italy! This was a word that brought forth the envy of others. With these types of cowards, a war could actually turn into a pleasure. And if you could see eternal Rome at the same time, that would be a bonus.

Behind Tauroggen, which now stood in ruins, we crossed the border, stopped at Lauxargen, and boarded the train. On the very same evening, we arrived at Elbing. At certain train stations, for example in Königsberg, people gave us cigarettes to welcome us back. However, food and delicacies were not in sight as they had been in previous times, and it already looked as though shortages were in effect. After war had been declared by Italy, many guessed that other countries would soon join in; at any rate that was the opinion of the concerned civilians we met along the way. We tried to calm them, because Italy was not to be taken seriously, and we pointed out that it would be easy to ward off an attack because of the great defenses found in the Austrian Alps. We acted as though we were part of the general's staff even though we knew nothing. But because we were now soldiers and it was a question of military strategy, we had to voice our professional opinion.

Early the next morning the train arrived at its destination. It was the staging area of the troops, Warthelagen, and very close to Posen.[13]

13. Then part of Germany, now Poznań is in west central Poland.

4

Kowno-Wilna-Duenaburg

For almost two weeks we stayed in wooden barracks that had only recently been constructed. It was a time of heavy work. The field guns and other vehicles needed to be repainted and taken apart. Every screw was carefully inspected to see if it had been worn. The axles were greased and the aiming scopes were newly calibrated. Then we moved on to mending our uniforms. In the first days we were subjected to a delousing so that our traveling companions would be eliminated. Now we could stop squeezing these lovely little beasts and going on a search and destroy mission before going to bed. So, in that way we didn't have as much to do. In the meantime, the other reserve regiments had also arrived in camp. The majority of them came from Hamburg or from the general vicinity.

The new regiment was ready, and Commander Major von Hamm could observe the individual batteries during their training. This is when we got a little introduction to what he would be like. Nothing was good enough; on each and every point he had something or other to criticize. It appeared he thought of us as peacetime soldiers who were simply going off to march in the Kaiser's Parade, and he apparently forgot that we had already endured eleven months of war on the front and that this experience had left its marks. Our new shoulder straps bore the number 223, a number that was so high that the older peacetime regiments didn't think much of us.[1] But even so, we continued to work as an active regiment and didn't have to use the dreaded word "reservists" when asked what our rank was. Not to let this good opportunity pass, I wrote to my parents that I would come and visit next Sunday because who knew how long I would still

1. Since units were often numbered sequentially as they were formed, this would give the impression that this was a unit of new recruits.

be here. Promptly, my wishes were fulfilled. After a few thankful hours of reconciliation, we needed to bid our farewells far too soon. It was lucky that this visit was still conducted in the last moments of our stay, as we received our marching orders for the next Monday. A great anticipation fell over us. Our Second Battery was the first deployed and showed the way for all the rest of us. Where would we end up? In Italy? But no, the train took an easterly direction. That was a real disappointment, but it was better than going toward the west.

With mixed feelings we saw how the crops were being harvested by French and Russian prisoners of war.[2] We only saw old men, women, and children. It appeared as though anyone capable of carrying a gun had already been recruited. We became reflective. As we reached Thorn, we continued toward Kowno near where we knew that our troops had been stationed for the past five months.[3] In Marianopol our trip was ended.[4] We departed the train and waited for the other formations to arrive and marched for the next two days a total of eighty kilometers by foot.

Then we had a day of rest and used it for an impromptu church service. On a meadow in the middle of a leafy forest, an altar had been erected. It consisted of a margarine crate over which a tent cover had been laid. To the left and to the right, cannon carriages had been placed, and around all this, green trees had been positioned. The whole picture was so unique and tasteful. As everything was finally completed, we all assembled in a large square in front of it, and the sermon began. After singing the first hymn, a volunteer non-commissioned officer named Hoff stood behind the altar and began the sermon. We were astounded by his theological expertise

2. While all the nations in the conflict utilized POWs for agriculture to a certain degree, Germany quickly became notorious for the extent to which they were willing to exploit involuntary labor. See Heather Jones, *Violence against Prisoners of War in the First World War: Britain, France and Germany, 1914–1920* (New York: Cambridge University Press, 2011).

3. Kovno to the Russians and now Kaunas in Lithuania. As events were heating up on the Western Front, the Germans had shifted troops from the Eastern Front, necessitating a drawdown in activity in the east, their major goals there having been accomplished. The push in which Schiller will now take part was one of the few large-scale offensives in the east after this.

4. Or Miriampol, now Marijampolė in southern Lithuania, southeast of Kowno.

and knowledge and the entire way his sermon was conducted, and we could not believe how he had so much understanding of a subject that he only attempted to preach about for the first time. We all thought he was a born pastor. We had no idea that he actually had been a pastor for the last ten years in the province of Mecklenburg. He didn't talk fire and brimstone, but he spoke plainly, as it should be for our audience. He spoke of those things that moved us, and he was well versed because he had also been at the front from the beginning. For this reason, we enjoyed listening to him. When he finished, we sang another hymn, and then the service was concluded. It was the only time we had a field church service that I participated in, and it always remained as a good memory.

The next evening, we were already positioned. This time we were in the most imposing forest that anyone could ever imagine. Everything here was so primeval and untouched by man, as though no one had ever entered there. We felt as though we were committing a great sin by felling trees in order for us to be able to have a visible field of fire. To our great joy, we heard that we would probably be encamped here for several weeks. With the help of giant trunks, to pass the time we built log cabins for us to live in, and each and every one was mightier and more beautiful than the other. We were very proud of the magnificent dwellings, but as soon as the first ones had been completed and occupied, we discovered that it was so hot in there so that no one could endure it. In addition, the houses were a gathering place for all manner of vermin. Then we complained about all the unnecessary work, left the rest unfinished, and crawled back under our tents.

Here it was still the best, as it was now midsummer and the sun was burning hot. A bit in front of us and half covered, the Jessia flowed and formed the border between the German and Russian troops. The enemy had it good because they were stationed in concrete trenches that were fortified against artillery that they could safely retreat to. They were positioned on the top of a hill and could overlook the entire vicinity. Our infantry in comparison had to burrow in on flat land and were visible to the Russians, so during the daylight hours could hardly move. Impatiently they waited for the signal to attack.

Our opportunities for fighting were diminished, as were those of the entire unit, because the enemy needed to be kept in the dark about our numbers and positions. The beginning of August [1915] things started to liven up. The reserve troops were guided to the front during the night; we could hear how very carefully several batteries nearby embedded themselves, and suddenly we were delivered an enormous amount of ammunition, the struts for the cannons were moved closer, and the general in charge, Litzmann, walked up and down and inspected our work. That was a certain sign that we were preparing for battle. Even the Russians seemed to sense the same, because suddenly their guns woke up and started firing at us. Now indeed our log cabins were good enough, if only as protection. Only one gunner was hit. He had sustained shrapnel in his shin. His leg was subsequently amputated all the way to the knee. After the end of the war, as we moved into Hamburg, he came to visit us on crutches.

Earlier than we even thought, decisions were made. On the sixteenth of August, we received the news that Hindenburg had started his huge offensive campaign; on the seventeenth of August, we received the news of the storming of Iwangorods; on the eighteenth the stronghold of Nowo-Georgiewsk fell; a few days later even Warsaw.[5] This news spread just like a wildfire, and it awakened our jubilation and fighting spirit. We didn't want to hold back the momentum.

Finally, on the twenty-first of August, the dance began. From three sides at once Kowno was attacked. Unfortunately, we were not able to see of any of this fighting. We could only continue firing upon the numerous targets ourselves, using our caringly stored ammunition. We continued firing without interruption until midday. One of the enemies' batteries tried to silence us. Their shells exploded not even one hundred meters in front of us. It was almost comical that they continued to fire exactly at the same spot relentlessly. In this fashion we escaped with just one wounded telephone lineman, who was injured when a tree trunk fell upon him during his repair work. In the meantime, the trapped bear still fought with frustration that one wouldn't have thought him capable of. In a wide semicircle the larger guns roared; the lighter calibers kept the battlefield under fire, and the constantly firing machine guns made every attempt to push further impossible.[6]

5. Iwangorods is now in Estonia. The fortress of Nowo-Georgiewsk (also Novogeorgievsk) was situated at a confluence of the Narva and Vistula Rivers and considered by the Russians and Germans as being critical to the defense or conquest of Russian Poland.

6. "Larger guns" here is literally "Schiffskanonen," or "ship's guns." Highly unlikely that there was any marine engagement intended.

Around midday, the order arrived to take the Jessia position. As the first members of the infantry left their trenches and tried to climb over the embankment, they were quickly swept away. The second and third waves of infantry suffered the same fate. Now we only had our reservists left. It would have been pure madness to sacrifice them unnecessarily before the enemy could at least be driven back. Then we received help from another side. In the north, Prussians and Bavarians had dispersed the enemy and had moved forward and taken two emplacements into their possession. Through this occurrence, we were able to enter the enemy's inner circle, and with that the day was ours. Kowno was not to be held. The commanding general was absolutely sure of this. Further resistance could only lead to having them be completely surrounded. We then received orders to depart our positions and head toward the east.

The repercussions of this order were soon felt by our units. The battery commander saw from his observation tower how many of the enemy had left their trenches, while the remaining continued firing relentlessly in order to make up for their reduction in strength. Now the division ordered the attack again. The reserves needed to come forth; the artillery had to take over protective fire by rapid fire without regard to bulging and bursting barrels. The next half hour was a record in the use of ammunition. Nearly eight hundred shells and shrapnel shells, whatever we could reach, we shot out of our guns. Every second we expected that one of our guns would explode. But they held together. Krupp had done a good job; excellent, in fact, considering that three hours afterward the barrels were still too hot to handle. As the order to stop arrived, the Jessia had been taken. It was a serious battle, man against man, and before it was all over, every embedded soldier and every trench had to be conquered single-handedly. Very slowly now, the Russians retreated. Very quietly and assuredly we marched forward. Now we received the order to follow. Using major detours, since the forest was impassible, we slowly neared the actual battleground, but the dusk camouflaged the slaughter that had recently occurred. We marched throughout the night.

The next morning the Russians tried one last time. They put all their resources together and mustered into a triangle: a last stand counterattack. The tip of their triangle was aimed directly at us. We hid behind a hedge of trees and positioned our guns. Even before we had aimed our guns we were overcome with fire. Two horses were hit and fell simultaneously. Here we were visible to the enemy. In time our commanding officer came galloping toward us and ordered us to move our guns two hundred meters forward. That was easier said than done, because the trees were as high as a man and needed to be cut first so we could safely drive over them without damaging our sighting equipment. The enemy must have had someone sitting up high in a tree because with every step we took forward we were immediately fired upon. His shells and their explosions accompanied us, as though they couldn't shake us.

This is where Lieutenant von Stempel fell with a shard in the forehead and was dead immediately. This is also where the commander of the Third Artillery, Officer Zinnon, fell with a stomach wound. The orderly who rushed to his aid received a shrapnel wound in his arm; the unit to the right lost a soldier and another was wounded. When we finally achieved our goal, we had not accomplished anything, as we now were even more surrounded and under fire. Just as soon as we started shooting, I received a direct hit to the head and fell over the tail of the gun carriage. At first I thought: "Now you have lost your head!" But that couldn't be or I wouldn't have been able to process this thought. But for sure I had sustained a hole in my head. I gripped my hand to my head and saw that there was no blood. So, therefore I could not be wounded. But something had to have happened to me! Then I discovered my helmet a few steps in front of me over to the side where during my fall it had landed. The ball on the top of my helmet had been blown off and disappeared somewhere, perhaps between the trees.[7] I had no desire to look around and find it as a souvenir. If the shrapnel piece had only been three centimeters lower I would have died a hero's death. Quite suddenly the enemy stopped shooting, probably because they were forced to retreat.

Captain O'Grady came running from his observation point and told us to hitch up our guns. The enemy had been pushed back; we could continue our pursuit. He had just had news that four thousand prisoners and over seven hundred artillery pieces were the result of the fall of Kowno. Suddenly we didn't think of our fallen comrades and were jubilant over our victory. Only the captain said sadly, "Poor

7. At this time, most German soldiers wore the iconic spike on top of their leather helmets, except for artillerymen, whose helmets were adorned with a symbolic cannonball. Steel helmets would soon replace leather, for obvious reasons.

Stempel; he was the only son." But I was also an only son. This battle of Chlebischki cost our unit three dead and six wounded, and from the observation area only the captain survived intact. We had directed our fire, without knowing it, toward the church spire of Schilowsta and had demolished it completely and had also taken out the observer in the tower with it. We were proud of our leader who understood how to aim and fire perfectly.

Without any rest we continued eastward. Without pause we were on the hunt for the enemy, from hill to hill, from village to village, from river to river. Wherever he encamped we forced him to retreat. We hunted him both day and night. It was an uninterrupted pace of hunt and shoot and attack. The ten weeks that followed were the most strenuous of my entire war experience. From the twenty-fifth of August to the ninth of September we followed the Russians in the Njemen Battle and crossed the Preny River and were victorious. And in the deciding battle at Wilma from the tenth of September to the fourth of October we were also victorious.[8] We battled against the Siberian corps at Orany and won and demolished the guard at Wilija.

With sore feet and without socks, bodies completely bitten by lice, without any warm food or water, this is how we crawled forward, this is how we positioned our guns, this is how we shot, this is how we left a dead or wounded comrade behind and just went forward as though in a dream over muddy ground so we could stay on the heels of the enemy. We had no capacity for thinking. We just operated as though we were machines. We only knew that we battled and marched and then battled and marched all over again. We drove through burning villages but didn't see them, we drove over corpses and didn't give them any notice, we slept while walking and didn't even know it. Every feeling within space and time was forgotten. We didn't even know where or how long we had been firing. It didn't matter whether it was day or night, if the Russians were firing on us or not, if the sun was shining or it was pouring rain.

We thought those who fell in battle were the lucky ones because they had found their peace. We covered approximately forty to fifty kilometers a day, which made it difficult for us to obtain our supplies. Even in the burned-out villages we couldn't find any provisions. So

8. Wilma, alternately spelled Wilna in this narrative, is now Vilnius, capital of Lithuania, and officially fell into German hands on September 19, 1915.

we ate potatoes that we dug out of the fields' furrows. We ate them raw because there was no time for cooking. We ate them as we marched. We cursed at our fate. Snail-like, one company crawled after the other company. And more and more infantry fell behind; soon, those left behind would outnumber those fighting! Everywhere you looked, emaciated horses lay with four feet facing upward and broken eyes. They had starved to death. There had been no food for them in a long time. In desperation, they ate the pine needles from the trees.

The casualties grew larger and larger. It was not even possible to obtain replacements because we had lost all communication with our homeland and drifted even further away day by day as we headed eastward. Some companies only had fifteen to twenty men remaining. And some only had one officer remaining. Dysentery was raging everywhere and sometimes we would lose a few men at once. We all had some form of it because our stools were bloody and our eyes were sunken and red-rimmed. We weren't an army anymore; we were living corpses.

The newspapers, however, painted a different picture, of an army that was enthusiastically conquering the east and was unstoppable. This is what we later read. As one of our sergeants said: "I never knew I was a hero until I read it in the paper." And everyone laughed when he said this because at the time he was known to be very timid and anxious. Could the commanding officers have been so blind as to not have known what was going on with us and continued to push us forward weeks and months? Even two- or three-days' rest would have restored us to a reasonably functioning troop. Suddenly an order from the command staff was read to us. It began with the words "Unbelievably great is our mission, but the sacrifices to achieve this are also unbelievably great. If you can endure then you have helped your Fatherland achieve the ultimate victory." We understood this and wanted to clench our teeth for the sake of the Fatherland. But on the other hand, we were just human beings. Even with our very best intentions, our bodies were at the breaking point, and there are certain physical limits you cannot overcome. And these limits had been reached.

Very early, winter had appeared. Already at the beginning of October, we experienced frosty nights. We had no shelter, and we had no warm food. The only thing we did have were munitions and that was the only thing that was delivered. We shivered deep in our bones. Almost everyone who had to endure this suffering became a sick man. We had no interest in knowing how the war was progressing.

We didn't even know what was happening with us. We only had one wish, that we could just have one day off. That we could just for once prepare a warm meal, but this wish was never fulfilled.

During this time, I became a messenger rider. At least I didn't have to proceed by foot; now I had a horse between my legs. But what a horse! It was a horse that had been found locally, a small and starving creature that the Russians had undoubtedly left behind because it was too weak. It could barely walk and appeared as though it would collapse as soon as I got on it. And with the horse's assistance I had a job to do that was almost more difficult than my prior one. I had to deliver orders between batteries and the command staff, a task that would be difficult enough in any event, but now in Russia, in unknown areas where there were no distinct paths, it was nearly impossible. The previous non-commissioned officer had been relieved because he couldn't understand how to do this job. That couldn't happen to me. I pulled myself together with all the resources I still had remaining.

In the dark of the night we stopped and found the gunners in half sleep, positioned by their guns. I still needed to ride to the officers' quarters in order to bring back the orders for the next day. But where were the quarters? If at least I had even known the name of the place where the quarters were supposed to be. But even that was unknown. Usually it was said: "The headquarters might be here or might be there. You need to ride about and look for it. You will be sure to find it if you travel westward." That was it. And with this orientation I was sent out in the dark of night without a map and without any further directions. If by chance I encountered bivouac camps and asked them if they had seen an artillery headquarters, the answer was almost always no.

The ones that knew more than anyone were the cavalry. During daylight hours they had already assessed the roads and paths and therefore at least knew where to travel. Often I could attach myself to patrols that were heading in the same direction. Sometimes I could find my way by aiming toward a burning farmhouse. These, however, were occasions of pure luck. Usually I spent hours searching, and when I finally found something like a town then I discovered the quarters somewhere very far away. Oftentimes I returned back to my battery the next morning and found they had already been marching for hours. Then I delivered the orders and laid my arms over my saddle and slept sitting on my horse until we started moving again. It was very frustrating.

But I couldn't give up because I saw the fruits of our efforts on a daily basis. Didn't we manage to throw the enemy back by over eight hundred kilometers? Didn't we destroy his biggest and most fortified positions and therefore rob him of his strongholds and bunkers? Didn't we destroy thousands of artillery units and capture hundreds of thousands of prisoners? Weren't his most important and strategic cities and train junctions destroyed—Warsaw, Wilna, Iwangorod—and had fallen into our hands? The only reason they weren't completely destroyed was because without interruption, fresh troops arrived that had not yet been in the war and therefore were able to throw themselves with new vigor at us. But what use was it! Even they were demolished as soon as they showed themselves.

Now finally, it was November first, and suddenly our forward march was halted. We had marched just fifteen kilometers short of Duenaburg and believed already that even this fortress would fall after a short battle.[9] But here the Russians had assembled every bit of manpower they possessed; here they had had ten weeks while we were marching to get prepared for our assault by installing Japanese-style fortifications; here they assembled their elite guards, and from this position they wanted to deliver a death nail to the Germans; and from this position, with this enormous mass of troops and supplies, the counterattack against them needed to be successful.[10]

Even so, the infantry threw themselves with all their remaining strength on the concrete bunkers with the machine guns, on the extensive barbed wire installations, on the flamethrowers, on the minefields.[11] But even with their best efforts in the first stages of battle, with soldiers that were dead tired and exhausted, they could not withstand the enemy's fire and did not get far. Whatever was still living dug in deeply, and there weren't many left. And yet we were able to withstand the enemy's constant firing. These companies with only fifteen or twenty men, led by a sergeant, let themselves be torn apart

9. Currently Duagavpils, in southeastern Latvia.

10. Schiller here uses the term "japanische Festungsgeschütze." It's unclear whether he would have used this term during the war versus the 1928 writing. From context and Schiller's next comments, this almost certainly means that the Russians dug in with well-defended trench and tunnel systems, a common Japanese tactic in conflicts leading up to the Great War, primarily the Russo-Japanese War in 1904 to 1905. Since such systems were also common on the Western Front in Europe, however, it is curious why Schiller would refer to it in this way.

11. "Minenstände," translated here as "minefields."

and died, but they wouldn't retreat. They held their ground that they had marched to beforehand. I was embedded with Corporal Bollmann, a telephone operator, in one of the front trenches. What we were doing here was unclear because we had no real communication with our superiors. The telephone line was shot at and destroyed at least ten times an hour. Even so, we had to stay put because retreating was impossible. All one could see was smoke and haze, exploding shells and fragments. You lay next to the dead and the dying, who pleaded for water. You were covered in dirt and constantly had to dig back out. You had but a simple infantry rifle and shot with it but you never aimed at anything in particular. Wave after wave of Russia's main assault came toward us. The crater in front of us was only one living mass that continued to surge toward us in order to completely annihilate us. We engaged in these twenty-four-hour waltzes that left the enemy standing in its same position and even pushing back a little. The burning village of Grangtal at our backs at least let us know where to aim during the night.

For ten days, without any pause, the enemy attacked us and then they stopped because their fallen comrades formed into a wall in front of us that was much too high to walk over. In six-deep stacked rows, the dead lay in front of us and in the dark looked like a giant wall. For ten days we had not had any orders because in this situation we could not have comprehended anything anyway. For ten days our fallen comrades served as protection for us. For ten days we only loaded our weapons and shot and knew that we would die here. But then the giant might of the Russian bear was extinguished. His pointless attacks were stopped. Only the guns still played their old song and we woke as from a nightmare. For every five of our men, only one survived. And the very air we breathed was contaminated with the stench of rotting corpses. From Hindenburg and Litzmann we received telegrams that the commander distributed to us, thanking us for our heroic service; he got the Pour le Mérite and said that he received this medal of honor through us and he wore it for all of us.[12] Four fresh enemy divisions were destroyed with only one

12. The Pour le Mérite, established in 1740 by King Frederick II of Prussia, was awarded for high personal achievement in both military and civilian life. Called the Knight's Cross by the older services, it was famously known among World War I aviators as the "Blue Max."

hundred men on our side! It was such a pity that our dead were not able to hear of this great honor.

As soon as things calmed down a bit, we started building shelters. My battery was assigned to camp in a very nice little area in a birch forest by the village Pokapine. The very few houses of this village were stripped down to their foundations, and this bounty of lumber then became our walls and ceilings. They were pitiful and damp dwellings built into loam trenches. We were proud of them nonetheless and at this point they seemed like castles to us. We were supposed to encamp here for a longer time, we were told. The drive into the east had ended. We were very happy. At last we had found some rest.

It didn't last long before I was ordered to ride to the headquarters. This would be the first time that I was not on the front line. The headquarters were stationed in a larger farm estate named Lipnischki. It was about four kilometers from the front line. The officers' quarters and military offices were located in the main farmhouse. The rest of us lived in the servants' quarters. The only furnishings we had at first were an old table and a few stools. About twenty men had to squeeze into three small rooms whose windows had been smashed. Most of the doors were missing or were hanging by a thread. The smoke came out of the half-fallen-apart chimney and burned our eyes and made breathing difficult. It transformed the room into a black cloud of smoke, yet one still felt heavenly to be able to sit upright and not get wet if it happened to be raining. It was hard to imagine that we could live like this again.

My work life primarily consisted of distributing the regiment and battalion orders that usually arrived around eight p.m. to the elegant quarters of the battery. They were located in the free zone about twelve kilometers from headquarters. My night rest was disturbed because I only arrived at the sergeant's at about ten p.m. and had to wait until the orders were written and then only could I ride back; therefore I was never back at my quarters until before two a.m. But I enjoyed this and took it all in stride because I liked the routine of the job. The only unpleasant part of this was that it was so incredibly cold in this winter 1915/16 where temperatures could be negative thirty degrees.[13] Nothing helped in this cold; not ear muffs, stomach

13. We are following earlier assumption that he was using Fahrenheit. If Celsius, -30 Celsius would be -22 Fahrenheit. Either would be possible in this case.

warmers, nor double socks or gloves. You could feel the icy cold through the stirrups through your soles even though we had wrapped them in straw. When I traversed through the silent and lonely night that was deeply covered in snow and hardly recognizable, I always wished I would get back in one piece.

During one of these nightly rides, I had an uncanny encounter; on this night the issuance of orders took such a long time that I wasn't able to depart until almost midnight. It was especially cold. The icy air hit me as I left the protective courtyards of Lipnischki. The old nag that had been assigned to me snorted loudly with every breath and almost sank to its stomach in the deep snow. With foreboding, I thought of the three or four hours it would take me to reach my destination. And every so often a huge snow drift would hit me across the cold frozen fields. At least I was lucky that there was a full moon that guided me on my way. If I could have laid the reins over the withers of the horse and put my hands in my coat pockets and lit a pipe because it would have been easier to endure. But all of a sudden, the poor creature sunk to its knees and could not get up again. It took a long time before I got the horse to get back up, but it was impossible to ride it at this point. So I had to pull the horse very slowly behind me because I was not allowed to leave it, nor would I have left this wretched animal there. However, it was a strenuous activity that resulted in the sweat pouring out of me. At least it put the danger of my freezing to death as a clump of ice to rest. Also an advantage!

At last in front of me I saw the straw roofs of a village through which I had to pass. This is where a heavy artillery unit was embedded. In a fruit orchard they had stationed their guns. A guard was not to be seen this evening; the commander had probably told him to come inside because of the extraordinary cold. There was not a light to be seen either in the five or six buildings in the courtyard. It appeared everyone was sleeping soundly. With envy I thought of the comrades that were sleeping so soundly because I had barely covered half the distance and probably wouldn't get any sleep this particular night.

I was nearly through the village when a figure in a sheepskin coat with a machine gun materialized out of a doorway and called out: "Stop, who is there?" It was the guard. I announced myself, told him the daily code word, and stopped. A very old soldier came out of the shadows and asked why I was dragging a horse behind me instead of riding it. I explained the situation. He proposed that I come into his quarters for an hour to refresh myself. In the meantime, the horse could have a bit of hay and hopefully get his strength back. Then I could continue riding and would reach my sergeant earlier than anticipated.

I approved of this suggestion. Because the guard had just been relieved of his duties and it was exactly one a.m., he took me to his room, prepared boiling water, and poured rum into a glass. Five minutes later I drank the most delicious grog of my life—at least it appeared to be such at that time. Newly charged, I continued on my way after one hour. The thermometer showed it was negative twenty-eight degrees. Two sorry hours were still ahead of me. To my relief, my horse was back on his feet. He had eaten every bit of hay in the trough. With thanks for the friendly interlude, I saddled back up and rode into the night and the frost.

I had traversed about two or three kilometers and was near the edge of a forest when I saw an animal that was crouching quietly but then started running toward me. At about ten meters it stopped and looked at me and my horse. It was a dog. How in the world did it find itself in the middle of the night outside? With this cold, every animal should find shelter and stay there. My horse pricked its ears and became anxious and started to gallop off. I couldn't understand why it was so nervous. The dog, which seemed rather large, decided to follow us and stayed just behind us. This continued for a number of minutes. Then I stopped and tried to entice the dog to come closer. However, it didn't come any closer but circled us instead. The dog seemed a bit shy. I suddenly felt very sorry for this poor creature, especially because I had seen how completely starved the dog was. When I realized that my entreaties had no success, I rode further on. However, my horse was having none of this; it was as though newly electrified and proceeded at a fast clip that was astonishing to me. After a very long time I turned around in my saddle and to my surprise realized that the dog was still following me at about ten to fifteen meters' distance. Not until I saw the first houses of another village did he hang back all the way and then disappear.

I delivered the orders and was told not to return to headquarters until the following morning. I was supposed to rest until then. I was so overly tired that no one could even wake me until about midday. Very quickly I saddled my horse and started riding back. When I reached the area of the forest where I had first spied the dog, I saw the snow was dug up and mixed with blood. I started thinking very hard about what this could have been but found no real answers.

In the village in which the troops were embedded, there was a lot of excitement. I found out that this very morning, right before sunrise, a lance corporal who always collected the mail was attacked by a wolf and seriously injured. The beast had suddenly and without warning bit him in the back and arm and thrown him to the ground. Only with a great effort was he able to reach his sidearm and stab the wolf in the ribs and stomach so that it soon died. Then he lost consciousness. About an hour later he was found nearly frozen and brought back. Just now the doctor had been with him again. It was a touch and go situation. I was soon ready to depart after my curiosity had been satisfied. Then I started thinking about the encounter I had with the dog the previous evening. I thought about the fact the attack had happened at the exact same spot where I first saw the creature. I also thought about the nervousness of the horse and that it was well known that horses could sense wolves.

I asked everyone if the creature had been brought back here. Yes, it was lying by the munitions wagons. I walked over there. As I stood before this dead beast I was suddenly gripped with the realization that for certain he was the supposed dog from last night. I remembered a distinct star on the forehead that I had noticed upon my encounter and proved that this was one and the same. It was definitely a fine example of a wolf, except that it had been quite starved, an officer who had suddenly approached explained to me. I told him that I had the distinct pleasure, a few hours before the attack, of meeting this beast myself. Soon I was surrounded and had to explain the entire sequence of events in detail. I acted as if I had had an earth-shattering experience. It was the only time that I ever encountered a wolf in his natural environment in Russia. Usually they avoided any sounds of artillery near the front and retreated. The military newsletter was quite occupied with this story and came to the conclusion that this wolf had separated himself from his pack and struck out on his own. In his starved condition he had made one last desperate attempt to attack something living and nourish himself from it. In a few nearby villages, the same story was repeated as well.

The attacked lance corporal did manage to survive his injuries, fully recovered and because of the incident was able to enjoy an extra-long holiday. However, from that day on, he never again ventured out to collect the mail. This business he left to others. He also received the nickname "Wolf Killer."

Soon in our newly organized unit, we received a regimented

schedule of duties. We allowed ourselves to accept this because through this our boredom ceased. From now on at five forty-five a.m. the non-commissioned officer punctually said, "Get up and feed [the horses]." After that was finished, we got fully dressed and had breakfast. Then we had two hours in which we groomed and cleaned the stalls. After that was completed, we started in on the saddles and tack. Then we had to split logs because there was no coal delivery. It didn't matter because in this area there was enough forest. By then it was already noon. We always had peas, white beans, and rice, and everything was cooked in one pot. On Sundays, however, we were served goulash. We almost killed each other for the leftovers in the pot. In the afternoons the work continued. That's when we built chairs and bedframes, built troughs, and then refurbished the ovens, doors, and windows of our accommodations. We built a real floor over the lime, painted the walls and frames, ripped off the old straw roof and built a new one. We also constructed fences made from birch trees and built arbors, latrines, and deep trenches to protect us from artillery.

For months we continued in this fashion. The only time our schedule was free was Sundays. However, we did accomplish something. A few months after we moved into Lipnischki, it looked so good that you could not recognize it from its original dilapidation. It had become a jewel that needed to be admired. The simple mansion had transformed itself into a palace and all of that was wrought with the most primitive materials and from people who had never done this kind of work. It was astonishing how inventive and practical humans could be if they were put into difficult situations.

But after we finished all the rebuilding, that wasn't the end of it yet. As soon as we completed the renovations we started in on the dirt roads. Where the mud was too deep we laid fascines. Over the streams we built bridges and laid platforms. We pulled electrical wire from a power plant far away from the front lines right to us and then to the front trenches. Soon every village and headquarters was now lighted. We built a delousing station that was as large as necessary in this lice-infested region; we built mess quarters and a theater. Our commanding officers had planned an ambitious program, and much of it was executed by us. The field post was newly organized and worked punctually and quickly. In forty-eight-hours' time in our hands we held greetings that had been written in our homeland. A military newspaper was printed in Wilna and kept us abreast of the current world news. The first trains that carried those on military leave began to depart and took those comrades first who had been on the front since the beginning. Our rations had improved, as had the feed for our horses. Once in a while you could even hear a gramophone playing that had found its way to the front. Spring had begun and the region was bathed in green. One could easily have forgotten that one found himself in Russia and with the enemy, except for the firing of guns.

I will never forget, due to the uniqueness of the experience, what Christmas 1915 was like. In all of Germany, many had made more sacrifices than in the year before so that we soldiers would have some small tokens of appreciation. Therefore, suddenly around mid-December, large and small crates and packages arrived. The most came from Hamburg because that was our garrison city. A senator from Hamburg had personally escorted the shipment and turned it over to our commander. The rumor was that it took up five completely filled train cars. No wonder that we were excited about the holiday, and just like children we counted the days until we could enjoy all these luxuries. On top of everything, all of our duties would be excused except for the most crucial items.

Two huge field wagons filled to the rim with Christmas trees drove up to our facility on the twenty-third of December. Adjutant Lilie had gotten them from a distant forest, because in the nearby forest we had no pine trees. We now needed to decorate these trees for our main receiving hall. Everyone who was dispensable was summoned and worked under the direction of a sergeant who in civilian life was a decorator and was thus in charge. Many walls were soon plastered with greenery that hid all the paintings and orders that belonged to a military quarters, but that didn't fit in with a religious holiday. Even the floors were strewn with twigs and needles.

In the meantime, the strongest comrades had dragged three of the heaviest cartons, puffing and huffing, into the room. That they didn't swear was probably due to the fact that they were occupied with all the treasures contained inside that we would divide tomorrow. It was such a pity that they were all still nailed shut. Therefore we could only guess at the contents. One thought he might have smelled Schnapps, as his nose was expert in detecting that. With great speed we positioned more Christmas trees into each corner and bedecked them with white candles. At the very end we festooned a ribbon around the trees that said, "Peace on Earth," which of course was paradoxical. But no one seemed to take any note of this. Then we put a long banquet table in the middle of the room and were dismissed by the lieutenant. At long last the big day had arrived. The midday meal alone was a pleasure. We had goulash with salted potatoes and in such an amount that everyone was amazed. You were allowed to go back two and even three times and did not risk being greeted and dispatched by the cook with a "glutinous carrion."[14]

The celebration and distribution of gifts was scheduled for six p.m. Long before the appointed time, all twenty-eight men stood outside the door in long lines and anxiously waited for the officers to arrive, who would enter first. We didn't have to wait that long. Everyone came: the commander, Major Jacobi, the adjutant, the aide-de-camp, the good-natured military physician Dr. Haarland, and the veterinarian with the melancholy look. Then we also entered the room, whose candles lit up the room with a bright glow, and the Christmas trees smelled fresh and earthy. The table with the presents was packed to the gills. We couldn't even determine what exactly was on that table. Around the table lay tags with our names. We stood in front of the chair with our name on it, and the "Old Man," our nickname for the commander, strode into the center and ordered that the song "Von Himmel Hoch" be sung.[15] The first verse went beautifully, but as soon as we got to the second, many did not know the words and just hummed along, making the rest of us sing even more loudly.

As the last notes were finished, the Old Man pulled the New Testament out of his pocket and read us the chapter about the birth of Christ. Afterward, we sung the song "Es Ist Ein Ros Entsprungen," and then he gave us his Christmas speech.[16] It was more or less a sermon. The room itself, with its decorations and atmosphere, appeared to look very much like a church. And we felt as though we were in church. I was overcome with a strange feeling as I saw the Old Man stand there with the book of books in his hand. To me he looked like a pastor who had accidentally been transformed into a soldier wearing a field gray uniform. The room looked wonderful, as though it had come out of a fairy tale. In the middle stood the long

14. "Verfressenes Aas."

15. "Vom Himmel hoch, da komm ich her," "From Heaven Above to Earth I Come," a nativity hymn written and probably composed by Martin Luther.

16. Commonly translated to "Lo, How a Rose E'er Blooming."

table, around it the men who had already experienced so much, sat in their old but mended uniforms, and in front the old major with the bald head and the white clipped short mustache, the oldest of us all. It was too bad that there wasn't a painter around who could have captured this picture, I thought. Besides the sputtering of the candles, the room was completely silent while the old man spoke. His speech was short, to the point, and didn't use complex words, but what he said came from the heart. A festive memory that would remain for all of us to remember into the far distant future.

He wanted us to tell our children and grandchildren of this night whenever we stood in front of a Christmas tree. Although physically we were separated from our loved ones, yes, but not in our hearts, as they were spiritually with us. Every German was thinking of their fighting men in the enemy's land, and this was proven by the presents in front of us. Then at the end he expressed all that moved us in this hour, and that was the hope that we would be back home next year. With the Niederlander Dankgebet we closed the official portion of the evening.[17] And now for most of us the main event could begin.

Everyone headed toward the presents that were spread in bountiful glory in front of us. What bounty there was to gaze at, taste or touch! Most of the comrades had never before been presented with such an abundant array of gifts. Everyone received nearly the identical presents. They had been distributed fairly. No one could be jealous or envious. Cigars, cigarettes, tobacco, pipes, wine and schnapps, chocolate and stationery, cakes and suspenders, sausages and books, pocket knives and gloves, socks, shirts, and hand and chest warmers; in short, everything one could wish or hope for was on display. The free city of Hamburg, which most of us only knew by name, had done right by its reputation and honor. We were full of praise and didn't even listen to the huffing and puffing of our cook, who had been hinting that he wanted a piano or even a grand piano or something along those lofty lines.

After we had spent enough time admiring our presents, the major explained that now he wanted to give some of us a special treat. And so he presented the Medal of the Iron Cross to one of the reservists.

17. "Dutch Prayer of Thanks." It is a melody similar to "We Gather Together to Ask the Lord's Blessing."

Everyone else was invited to a hearty shot of alcohol. "Rum and water I will provide. However, you need to bring your own chairs and glasses." We didn't need to be told twice. Very quickly we secured our presents, ran over to the barn, and gave our horses two and even three rations of hay in their troughs so that even they would experience Christmas. Then we could cozily relax. At first it was a bit awkward, but then the officers relaxed, and we drank and sang and then drank and sang some more for hours.

In the interim, some small skits were performed and jokes were told. Some of them were so funny that you laughed so hard until you cried and quickly had to down another shot to calm yourself. How was it possible that the supply didn't dwindle? We really tried hard! It was maybe the commissary officer's fault. Although he was usually an exacting individual, he operated from his heart and not his head on this holiday and was more than happy to distribute his carefully saved alcohol stash. There wasn't a drop left over, even though he privately thought there would be. We didn't recognize our major; he was so open and humorous. He toasted everyone in sight and led the party. Today nobody was offended. All the superiors were teased about some of their weaknesses and probably for the first time realized this.

A small orchestra had materialized, made up by an accordion, violin, trumpet, and drums, but the deafening music gave the doctor pause to ask them to cease because he feared he would have to treat cases of hearing problems. About two a.m. a few comrades who had already partaken of a bit too much disappeared. Some said they were merely admiring the wintry landscape, propped against trees, and were testing the depth of the snow at their feet. We actually believed that. Others followed. At four a.m. the officers departed, propped up by their valets.[18] Only the major was seen departing to his quarters as erect and stiff as ever with no assistance. We had a lot of respect for him, but as the dawn arrived, the last group of officers finally departed the festive hall. There were still men to be found under tables and benches, as you could see arms and legs sticking out. Those remaining most likely thought they were actually in their own beds. All four of us messengers stayed together the whole evening and drank

18. Valets were normally enlisted men assigned to officers to assist them with day-to-day tasks. Schiller will employ valets later in the narrative.

to our brotherhood and spoke to each other in a familiar way.[19] That is why we now helped each other to bed and then looked disdainfully at those sleeping under the tables. Did we even have the right to judge them? That was the Christmas fest of 1915 at the front in Duenaburg. It started as a solemn and serious religious celebration, and it ended in a drunken blur. The contrast was very powerful but, after all, it was war.

In the first days of March [1916] I was reassigned to the artillery unit as a gunnery captain and was assigned as a lookout in the most forward trenches with the duties of a corporal. The unit had changed dramatically since we had stayed on the river! I only discovered this now that I had come back. I only saw about one-third of the old familiar faces, even though it had only been a scant eight months. I wondered how it would look in another eight months down the line. I forced myself not to think about it.

My service was suddenly quite varied. For two days I was assigned to the gunners and supervised the work of the soldiers of the Second Artillery, then I was assigned two days as a lookout for the infantry. One hundred meters in front of us, the Russians were embedded; in between there was a large trench. I needed to acknowledge that our trenches were very well outfitted. The machine gun stations and the mortars were fortified on concrete platforms, the breastworks were further fortified by tree trunks, foxholes and tunnels were plentiful, barbed wire and wolf traps were laid up to forty meters ahead of us, and positioned in between were various listening posts and concealed entrances, including telephone lines, reserve trenches, and sappers.[20] If the enemy shot at us, they would have to release a powerful barrage lasting many hours to make an impact. I really enjoyed watching the enemy's trenches and beyond through the binoculars. As soon as I saw any supply wagons, I would raise the call to the troops to shoot in that direction and watch intently as the Muscovites fled in all directions. Once in a while one or more would fall. Then the objective had been achieved, and I allowed the firing to cease

19. Using informal German speech reserved for family, friends, and children (du) instead of formal address (Sie).

20. "Wolfsgruben," literally "wolf pits," were covered pits that enemy soldiers would fall into while advancing. In back-and-forth fighting, an enemy's trench could be converted into a trap if the occupying army needed to retreat. Wolf traps were one of the many booby traps that the Germans and others employed.

because to shoot at the wounded was not fair. The same philosophy was employed by the English. However, the French did not acknowledge this, as I discovered later on the Western Front, and neither did the Italians or the Belgians.[21]

At the same time as my return to the unit, a course for graduates was offered, and about twenty men took part in it. I had been recommended by the unit leader to attend and now had the pleasure to listen to the lectures of the most hated officer of the regiment, adjutant First Lieutenant Richter.[22] Twice weekly we received five hours of instruction in the firing range in military protocols, map reading, and map drawing; we were schooled in maneuvers and tactical operations, so that we believed we were now more qualified than any general. However, riding was the passion of the regiment officer, so I honed my equestrian skills through an intensive riding program. Here we had a former sergeant and later a sleeping car conductor as a teacher, who now had the rank lieutenant sergeant and was named "Stahlkopf."[23] That this particular Stahlkopf was himself an excellent equestrian and that he knew how to handle horses could not be argued. However, he had no idea how to teach and that was just as evident. We didn't take it too seriously, because at the end of the course the commanding officer wanted to test us. However, when the test was performed, it turned out to be a huge disappointment.

Major von Hamm was known to be moody, grouchy, unapproachable, and had a very negative attitude overall. On the testing day, he appeared to be in a particularly foul mood. Without even giving us a greeting he approached, carefully checked the saddle and tack of every horse, and made quite a few criticisms while angrily waving

21. The only major work on the "live and let live" system, which included the courtesy of letting the opposing side remove wounded and dead from no-man's land, is based exclusively on British sources. Schiller's reference to the French, Italians, and Belgians not allowing the practice opens up a potential avenue of research. See *Tony Ashworth, Trench Warfare, 1914–1918: The Live and Let Live System* (New York: Holmes & Meier, 1980).

22. What we translate as "most hated" here is "bestgehastesten," a strange construction. It may be a spin on "verhaßtesten," which would be "hated." "Most hated" does fit the context.

23. Tongue-in-cheek, but possibly his actual name, literally, was "Head of Steel."

his cane around. Then he told Major Stahlkopf in a very unfriendly fashion: "You need to get the entire company on the horses and then start parading them." Then we got the order: "Stand at attention, get ready to mount, mount, form a line to the right, trrrarab."[24] However, as we made our first circle in the open arena, a tremendous thunderstorm accosted us with such force that both the horses and riders became very skittish. "Damn it, you are hanging in the saddle as though you are a grandmother and you appear to only have ridden donkeys before. Do I need to build a fire under your ass before you can do any better?" This is how we were tested until he had gone through all of us. Everyone was equally criticized. To me he said the way I was seated was an insult to the horse.

At the end, poor Stahlkopf also received a ration of insults. He should be held accountable as to why he would dare to present his commander with such an undisciplined band of riders for his inspection. He couldn't find his answer, though, because he was so terrified he was struck dumb with shock. Lastly we were chased out of the arena with this: "You want to become officers and yet you know nothing. Go back to your units and return when you've actually learned something." We listened with stony expressions and showed absolutely no emotion. Silently we rode off, but when we had made some distance from this ghastly testing arena, then suddenly our humor broke through. The weird old man had in his anger made a funny impression on us. Maybe he would be in a better mood the next time.

Soon after this catastrophe I received my very first vacation in April. What a delight it was to be able to sleep in a real bed after fifteen months. Unfortunately, the three weeks flew by far too fast, and before I knew it I was back on the train and then back at my unit. Then things were once again less tolerable.

On the fifth of August [1916] I needed to appear in my dress uniform in front of the regiment commander, as the battery needed to induct me as a corporal. I was not looking forward to this examination because of who would be administering it. There were seven other volunteers who had taken the first examination with me as well. We made unofficial inquiries if the old man was tolerable

24. Transliteration of the actual sentence ending in German. Probably onomatopoetic, like "harrumph."

today. No, he already caused an uproar at the main office in the early morning hour.

When this news was relayed, we tried to console each other because we already knew what was in store for us. He arrived with his entourage, and we stood next to the horses as though we were made of stone. Today we started with the theory part. Already, as the first questions were posed, the swearing began that was now well known to us. I was given questions in field service regulations and then needed to explain how to work with several levels of artillery operations. That actually worked for me because I had already practiced it at least a few dozen times. With a nod of his head that one could take as positive affirmation, the strict gentleman left me and turned his attention to the next candidate. Now the riding began. At first in a trot and then a canter and then we jumped over hurdles. The lead rider was chased out of the arena and I became the lead rider. This time I had an officer's mount between my legs, a mare named Minna, who carefully listened to all of my cues and belonged to Lieutenant Schleiffen. The cursing became more pronounced, but it wasn't aimed at us. By and by, six riders were thrown out of the arena. Two of us remained, and we continued riding until we received the order to halt. "You two come here," said the major. We galloped over as though we were going to run him down. Three steps in front of him we suddenly halted. "You two have passed. I now promote you to the rank of corporal. Dismissed!" We rode away so quickly that the dirt flew out behind us. Minna received many pieces of sugar that day. And then I had my new golden braids sewn onto my uniform.

This summer too ended and eventually the leaves fell from the trees.[25] Then winter arrived. When I returned to the front in December after my second leave, the big Dryswiati Lake was frozen over.[26] But this time we were prepared for the bitter cold and had a different view of it than in the previous year. Now we had well-built shelters with heating stoves; now we had tables and benches, beds, and electrical light. After working for many months on our gun emplacement, we had constructed a giant concrete and iron block, which was the talk of everyone. It didn't hurt that our commander,

25. Romania had entered the war with the Allies in August. While there was a good deal of action in the south on the Eastern Front, the northern area where Schiller was stationed remained relatively stable.

26. Lake Drūkšiai, now in northeastern Lithuania on the border with Belarus.

First Lieutenant Menzel, had been in the government construction business. We weren't impressed with his military skills, but he knew how to build things. It was his ambition to construct the most sturdy, the most practical, and the most beautiful gun emplacement in the whole division. And he was successful. Even the commanding general, his Excellence von Heineseins, came especially just to inspect this achievement. Here in this cozy birch forest we could easily stay a little longer. Sometimes the enemy shot at us, and sometimes very close to our location and took with him a few dead and wounded who couldn't run for cover fast enough, but they didn't have it in them to do much more damage. Even though the enemy's air command knew of our exact position since we had been there for one and a half years, they still somehow never managed to drop a direct hit.

The fighting was not too extreme here. There were even days when we only shot our guns four or five times. But there were also times when we barely left our artillery positions. The Russians loved to take advantage of the dark winter nights to try to attack us and move forward. In order for us not to see them, they put on white coats so they could crawl up to our trenches in the snow. Even though we always had no-man's-land illuminated by spotlights and set off flares, it was only possible to see them when they had approached at less than ten meters. This is how well the snow coats blended into the environment. It was only through the attentiveness of the infantry that no one actually broke through. And it was only because of the barrage of firing from the artillery that no Russians ever got back alive.

During this time, something happened that would have been a sensation under any other circumstances, but here it was quickly forgotten. For me to start at the beginning, I need to go back. From my observation platform not too far away, another observation platform could be seen from the neighboring unit. One day I had a visitor from there. It was a young corporal, a volunteer like myself. He couldn't have been more than twenty years old. It was only a few days ago that he had arrived here as a replacement and for the first time had looked through the binoculars and saw the enemy's trenches. We became friends quickly. He was full of life, humor, and jokes, and he lightened the mood whenever he appeared. Because he was so open-hearted, I immediately found out about his family situation. His name was Wisotzki, the son of a widowed government official, and though his mother only had a widow's pension, she made sure that her only son went to university. Because he was interested in architecture, he went to the University of Charlottenburg two years ago, but then he left because he wanted to serve as a volunteer in the war. Now he was here. As we left each other, we agreed to meet as much as possible for a nice chat. It didn't take long before my new friend had also gained respect and admiration from his own comrades. They all loved him because he was handsome and had a fine aristocratic smile, and wherever he went he lent a sympathetic ear.

Seldom had I ever seen anyone with more tender limbs or a more delicate frame. It appeared that he was not suitable for the rough and ready life of a soldier at this unwelcoming front. And yet he was a hero. Once the Russians attacked us on a hill and wounded a member of the infantry severely in the legs so that he couldn't get up. We then saw the delicate comrade hurry up the hill. He didn't seem to appear fazed by the shells exploding about him. In a very calming way he tended to the wounds, and then he carried the heavy comrade out of the danger zone.

That he survived was an act of God. He received the Iron Cross and the compliments of the battery chief as a reward. Soon he became a sergeant major second class and was recommended to become an officer. The regiment's commander was in agreement, and not even four weeks later my friend was transferred to an artillery school for a quarter of a year in Warsaw in order to receive all the necessary training required for an artillery commander. Three other comrades of the regiment accompanied him. They were the first of our regiment because the advancement in my unit was very lengthy and slow. That was the regimental commander's fault because of his strange views and opinions.

Laughing, Wisotzki bid his farewells to me and everyone else. The whole world seemed to be at his disposal, and his very luck shone from his sparkling eyes. He knew he would do well and that it wouldn't be long before he received lieutenant's stripes. Everyone thought he deserved it, because he was so exceptional. But it wasn't meant to be!

From the very short military postcards that he sent, we discovered that a lot was asked of him. Almost every single piece of news spoke of a new achievement, and we knew he was not prone to any exaggeration. His character was so pure that we knew he would never even think of stretching the truth. The proof was also that the other three comrades supported these facts. It almost sounded as though they were jealous of him.

With a glowing record and recommendation, he returned to our regiment after he completed his courses. He brought with him the best of all grades. But there was one blemish on his record. One night he did not return on time to the barracks but instead had spent the night partying on the town with Warsaw women. Was that such a crime? He had been deployed for months on the front and only saw horror and destruction, deprivation and death, and he was young. Why should one condemn him for a few days of costly freedom? After all, far too soon he was to return to the same miserable circumstances. The officer of records had noted his absence and recorded it dutifully. Now this lapse became part of his record. Every other commander would have laughed at this and recalled his own youth. However, that was not the case with Major von Hamm.

Shortly after their return, these four officers were called to report to him. He found a few words of praise for the other three, even though they had completed their schooling as just average students. But Wisotzki was looked upon as though he was a criminal, although he was the best of all of them. It was a scandal that he dared to insult his own commander with such behavior. This act had vanquished the major's former good opinion of him. The rest would be discovered. Then my friend knew the bell had tolled for him. Hoping for a good future was no longer an option. From this hour on he did not laugh again and acquired a stern expression that didn't even fit on his delicate face and was firmly etched around his jawline. Officers and everyone else tried to cheer him up, but he remained silent and withdrawn. After that we gave up.

This is how several weeks passed. Then the news arrived from the king's cabinet that the other three comrades had been promoted to lieutenants, and on the same day an order was received that Wisotzki was no longer under consideration to become an officer. The only reaction he gave was a stony-faced nod when he received this news from the battery commander, who tried to console him as he delivered this news with a sympathetic squeeze of his hand. Silently he left.

But a few hours later, the Wisotzki we had known in earlier times broke through. We finally thought to ourselves that he had now gotten over the earlier disappointments and that he would have again returned to us as the charming little Wisotzki. On the very same afternoon one of the new lieutenants, already dressed in his new uniform, went to the daily mustering, and Wisotzki was not accounted for. In his present mood he had put on a phonograph record of *Carmen* and was playing "Off to the Battle, Toreadors."[27] Just as they were about to call him to his duties, a shot rang out inside. Everyone rushed to the room, but it was already too late. He had shot himself directly through the heart. And as we lifted him to his bed, the machine, unconcerned about all this, calmly continued to play "Off to the Battle . . ."

I had already seen many fallen soldiers upon whose faces you could see bitter need, pain, and sorrow, but such an expression of sorrow and melancholy I had never before seen as on my dead friend. We also found two farewell letters. One was addressed to the comrades of the battery. As this letter was passed from one to the other you could see tears in our eyes. What was in the letter to the regiment commander no one ever knew.

Until April 1917 we still remained in our lovely birch forest near Pokapine. Then we departed and went to Wileyka, a place near Wilna.[28] Sadly we took leave of our quarters and observation platforms, which we had constructed with unbelievable efforts and that we almost considered our home after one and a half years. None of us would ever again lay our eyes on this place that had given us so many happy but also very sad memories. That was not easy. In Wileyka we were just a reserve army. Here we found ourselves embedded in the farthest position from the front lines, which had its advantages and disadvantages. Now we wished we could be back at the front. The mighty buildings of the large insane asylum were now our headquarters. We were always hungry because the rations had been reduced. However, we were constantly engaged in training activities that were quite strenuous. It didn't make any sense that we worked so hard but were not on the front. A community gathering place for soldiers in the town that we were allowed to visit in the evenings was our only source of relaxation and recreation.

A few weeks after our arrival I received orders to go to the equipment depot in Wilna, approximately one hour by train. I was very

27. Schiller's German here is "Auf in den Kampf Torero." This particular German translation of the chorus from Bizet's French opera *Carmen* is not exact; in English, it is most often rendered simply "The Toreador Song." We have remained literal because of how Schiller ends the paragraph.

28. Now Vilyeyka in Belarus.

happy with this assignment, because until now I had never had the opportunity to get to know an enemy's larger city. However, what I did see was so depressing and abhorrent that I only look back upon every hour I spent there with disgust and revulsion. Right outside the train station, the misery began. I had just passed the platform barrier and walked upon the square. I was immediately surrounded by adults and children, who begged me for bread. They stood very close to me and were very aggressive so that it made it impossible for me to move further. I explained that I had no food items with me and attempted to push the nearest to me away. I couldn't do it. I was held fast by my arms and waist, and all around me I heard only plaintive begging. "Please good soldier, just give me one little slice of bread; sir officer, please take pity upon me, I haven't eaten for two days; Mr. Soldier, my mother is at home dying and will die unless she gets something to eat soon." And so I was surrounded on all sides by ten, twenty, or thirty persons.

I looked at these people a bit closer. They were starved to their bones, and their eyes were set deep within their shrunken faces. They shivered when they spoke but couldn't be cold as it was June and the sun shone brightly. I wanted to give them money. They didn't want any money because there was nothing edible they could buy; just bread, just bread was what they wanted so they could fill their stomachs. I would have been hemmed in there a good long time, but just then a patrol happened by and forced the crowd to disperse. So now I was free again. I asked the leader what all of this meant. He said: "The inhabitants are being starved, because they are only getting one hundred grams of flour a day and nothing else. Every week between six and seven hundred are dying of starvation. They accost every soldier because they believe they might get something to eat, but they don't understand we don't even have enough food for ourselves. Look over there on the curb—there's a woman who can't get up. She's been lying there for over an hour. Perhaps she has already died. It is so distressing to have to watch this. And I have to witness this suffering every single day for six hours at a time, moving these skeletons aside to keep the roads clear. I'd rather be at the front." It was unimaginable, what I was told.

I made haste and continued. This first impression was heart-wrenching, but maybe as I continued into the heart of the city the suffering would ease. However, I was wrong. Every other resident who approached me asked or begged me for bread. Some very shy, as though they were ashamed, but these people touched me the most. Others, you couldn't shake. They followed me for streets at a time, as though I could cut bread from between my very own ribs for them. I saw the old glorious churches with their gold cupolas, I saw castles and palaces, I saw the commanding and magnificent government buildings, but I also saw that in front of and in these churches hundreds of half-starved inhabitants lay on their knees begging for salvation. I was suddenly overcome with a furious hatred for our enemies, who had wrought this atrocious suffering upon the innocent townspeople with their blockade.[29] Why couldn't they bring themselves to fight honorably? The ministers should be forced to come here and witness for just one hour the suffering and dying that their actions had brought. They would forevermore be rewarded with these haunting images.

I was accosted, on every street, sometimes three times, sometimes four times, continuously, from every side. And every time I heard the same plaintive cry: Brot or Klabba.[30] I had had enough of this wealthy government seat of Wilma. I had wanted just one afternoon to amuse myself in this city, and before I arrived I had thought of one afternoon as being far too short. However, after these impressions I couldn't reach the train station fast enough to return to my regiment. The sergeant observed me open-mouthed as I arrived back at his station around noon. "Well, you're certainly back here early. Why didn't you stay until evening since you had the whole day off?" "I saw death everywhere lurking under gold cupolas and between marble statues. You ought to go there yourself and you will learn quickly enough to hate England." To that he said nothing, but just nodded in agreement.

A few days later, by complete surprise, our regiment was reassigned, while the rest of the group remained in Ruhe. What could that possibly mean? We all tried to figure out the reason. Just before Illuxt, another regiment invited us to stay with them, and this

29. Here Schiller blames the British total blockade of all shipping for the famine in the Baltic, as many did, seeing it as an unethical war practice. German policy, however, which placed military needs above all others, also played a role in the collapse of agricultural production. See Vejas Gabriel Liulevicius, *War Land on the Eastern Front: Culture, National Identify and German Occupation in World War I* (New York: Cambridge University Press, 2000), 181–83.

30. The German and Polish words for "bread," respectively.

assignment became the most peaceful I experienced during the entire war. The enemy was entrenched almost two kilometers from our infantry, and between us lay huge swamps that provided additional protection from approaches toward us. We received orders to use munitions sparingly, and we took this order most literally. It appeared that those over there had received the same orders and reacted likewise, as it was quite seldom when a shot was fired by either side. Only the infantry made itself known from time to time. However, that seemed more just to prove that they were still in position.

For us it was just a continuation of our peaceful encampment. If only the abominable enemy did not exist! Again, our rations were reduced, and the little bits we got were just enough for one decent meal a day. But then we discovered that the ration was to last for two days! We looked for the orachs that were plentiful along the paths and cooked them so our stomachs were filled.[31] I wondered what the conditions were like at home when next to nothing was sent to the front. I tried not to think about it, but memories of Wilma kept appearing to me. I wanted nothing from back home and wrote that we were well supplied with food.

But even this time was to end, as we suddenly received the news about a huge breakthrough battle in the vicinity of Kowno-Smorgan that the Russians had undertaken with a massive force. The push was so large and so surprisingly executed that the frontmost trenches and many gun emplacements were lost. With enormous force, the enemy pushed forward in a way that had never before been experienced. Was this the last act of desperation that would be waged, in order to quell the threatening revolution? Even battalions of women were said to have participated in this maelstrom, a circumstance that made the entire situation even more interesting and thought-provoking for us.[32] The circumstances must have been very grim, because the next morning we received our marching orders. In the course of the years, our fascination with the glories of war had diminished greatly and we didn't have any yearning for large battles, but this time we were happy nonetheless about getting to the

31. The leaves of the orach are the most edible part of the plant, used like spinach.

32. On the use of women soldiers, see Laurie S. Stoff, *They Fought for the Motherland: Russian Women Soldiers in World War I and Revolution* (Lawrence: University Press of Kansas, 2006).

battlefield, as there we would be getting double rations, referred to as engagement rations.

This wish was fulfilled. There was a lot of butter, sausages, and bread, but at the same time there were lots of wounded and dead. That's because the battle was in full swing as we were called out. The newly arrived reserve soldiers were tasked with removing the enemy from the artillery positions they had taken over. Now we focused on taking back the lost trenches. Only Militia Regiment Number Two held the front line and bled to death in the process. And that's why it needed to be freed to carry on the name "von Hindenburg." For nine days we stood in open fields in a firestorm we hadn't experienced since the days of Praznicz and Gdangtal. For nine days new Russian forces attacked us and were repulsed. For nine long days the planes dropped bombs next to us and into our positions, without any anti-aircraft fire from us because we had no equipment and only a few planes. And on every one of these nine days we hauled the dead and the wounded out of the fields, so that in the end we only had three men remaining to operate every gun. Reserve troop after reserve troop crept by us toward the front in the light of the dawn, filling in all the gaps in the trenches. Thousands found their way to the enemy, but less than a hundred found their way back, and these men were silent and mute because of the horror and the misery that had sucked the very life out of their souls.

I received the order to install an observation post in the front trenches and worked the evening before in preparation. In the morning I only saw shell craters in which the field gray soldiers were positioned, who ducked down with every explosion. Far to the right a machine gun shot regular bursts of fire in short intervals. The earth around me was but a crater of flying pieces of shrapnel and sand along with dense thick smoke. That was our foremost front position! A lieutenant, who was leading the battalion, showed it to me. I saw shelters that had been obliterated, along with their inhabitants, with a single direct hit; I saw the remains of artillery that was completely destroyed amid a large circle of debris; I saw convoys, both human and horse, whose remains were just piles of bloody, pulpy mass, while the vehicles lay next to all completely shattered to pieces. As I passed the destroyed trenches I saw single arms and legs and half corpses flung about, and as I crawled forward it was over stiffened bodies and animal remains.

The air was filled with a hideous stench and the cries of the wounded that no one could bring back and that were slowly dying where they fell. One could hear them screaming, but you couldn't see them, because the smoke was too dense. And that was actually a good thing. As I moved further toward the front it seemed like everything we passed was lifeless. I told this to the lieutenant and he said: "My battalion only has sixty men remaining, and those are dispersed about one kilometer apart. I am the only remaining officer. If these Russians try to advance just one more time, they won't find any resistance. That's why our artillery is constantly firing a barrage of shells." Yes, would the Russians please just advance one more time!

But he wouldn't do it. His resistance was broken. The huge revolution stood at the door! Kerensky had failed, now Lenin had the last say![33] The danger from Smorgon was removed. Our regiment was battle weary. Success was not achieved. The west took everything that was still remaining in the garrisons. So we were removed from here and put under the jurisdiction of the commander in chief of the east. This was a frustrating assignment because from then on, we were moved without any rest from one position to another.

We put hundreds of kilometers behind us in the next few months. Our marches led us through both the most desolate landscapes and the most unforgettable scenery that made huge and lasting impressions. The most beautiful of all was the city of Lwir that lay on the edge of the large Swir Lake.[34] It lay before us, untouched by the war, nestled in a deep valley filled with a forest of broad leaf and pine trees. Many gold cupolas and the ancient tower of a castle draped with ivy glittered in their reflection upon the still and clear lake. Many regal villas were built along the shore. Gondolas and fishing boats looked invitingly outfitted just for a vacation spin. The sun shone brightly over the entire area as we beheld this jewelry box of a valley from our vantage point in the mountains. We immediately took an extreme dislike to the fat commander of the eastern forces who sat on his opulent veranda and observed us in passing with his greasy grin, full of amusement for our plight. What an abomination this pig was!

33. Alexander Kerensky participated in the 1917 February Revolution, which deposed the Russian monarchy, and eventually led the provisional government. The provisional government was overthrown in turn by Lenin and the Bolsheviks in the October Revolution.

34. Just east and slightly north of what is now Vilnius, Lithuania.

In the meantime, Kerensky destroyed the Russian government and brokered a peace agreement with us.[35] We discovered this as we were being transported on our way to Grodno in order to build a siege artillery fortress there. This happened in the first days of December [1917]. Because of this, I was granted leave, and for the first time in what seemed the longest time, and was able to celebrate Christmas with my family at home.

Before leaving Grodno, we were able to have a little free time to explore this big city, in which life was pulsating. We saw a lot of fine people and the polished boots that the decorated officers wore, but we were most mesmerized by the high-heeled and fine boots of the ladies that had suddenly become the fashion. I had never before seen such extremes of both poverty and wealth as in Grodno. However, it could be that young eyes have a different outlook than older ones. Every day we waited for our marching orders to the Western Front. By now it had reached mid-March [1918]. The spring offensive of the English and French certainly must be near.[36] Had everyone just forgotten about us? We knew what was awaiting us in the west. There were fierce battles fought daily there, which we only had from time to time here. We knew this interlude that we were given was brief and so we made the most out of every minute. We drank a lot of watered-down war beer and thought about our futures, which seemed dark, foreboding, and as of yet unknown. Then we received our orders.

35. Schiller's reference to Kerensky's role in the late 1917 armistice, which took effect on December 15, 1917, is probably a conflation of events. Though Kerensky's government had indeed negotiated possible peace terms with Germany, these talks had broken down by the October Revolution. Lenin brokered the final cease-fire.

36. After victories in 1917, Romania was in the final stages of resistance and would come to terms with the Central Powers in early May. Germany shifted its efforts to the Western Front.

Schiller with his parents shortly after basic training, 1914. Courtesy of the Schiller family.

Schiller with his artillery unit, 1914. Courtesy of the Schiller family.

Schiller seated on a cannon with comrades, 1914. Courtesy of the Schiller family.

Schiller in enlisted dress uniform, 1914. Courtesy of the Schiller family.

Schiller in artillery uniform, 1915. Note the cannonball on the helmet. Courtesy of the Schiller family.

Schiller in a noncommissioned officer uniform, 1916. Courtesy of the Schiller family.

Artillery line on the Eastern Front, 1917. Courtesy of the Schiller family.

A Pokapine birch grove in winter with shelters, 1916. Courtesy of the Schiller family.

Schiller with company comrades at the front, 1916. Courtesy of the Schiller family.

Schiller with a friend in a horse-drawn sleigh, winter, 1916–1917. Courtesy of the Schiller family.

Schiller as a mounted messenger, 1916. Courtesy of the Schiller family.

Company feasting, 1917. Courtesy of the Schiller family.

Schiller in his field uniform at Eastern Front, 1917. Courtesy of the Schiller family.

Schiller and comrades, 1917. Courtesy of the Schiller family.

A postcard sent from Schiller to his family in Bromberg, 1918. Courtesy of the Schiller family.

Relaxing with Freikorps comrades, 1919. Courtesy of the Schiller family.

Schiller in his Freikorps uniform, 1919. Courtesy of the Schiller family.

Schiller with Freikorps officers, 1919. Courtesy of the Schiller family.

Schiller wedding party, May 1921. Courtesy of the Schiller family.

Schiller leading a holiday parade, July 1920. Courtesy of the Schiller family.

Schiller with a police unit, 1922. Courtesy of the Schiller family.

Schiller with his family, 1926. Courtesy of the Schiller family.

Schiller family, ca. 1929. Courtesy of the Schiller family.

Official police photo, 1926. Courtesy of the Schiller family.

Gisela, Margarete, Hans, and Ingrid Schiller, ca. 1930. Courtesy of the Schiller family.

Schiller with horse, ca. 1938. Courtesy of the Schiller family.

Schiller and horse on jumping course, ca. 1938. Courtesy of the Schiller family.

Schiller leading a police company, 1932. Courtesy of the Schiller family.

Schiller and officers relaxing with beer, ca. 1938. Courtesy of the Schiller family.

Battery 7 firing position, France, June 1940. Courtesy of the Schiller family.

Advancing through the Maginot Line, June 1940. Courtesy of the Schiller family.

Schiller in February 1936. Courtesy of the Schiller family.

Schiller cooking a meal during the advance on France, June 20, 1940. Courtesy of the Schiller family.

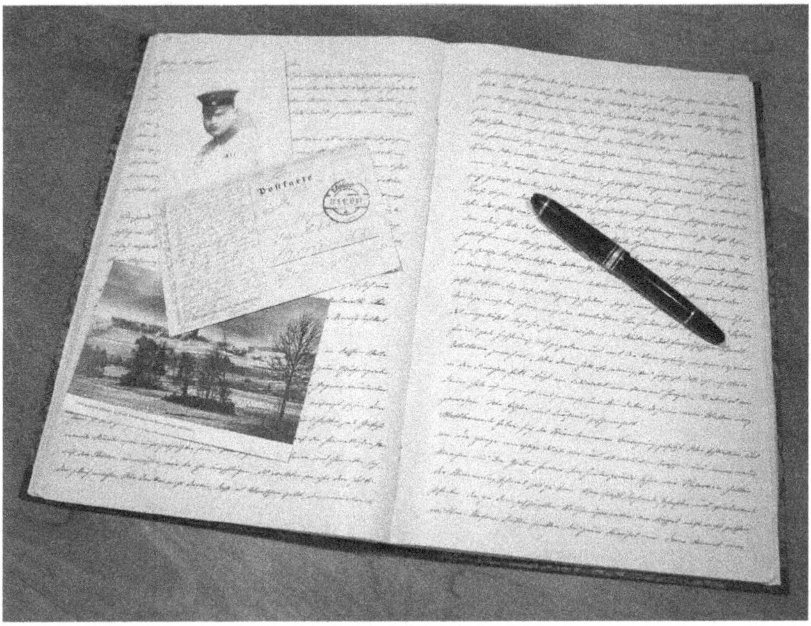

1928 manuscript with postcards sent from the field.

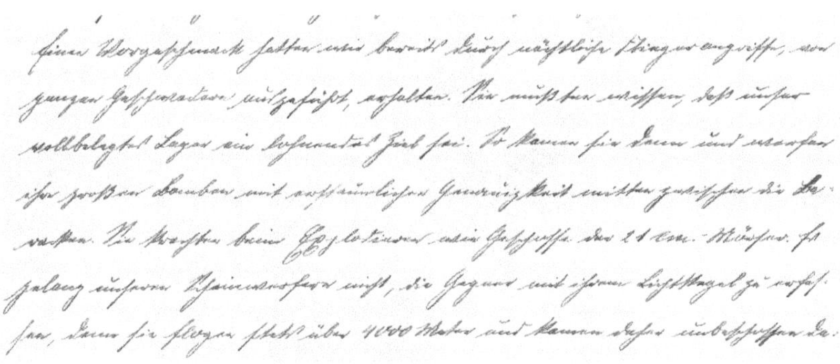

Close-up of a manuscript page.

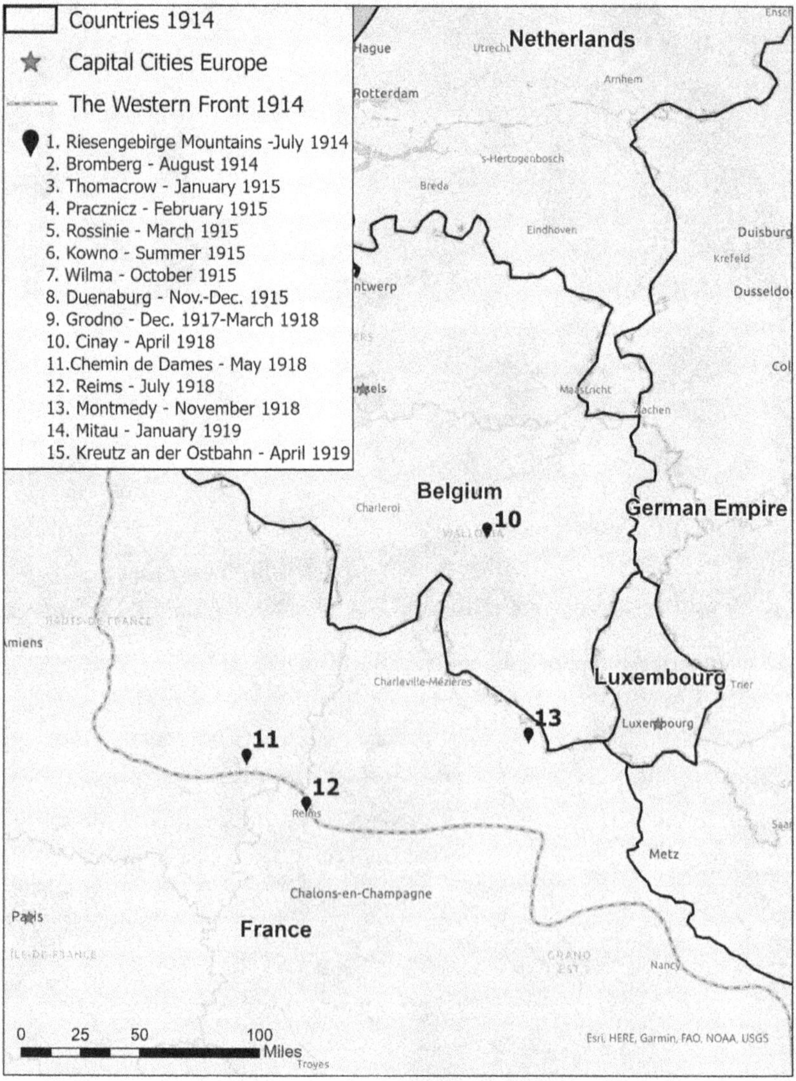

A map of the Western Front locations.

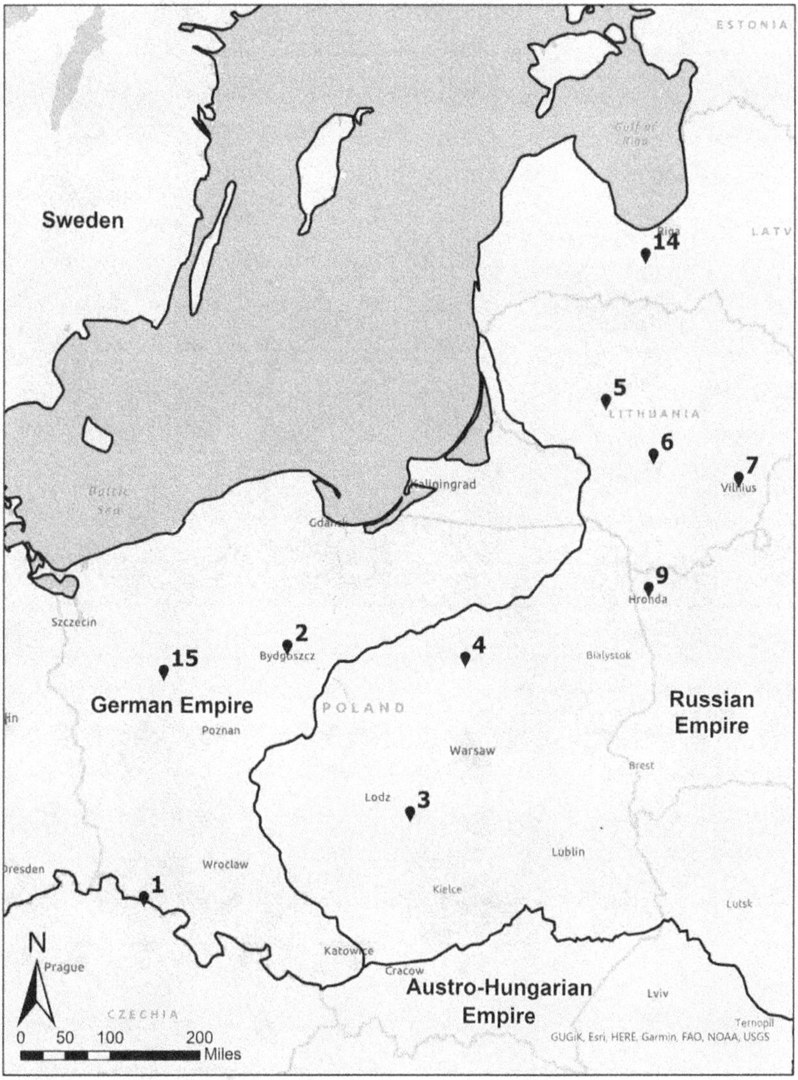

A map of the Eastern Front locations. Map by Jack Humason.

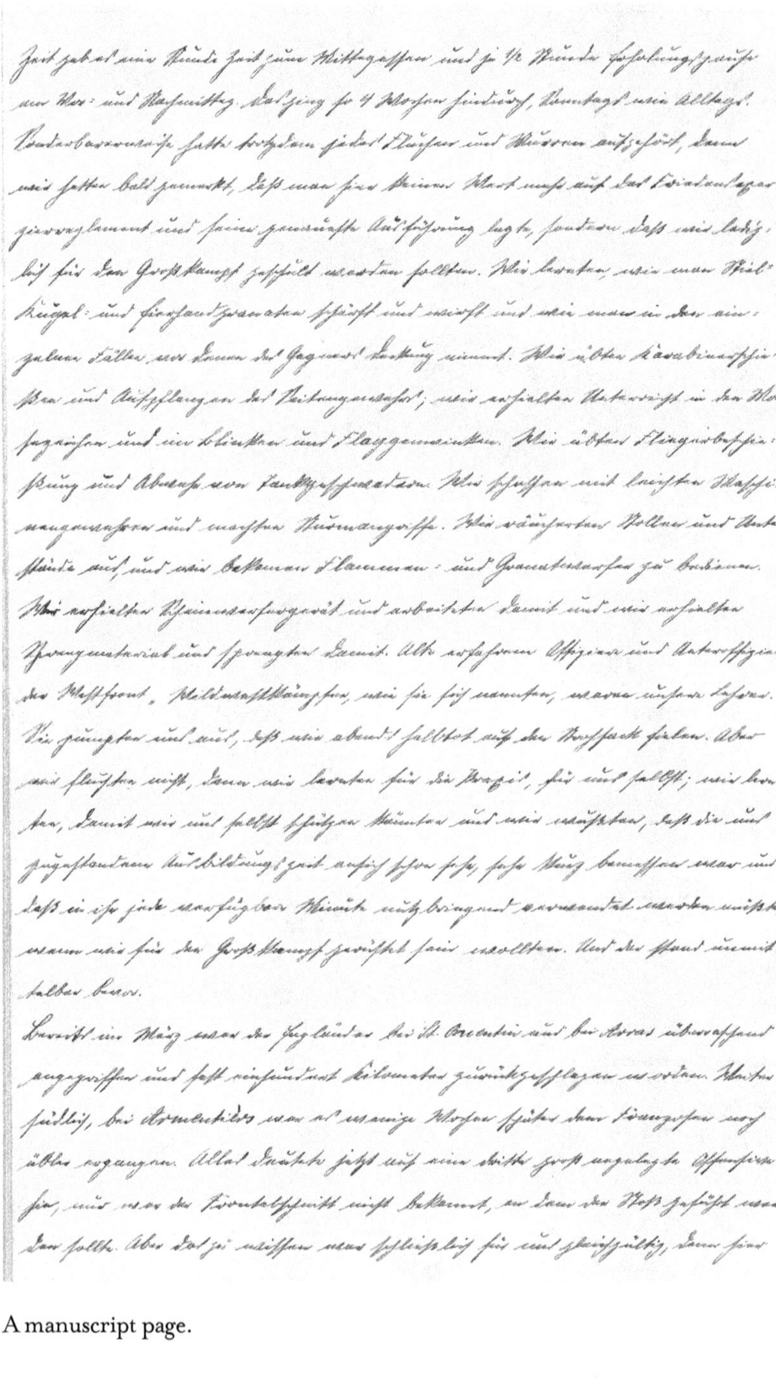
Zeit gab es eine Stunde Zeit zum Mittagessen und je 1/2 Stunde Erholungspause am Vor- und Nachmittag. Das ging so 4 Wochen hindurch, Sonntags wie Alltags. [illegible] hatte trotzdem jedes Fluchen und Murren aufgehört, denn wir hatten bald gemerkt, dass man hier keinen Wert mehr auf das Friedensexerzierreglement und seine genaueste Ausführung legte, sondern dass wir lediglich für den Grosskampf geschult werden sollten. Wir lernten, wie man Stielkugel- und Eierhandgranaten schärft und wirft und wie man in den einzelnen Fällen vor denen des Gegners Deckung nimmt. Wir übten Karabinerschiessen und Aufpflanzen des Seitengewehrs; wir erhielten Unterricht in den Morsezeichen und im Blinken und Flaggenwinken. Wir übten Flugzeugbeschiessung und Abwehr von Tankgeschwadern. Wir schossen mit leichten Maschinengewehren und machten Sturmangriffe. Wir räucherten Stollen und Unterstände aus, und wir bekamen Flammenwerfer- und Granatwerfer zu bedienen. Wir erhielten Minenwerfergerät und arbeiteten damit und wir erhielten Sprengmaterial und sprengten damit. Alte erfahrene Offiziere und Unteroffiziere der Westfront, „Materialschlachtkämpfer", wie sie sich nannten, waren unsere Lehrer. Sie [illegible] uns aus, dass wir abends halbtot auf den Strohsack fielen. Aber wir fluchten nicht, denn wir lernten für die Praxis, für uns selbst; wir lernten, damit wir uns selbst schützen könnten und wir wussten, dass die uns zugestandene Ausbildungszeit an sich schon sehr, sehr knapp bemessen war und dass in ihr jede verfügbare Minute nutzbringend verwendet werden musste, wenn wir für den Grosskampf gerüstet sein wollten. Und der stand unmittelbar bevor.

Bereits im März war der Engländer bei St. Quentin und bei Arras überraschend angegriffen und fast einhundert Kilometer zurückgeschlagen worden. Weiter südlich, bei Armentières war es wenige Wochen später dem Franzosen noch übler ergangen. Alles deutete jetzt auf eine dritte gross angelegte Offensive hin, nur war der Frontabschnitt nicht bekannt, an dem der Stoss geführt werden sollte. Aber das zu wissen war schliesslich für uns gleichgültig, denn hier

A manuscript page.

Hans Schiller in 1943. Courtesy of the Schiller family. Photo by Rachel Satterfield-Masen.

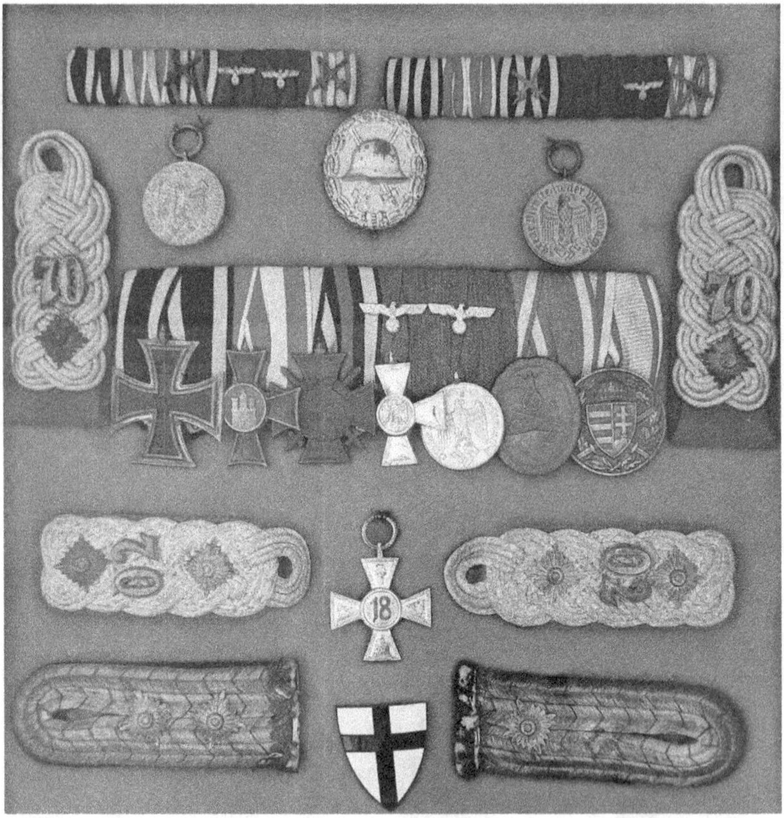

Schiller's World War I and World War II medals and insignia. Courtesy of the Schiller family. Photo by Rachel Satterfield-Masen.

Portrait of Schiller drawn by a school colleague, 1918. Courtesy of the Schiller family. Photo by Rachel Satterfield-Masen.

5

Battles at the Western Front

The transit to the German border and straight across the whole fatherland became a real adventure that we should have paid more attention to. We travelled over the rivers Weichsel [Vistula], Oder, Elbe, and the Weser; Thuringen winked at us and now our train found itself in the middle of Westphalia's industrial district. However, we didn't notice any of this in our compartment. The longest Dauerskat of my life was to blame![1] Three days prior, shortly after our departure from Grodno, it had begun and not stopped except for very short forced periods of sleep. And to think we had agreed that this little game initially was to take no more than two hours to conclude. But who would have known that there were so many different ways to play a hand!

It was only when the Rhine became visible that we allowed ourselves to be diverted from our grueling task, as only this old, venerable, and steeped-in-legend river was capable of doing. Even though we were holding great unplayed hands, it was time to put away our interesting game of Skat. This decision was not regretted by anyone, and from that point on we were very observant of our whereabouts. We looked over the landscape that was covered in the first green of the nearing spring and it lay softly and beautifully in front of us. Would we ever be able to return to this? That was the question that occupied all of our thoughts. We guessed that this summer the decision would be made, and we also knew that in this last push, many sacrifices would need to be made first, battles with a ferocity that had not been seen before in this battle-weary war. And our regiment was to be a part of this! It was no wonder that we became increasingly

1. Dauerskat is a trick-taking card game popular in nineteenth-century Germany.

more quiet than we had ever been before during any train transport. How would it all turn out? The overall mood was neither good nor bad; it was more cautious.

At Cinay in Namur we received our orders to disembark.[2] We marched over to the nearby training area, where we were to be trained for four weeks to fight on the Western Front before we were actually sent to the enemy. As the commander gave us our instructions, we accepted them without any emotion because we had already had enough of all of those types of lessons in Grodno. What was there still to be learned? All of the mundane details now bored us, including the never-ending inspections by the senior and then even more senior commanders, who each had their own peculiarities that you first had to get to know before dismissing half of their critiques regarding whatever it was you were doing incorrectly. And this was all to go on for another month? We started swearing, went to bars, and drank heavily. Suddenly we wanted to go to the front where at least you had some peace. However, we then thought back on Russia and needed to take into consideration that even stalemate trench warfare was likely going to be much more unpleasant and the toll on body and soul higher than in the east.

The training area was fully occupied with troops of every branch of service, particularly the infantry. What stood out were the very young recruits, who you could pick out immediately just by virtue of their shy demeanor and clumsy greeting. I stopped a number of them and asked their ages. Eighteen years. I asked if they had been drafted or volunteered and received this answer: "We were called to duty and were inducted as soldiers even though some of us have disabilities. Now they are taking everything, sir, because these days there isn't a person in Germany who would volunteer."[3] They made an undernourished and childish impression. Their uniforms were

2. Currently the city of Ciney in the Namur district of Belgium. Germany had taken Namur in the initial onslaught of the war in August 1914.

3. Schiller's description of the manpower shortage, as well as his earlier mentions of food and other resource scarcity, are common themes among those who survived the war years. By 1917, Germany was facing a major crisis as there were not enough men left to replace casualties. On the challenges of conscription, see Richard Bessel, "Mobilization and Demobilization in Germany, 1916–18," in *State, Society and Mobilization in Europe during the First World War*, edited by John Horne (New York: Cambridge University Press, 1997).

far too big for their small bodies and hung loosely on their thin frames. The heavy and wide army boots fit their feet like washtubs. I asked them if they wanted to go to the front, but they answered only with embarrassed laughter, that likely meant: "You could have kept this silly question to yourself." These were Germany's youngest infantry replacements, who were tasked with the great battles that were to determine the outcome of this war and win![4]

The very next morning we began our prescribed lessons. We started at six a.m. and finished at seven p.m. During this time, we were given one hour for lunch and one half hour break in the morning and the afternoon. This was our regular routine for about four weeks, Sundays included, as though it were just another day. In spite of this schedule, every complaint and swearing had ceased because we soon observed that no one gave any credit to the drill book that was written based on peacetime military rules, with all the minute details of the etiquette of war. It was clear instead that we were being prepared for a very large battle.

We learned how to prepare and throw both stick hand grenades and egg hand grenades and how to protect ourselves when the enemy used these weapons.[5] We practiced firing carbines and how to properly fix our bayonets. We were instructed in Morse code and in flash and flag signals. We practiced shooting at airplanes and repelling tanks. We shot with light machine guns and practiced assaults. We smoked out tunnels and shelters and we were schooled in flamethrowers and mortars. We received headlight gear and worked with that and also with dynamite that we detonated. Old and experienced officers and non-commissioned officers from the Western Front were our teachers; they called themselves the "Wild West Fighters."[6] They worked us so hard that in the evenings we fell dead tired onto our straw mattresses. But we didn't complain; we were grateful for the practice, simply for ourselves, for our preservation, so we could protect ourselves. We also knew our practice time was

4. And of course, Schiller's incredulity as to their age and boyishness is ironic, given his own entry into the war at seventeen. He is now barely twenty-one.

5. The specific grenades here are "Stielkugel- und Eierhandgranaten," the first being cylindrical grenades with a wooden handle, also known as "potato masher" grenades introduced in 1915, and smooth egg-shaped grenades introduced in 1917.

6. Literally "Wildwestkämpfer." Novels about the American West were popular in Germany.

severely limited and that we needed to utilize every available minute if we wanted to be prepared for the large and looming battle ahead. And that was imminent.

In March, the English had already been attacked by surprise at St. Quentin and Arras and had been pushed back almost one hundred kilometers. Further south near Armentiers, the French were defeated and pushed back even more. Everything was now pointed in the direction of a third huge offensive; however, where exactly on the front this battle was to be waged was not yet clear. But for us to know this was immaterial because in the west it really didn't matter where one eventually fought, as every battle was equally fierce.

We had a preview of the fighting through nightly air strikes carried out by entire flight squadrons. They must have known that our fully occupied encampment was a good target. So they came and managed to drop their bombs with great accuracy right between our barracks. They roared while exploding, just like the shots from a twenty-one-centimeter Mauser.[7] Our searchlights could not track the planes because they flew at an altitude of over four thousand meters and therefore no shots could reach them. This emboldened them even more. Soon we had to flee once or twice nightly into the shelters to take cover. In these weeks through these attacks, our regiment lost six men and suffered twenty casualties, not counting the many more horses and pulverized vehicles. However, heavier casualties were suffered by the infantry, which lost an entire block of barracks when it exploded into flames, as well as three of their shelters that buried everything in them with it. And that was a huge loss. After that, the most well-known fighter squadron Richthofen was put into service. And our fighter squadron only needed to pursue these enemy vultures twice before they gave up bombing us for good.

Higher sausage and butter rations and more meat with our dried vegetables were the first signs of our impending leave to the front. And now it was already the middle of May [1918]. One evening, after darkness had fully set in, our regiment set off. After a march of eight hours straight and as the morning dawned, we finally stopped in a forest and, among the green trees and bushes, we hid our cannons and vehicles from the sight of airplanes. Then we built huts covered with leaves for our horses and troops, under which we finally crawled

7. A very effective heavy howitzer used by the German military through World War II.

to rest ourselves. This went on for four days. At night we marched; during the day we slept. We were never alone on our troop advance. Artillery units and infantry divisions unknown to us now fell in with us and marched in front and behind us. In between rolled the munitions and supply wagons, field ambulances, and steaming portable kitchens. It was an ear-deafening noise that reigned amid the constant swearing when one division tried to overtake another. It almost appeared as though an entire army was on the march. However, as soon as the sun rose all it saw was a peaceful countryside among villages and open fields, where you might see a few farmers working. It was almost as if the moon, as it set, took all the weapons that were under its guard and, waltzing toward the front, just rolled them up. During daylight you couldn't see a field gray uniform, and even the vehicles turned into foliage-covered mounds. Even if the devilish fighter pilots had grown the sharpest of eyes they wouldn't have been able to locate us as we moved ourselves ever nearer to Laon in order to break through the enemy's lines.

Very close and southwest from the city, our position was discovered, and as silently as possible we embedded ourselves during this fifth night. We only had a very few hours in which to position our guns and dig trenches. The earth was so hard here that our shovels broke. However, officers, non-commissioned officers, and other personnel worked together so that the next morning no one within fifty meters could tell an entire battery was stationed here. We were under the strictest orders not to move during daylight hours. However, as darkness set we turned into moles, digging underground trenches and shelters for the troops, dugouts for the two thousand-odd round munitions dump, and underground telephone wires that all needed to be invisible. I was asked to become a battery leader and consulted with the officers about how many rounds would be needed to take out particular targets. The division's artillery commander later examined everything and found nothing wrong. Test firing, as was usual and simple, was not possible, mainly because then the enemy would detect our large artillery positions that were embedded here. And their artillery and sound-ranging parties were highly qualified, as evidenced by the many destroyed gun emplacements we encountered.[8]

8. Sound ranging was commonly done but had developed into a complex technology for the time on the Allied side, consisting of an array of microphones and a

It appeared as if we were in luck. Nothing pointed toward the French having gotten wind of our preparations being made to destroy them. Their artillery fired all over the general area and also shelled our approach routes, but it was nothing to be worried about, as it was just routine. And some of our batteries fired in return. They allowed themselves to do this, as they had been permitted to do so in the past. And so the week went by.

In the early morning of the twenty-sixth of May, the battery commander told me in great secrecy that the battle would begin in earnest the next morning at six a.m. In order to prepare the enemy positions high up on the Chemin des Dames for attack, our entire artillery was to put the enemy under increasing fire starting at 1:45. I was asked to be the commander of the signal squad and accompany the regiment's infantry liaison officer to position ourselves in the front line to set up communications from the conquered heights. It was a position of trust that he held in me. He shook my hand and wished me a happy return.

At ten p.m. I stepped forth toward our trenches with Second Lieutenant Nelken as well as my six men. After five kilometers, we saw the Chemin des Dames that looked like a huge looming vertical mass. Up there, one hundred and fifty meters above us, sat the enemy.

They had a huge advantage over us with this fantastic view of our positions across the entire landscape. And these nearly vertical and crumbling rock faces sprinkled with some challenging areas of support we were supposed to climb tomorrow? It was crazy just to think about it. How did the leaders determine to start waging this battle here, exactly at this spot that was through nature itself an advantage for the French? Nowhere else could an attack be so difficult to stage. I asked the second lieutenant to explain. He had heard that the front had advanced so far to the south, that we could stop them not only on this mountain but also at the Soisson-Reims railway, a primary position, by using this tactic. Here, at this elevation, that the enemy considered impossible to seize, they would never see us coming. Only here could we bring about a planned and surprise ambush.

We could only move forward very slowly, and because of the dark-

---

forward observer who would mark the flash of the guns. The time between the flash and the sound reaching the various microphones could then be used to pinpoint the location of gun emplacements.

ness we constantly stepped into barbed wire and also large shell craters filled with water. Oftentimes we had to throw ourselves down because some battery was firing harassing shots in our direction. Every few seconds we came upon guns that were being readied for the impending battle. Through the vastness of this we first got an inkling about the meticulous planning by the general's staff for this offensive, and this knowledge made us feel more secure in our leaders. High above us an enemy squadron flew near the vicinity of our vacated position. It is OK to fly out over there, we thought—go ahead and drop your bombs; the only things you'll hit are empty barracks. "If only they could see what was playing out right here at their feet," said the lieutenant. And as he was still speaking, the entire route lit up with an ear-piercing bang. The sleeping column took on a life of its own and spewed fire kilometers long. This radical change was so unforeseen and done with such force that we had little time to even throw ourselves to the ground.

In the next few hours it roared and pelted all around us as if the gates of hell had opened. We were so dazed that we couldn't even gather our thoughts; we could only lay there without any willpower to move, exactly where we had thrown ourselves. Just don't stand up, went through our heads, because that would mean certain death. And I tried not to think that death could easily snatch me here. The lieutenant next to me poked me and then screamed in my ear: "We must seek shelter." I nodded and looked around. But where? We found ourselves in a fire storm; if we looked backward, forward, or to the side we only saw explosions and streaming flames; we only heard the hissing and the clapping impact of shells. And where were my people? I didn't see a single one of them. Then I screamed with all of my might: "Assemble here!" I didn't even think that my voice would be lost in all of this terrible noise. No one retorted, no one came. What did that mean? As this concert had started, they couldn't have been more than ten meters behind me? Then I remembered that we had passed a huge shell crater. Maybe they jumped in there. I proposed to the lieutenant that we run back to that point. We immediately agreed. We took off as fast as possible and not even five minutes later dove headfirst into the crater. Our heads hit hard metal. Those were the helmets of our people. They crouched down there, up to their stomachs in water. We joined them.

A number of signal flares were shot over our location and for a few seconds lit up the area. I crawled over the edge of the crater and discovered that not even fifty meters to the side there was an entrance to the trenches. We needed to reach this shelter. However, the path toward it lay under heavy fire. We decided to try it in groups every thirty seconds. This quick pause in fire had to be enough. We kneeled, ready to spring out. In the very second that the next four shells exploded we sprang up and raced as fast as our legs could take us through the dense smoke. No one gave any notice to the other, everyone just had one goal in mind, each of us only cared about their own preservation, to only land safely there. And we made it. Exactly as the enemy's new round began, we darted into the entrance.

It was a deep tunnel, in which the staff of a large infantry regiment had set up its command post. Here we were buried for the interim. Thanks to God! Just then our lance corporal Stabe noticed that blood was seeping out of his armband. We removed his coat. He had shrapnel in his upper arm. A young assistant field surgeon examined him under the light of a flickering candle and discovered that his bones were intact. That meant casualty time at home. Who was more blessed than our Stabe? "This is the first blood I've had on my hands today," said the doctor, "and how many more liters will it be before this night is over?" I found this comment to be very insensitive and tasteless but this doctor had just graduated from university only to come here. I could forgive him for that.

I climbed up to the entrance of the tunnel with the lieutenant. With unforgiving anger, the fire outside raged. It must be destroying all. Our front line that was still one kilometer away looked like one long bloody red stream of fire. I could not imagine that anyone could still be breathing in there. The battery positions didn't fare any better. While hundreds of shell shots in conjunction with light artillery fire blew apart our shelters, the well-equipped enemy's artillery attacked those that were marching in the rear. Huge columns of fire accompanied by intense explosions meant that ammunition supplies had been blown sky high. And this went on for onward of a full hour! And it wasn't possible to predict any end! How would all of this pan out?

The regiment's aide-de-camp approached us, looked around for a second, and then said to our lieutenant: "We wanted to exterminate the Frenchman, and now he's exterminating us. An assault is not even possible in these circumstances. This is due to nothing but pure treason in this game." His assumption was proven to be correct, as we later learned from prisoners. Two Saxon engineers, who had been sent as lookouts, had been captured by the enemy, and they revealed the impending storm.[9] Immediately thereafter, the French general brought forth annihilating fire so that our assault could be nipped in the bud.

The clock showed it was now twenty minutes before two a.m. If we were still able to do so, our return fire would have to begin at any moment. But wasn't it an ill omen that until now not one of our regiments had returned any fire? Only one more minute remained before the firing was to begin. Our nerves were shot to pieces. The decision neared; it was at hand: a sea of flames as wide as the eye could see, thousands of flashes over us, and then over there loud crashes and shattering. I felt the tunnel shake, and the mortar and sand came down on us. We were blinded by the firestorm, and we were pressed to the ground by the air pressure of the shells.

For the longest time we couldn't even speak one word, and if we had, no one would have understood it. It took a while to adjust to the situation. It was both horrible and exhilarating at the same time. It was the huge volley that was supposed to mean the end of this world war, and it was also the greatest show of firepower ever used in any war, and who knew if it would be the end of all.[10] I felt lucky that I wasn't a witness in this giant production. Four hundred enemy batteries had wanted to finish us off, but one thousand one hundred batteries of our own crammed into the most narrow space now returned the answer to the other side. Six thousand fiery hot gun barrels and two thousand flaming mortars were at the ready at this hour as well as over twenty thousand artillery shots that zig-zagged against the skies every minute. How many could this amount to in just one hour? How was it possible that anyone under such a ceiling of deadly steel and iron could survive? It appeared as if humanity had prepared for hundreds of years just in order to be able to wage a total war of such might to test and reach the unimaginable limits of human capacity and destruction.

9. Here is a point in which Schiller's memoir challenges our assumptions. Alexander Watson described the attack at Chemin des Dames, which was a diversionary assault on the French to conceal his main attack against the British, as a complete surprise. See Alexander Watson, *Ring of Steel: Germany and Austria-Hungary in World War I* (New York: Basic Books, 2014), 522.

10. This was, according to Watson, the largest artillery barrage in any war up until this point. See Watson, *Ring of Steel*, 522.

And look here: all of a sudden the enemy's fire stopped. How could it have turned out any differently when they were outnumbered two to three times by our fire? How could they fire back at us with mortar shells when their positions had been reduced to a pile of smoking rubble and the skies above them were torn apart by innumerable shell fragments?

At three thirty a.m. you could safely say the French artillery was annihilated. Only a few of their most powerful cannons were still firing. These were so far back from the front that our sound ranging party could only estimate their position. So therefore, our fire was not going to be of any effect. But there really were no more obstacles to the offensive.

And over and over, without pause and unabated, we shot our steely greetings in their direction. As the early morning of the twenty-seventh of May drew over us it saw only shattered trenches and shelters from the impregnable Chemin des Dames; it saw shell craters and holes, it saw shelled-out artillery; it saw no machine guns, flamethrowers, or mortars—it saw only bits and pieces, blown about and scattered; it saw only the dead and wounded; it saw a seemingly unending long and wide gas cloud that lay over this great expanse of ruin, and it made the still-living catch their breath in awe.

The lieutenant told us to ready for departure. As we passed a pile of stones, at which spot a village named Cohertelle had stood, we made our way to the trenches. We climbed past a range of hills and over a meadow that the enemy had maintained an unobstructed view of, but we were not shot at, even though we were moving upright. That's because above us the projectiles were still passing and protecting us from any danger. It almost seemed like a walk in the park that we were making here, almost like an outing on the promenade and just as safe. We saw how the projectiles and mortar shells were flying about the Chemin, as if they wanted to smash the mountain to the ground. We didn't want to think about those who were condemned in this hellhole to a certain death. We were mesmerized, staring at this view that the mountain offered us. It looked as if it wanted to bury itself. And then after a very, very long time it came over me, a certain pride to be a member of an army that could achieve such a feat.

Now we arrived back at our own trenches. The infantry had just climbed out and, almost beside themselves with emotion, assembled in a long and uneven line facing the storm. We checked in with the battalion commander, a young captain, who was called by his people "Esteemed Count."[11] I wondered about this title at first, that such high-born men would enlist and put themselves at the front, because I had never seen anything of the kind before. Then it occurred to me that we found ourselves with the First Regiment of the Guards, comprised of the most elite of Prussian forces. We put the severely wounded on canvas and straw mats; others were carried out on stretchers. A group of lightly wounded non-commissioned officers stood on the embankment and observed with great interest the workings of our artillery. "It looks like we're giving these dogs such a battering that it's making them want to be done with this world," said one through clenched teeth. I asked them about our casualties. It looked as if half of the shelters were destroyed. And during the height of the French onslaught, we had given up all hope of survival and had reckoned with the destruction of our artillery. "But then at least we showed we still had some fight left in us," a sergeant added. "I have never experienced such a firefight and yet I've only been on the Western Front." We felt very flattered by this.

In the meantime, the line had put itself back in motion. We attached ourselves to it. The whole boggy field was full of troops in front of us, and more kept crawling out of their trenches. In the background we saw the reserve troops halt. The mood seemed to be very good. You saw laughing faces and heard whistling as we fastened newly prepared grenades to our waistbands. Our feet sank up to our ankles, and then we came to a stop. We soon came to the Aijette, a small river that was about ten meters wide. A few moments later we continued on our way. Now we were only about a half kilometer away from the foot of the Chemin and the first of the enemy's positions. We had already encountered "Spanish riders," wolf pits, and barbed wire.[12] With astonishing speed, these obstacles were cleared away by the infantry. They had been tested many a time before. How often had they experienced such an assault? I saw many a gold medal that signified they had been wounded before.[13] How much pain and how much blood was spilled and sacrificed by them?

11. "Herr Graf."

12. "Spanish riders," literally "spanische Reiter." From context, some form of booby trap or defensive installation.

13. These "wound badges" (Verwundetenabzeichen), which were awarded beginning in March 1918, came in three classes: Iron (third class) represented one or two wounds; silver (second class) represented three or four wounds; gold (first class) represented five or more wounds.

A few companies were shooting off red signal flares, as well as a fighter squadron that was circling over us. That was the signal for the artillery that we had reached the French line and that the assault could now be halted. Now the creeping barrage could begin, under whose protection we could start climbing up the mountain. Every four minutes we sprung one hundred meters ahead. The bullets zoomed almost overhead and nearly at our hairlines. They hit their targets so close to us that part of their shrapnel ricocheted back into our lines. We crawled and climbed further. The first of the dead became visible in their cornflower blue uniforms.[14] They lay half buried in between iron rods and still-smoking woodpiles. Here we discovered shell crater upon shell crater and some that were the size of a large living room. Those were the business cards of the twenty-one-centimeter mortars. Step by step we moved further along. By now we had already taken over half the mountain. The higher we climbed, the more we saw bodies lying on the churned-up boulders. The only resistance we noticed is the impact of a few heavy shells on a battalion to our right.

We finally reached the summit and with this the main headquarters. It was nearly unrecognizable. Concrete blocks were scattered about, and there were signs that a gun position or a tunnel must have been here. We didn't see any shelters; we only saw shell craters alongside shell craters and destruction as far as the eye could see.

Systematically the line sprang back into place. We ran into place at the rear. A shot that fell short of its target exploded into one of the lines. Some died and others were wounded. The infantry swore and threatened us, as if we were the reason our troops suffered casualties. Well, how could it be any different since the barrels were bulging and the scopes worn out? And what else could you expect when you've been shooting, for almost a year, every day, without ever being able to completely recondition your gun? Krupp only guaranteed the guns for ten thousand shots each, and these good machines had lasted for at least three times longer.

And so we continued pushing forward. Soon we got to the enemy's reserve lines, where just shortly before they had led their assault. We got up and were in the middle of running toward the line when we heard machine-gun fire go off right in front of us. At this close range

14. Indicating French troops.

every shot will hit its target. We threw ourselves down and waited to see what the infantry would do. This resistance was so unexpected! At our left a company sprang up and ran toward them with bared bayonets. Apparently, they wanted to catch them in the crossfire. They didn't get far. Two new machine guns fired and blasted anything that was not on the ground. And once again, the remainder sprang up just seconds later to throw themselves against the enemy's fire. Very close to us we heard the voice of one of the officers. It rang loud and clear: "Get up; march, march." And so we set off, just like all the others to the left and right of us. As the first of them climbed to the top of the trenches, the French showed themselves with raised hands. But their guns were still smoking; a hand grenade tore one section to pieces; the others we took as prisoners. There were about forty men.

The reserve pulled past us. We remained right where we were. I felt something wet running down my leg. As I investigated, I saw my water bottle was empty. A shot had gone right through the middle of it. Of my five men, only three were still with me. The lieutenant asked about the others. No one knew anything. Then we threw a glance back on the short path that we had run through during the attack. It was covered with the dead and wounded. The volunteer Stangel we soon found. He was lying on his back and had received two shots in the chest. The shattered case containing the broken signal devices likely rolled backward a few steps as he fell. The artilleryman Niemeyer was sitting further behind on a rock and waved us toward him. He was bandaging his leg. We carried him carefully back to the trenches and turned him over to a medic. The commanding officer was occupied with counting the troops. We heard from him that out of ninety men only thirty-eight were still accounted for. The others were lost in the assault. I hadn't noticed anything! I only ran with the rest of the men. Then I thought to myself, how quickly one can die out here!

I let Lieutenant Nelken know that the signal apparatus was no longer operable and therefore we couldn't establish any communications with the regiment. I suggested we return to the battery. However, he did not want my advice. "The first thing we're doing is a thorough inspection of these trenches," he said, and, "I have the feeling that we will find all sorts of delicacies that back in Germany exist in name only." Now there's a thought! We stepped out of the trench, and then discovered our luck was not to hold. Every one of the shelters that we could see had been shot to pieces by our large-scale artillery fire. And just when we were going to give up, we detected in a nearby trench an entrance that one could still just barely squeeze through if put to the test.

The flashlights shined brightly as we stepped onto a ladder leading us to the dark underground. Down below we bumped into two fallen soldiers from the Thirteenth Infantry of Breton that had occupied the Chemin and bled to death just a few hours earlier. A week ago these fellows were relaxing in Kemmel along with many of their men, as they had been given a well-deserved leave to rest. Now they would rest forevermore. In one corner of this stinking room we found a number of boxes, which we opened with our sidearms. What did they hold? We had to look twice to believe our eyes: tinned meats, sardines, ham, sausages, and chocolate. And everything in field-ready usable cans beautifully prepared. We searched a bit more and found two numbered barrels, "25 Liter" written on both. As we opened them we were in total awe. It was an excellent French wine! The only thing that could not be found was white bread, but under the circumstances one could easily do without it. With gaiety seldom expressed, we hoisted the treasures upward. Now the eating could begin.

We didn't stop for quite a while. However, in the middle of this feasting I discovered that very close to me lay a fallen guardsman from the Fourth Regiment. His vacant eyes were directed right at me. Suddenly I completely lost my appetite. I went over to him and turned his head to the other side, so he wouldn't be jealous. Then I opened another tin.

In the interim, the sun had risen so it was directly over us and signaled it was now noon. For a long time, the sounds of battle had grown ever weaker and further away. Endless numbers of prisoners shuffled by. Looking at their stricken faces, you could see that they were relieved to be done with this bloodbath. The wounded that were being carried forward advised us that all was going according to plan. The French were defending themselves, but everywhere their positions fell. Far on the horizon you could make out an artillery division that was moving on the only path over the Chemin in order to establish their new positions. And we were told our battery needed to join them. That was our signal to break camp. However, first we filled our duffel bags with all the delicacies and looked for every available canteen to fill with wine. Even so, we had to leave a full barrel behind. Then we decided to pour it in a washbasin and used it to wash ourselves, as water was in short supply here.

It was late afternoon when we finally met up with our regiment that had found itself on the march. We discovered that the field assault during the previous night had resulted in heavy casualties. I was soon able to convince myself of that. My regiment lost one officer and eleven men. As we passed a little ravine, we saw pressed against the side an important officer had stopped there. It was the division commander, Prince Eitel-Friedrich, who allowed the various divisions to pass him. He called out to a few in a friendly manner and offered some words of acknowledgment. However, as the Second Battalion of the Third Regiment of Guards passed him he was said to have taken off his field cap. That was the honor he bestowed upon the seven groups that were left remaining out of four hundred.

We kept on moving the entire night. We could only move back and forth, because the street was filled with troops and supply wagons. To the right and left of us, hidden behind fake bushes, the mighty guns of our opponents stood silently, even though just yesterday evening they had shown their unfriendly activity. A few batteries were only lightly damaged; their mighty concrete barriers saved them from complete destruction. We were amazed! Every single position had its own enclosure. This must have taken months and maybe even years to build in their present form. We could easily see this from Pokapine. How hard must it have been for the gunners to realize that all of their efforts had been in vain! A serious resistance by the enemy had not even been considered here, because any signs of hand-to-hand combat were not detected. Everywhere you looked you found carbines, helmets, sidearms, and empty or half-filled ammunition cases. We carefully checked the bunkers, as we'd already had a lot of practice doing that. A big fight broke out over a beautiful yellow leather suitcase. Everyone thought they had spied it first. The strongest was the victor, as usual. I snatched a lovely silk blanket that I thought would be very useful for the cool nights and fastened it to the horn of my saddle. However, as I returned from another newfound conquest I discovered that someone else had already made off with it. After that I stopped pillaging about since it didn't seem to be worth the effort.

In the first light of dawn, we crossed the Aisne. Around the narrow wood bridge, a lot of heavy fighting had occurred, and we found huge numbers of the dead. The battlefield was quite close by, as we saw by the clouds of shrapnel that quickly dissipated. The infantry next to us was asked to move forward. In a frenzied crisscrossed gallop, three riders neared. As they moved closer, we could see that the leader was the division commander Captain von Garnier. He gave orders to the battery commanders to get ready. Immediately thereafter we trotted into place. I was called over to the first lieutenant Wenzel and received the following order: "We are going to travel in a westerly direction behind Hill 209 at Cermont and there position ourselves. You are to install a lookout position in the church tower and then open fire on the adjoining trenches with the battery. I will follow you directly." With two other corporals and two telephones I hurried toward the village.

We had almost reached the first houses when simultaneously the first heavy guns were fired into the village streets. We couldn't go any further, so we tried to maneuver sideways through gardens. That worked. Pretty soon we were tripping up the narrow and dark stairway leading to the church tower. Until now this position had not been damaged. We hoped that it would stay that way as long as we were there. In a small slit we installed the telescope, while the line to the command center was laid. Would we even get any reception? That was the first order of business. I had an unparalleled view over the entire area. Although our infantry was obscured by a range of hills, I can see the French all the better. They had embedded themselves on the edge of a cornfield. The distance was thirteen to fourteen hundred meters! Next to me the field telephone rings. Thank goodness! The battery was on the line! I called into the receiver: "Cannons: impact—entire battery—fix course—position one up—two hundred—fire." Every word by regulation was then repeated back from over there; a few seconds passed, and then it hissed overhead us, and in almost the same instant right in front of the enemy's line you could see them burrowing into their trenches. "Increase fifty meters. One group." It is too far away, but in this fashion we had the enemy pinned in. In quick and even succession our artillery fire exploded. I discovered that the French were now evacuating this part of their trenches so they could better position themselves on both sides. Did they think this move would benefit them? Shortly thereafter we had them back in our sights, and soon they wouldn't have any recourse but to flee.

Suddenly there was a terrible crashing, splitting, and rumbling. We felt the tower shaking. Limestone and mortar fell down around us. We suddenly thought: now we're going to plunge into the abyss. We looked at each other shivering. "What was that?" the telephone operator asked, trembling a few seconds later. "A bull's-eye," a corporal answered shortly. It had landed in the middle of the church and the roof collapsed in half. Even now a few beams and bricks were still falling. A huge dust cloud materialized. However, the tower itself did not appear to have been hit. It stood. But for how much longer? All of a sudden it started slowly gurgling heavily again. We ducked, as if that would help us from this new threatening danger. And once again an ear-splitting crash. Once again the tower started shaking, and once again mortar and limestone fell upon us. This time heavy gunfire exploded near the door.

Now there couldn't be any doubt. The enemy was shooting at the tower because he suspected that there was a lookout position there. Our telephone line was blown up; it would be impossible and useless to try and fix it. Our people became restless; they wanted out of here. I hesitated because I had been ordered to wait for the battery commander at the tower. "Well, by the time he shows up in this thick smoke, you can turn old and gray," Corporal Baerbohm offered. And for the third time the assault neared, eerily, inescapable, deadly. Once again a shot landed in the middle of the church, but this time almost instantaneously a bright wide flame shot forth. It caught fire. To stay in this position further was suicidal.

We dismantled our gear with trembling hands and ran back down the wretched stairs, and with each step we touched we thought only of getting to the ground. And we managed to get ourselves free still fully intact. Now we needed to seek out a new lookout position. We ran along the village street as fast as we could, weighed down by our heavy equipment. We jumped over a couple of dead people who were lying in our way. They were mostly French. In front of us and behind us were heard the crashing strikes. Various farmhouses were burning.

Suddenly we received a call. It is First Lieutenant Wenzel, who had been hit in the leg and was unable to move as he had tried to get to us in the church. His valet was lying ten steps away from him. We didn't need to bring him back because shrapnel had blown away the entire back of his head. While two men assisted in getting the battery commander out of the line of fire, the rest of us nestled into a gable of a nearby house. The view from here was limited, but to cut off the troops it was still enough.

Our infantry was still at the same position. The poorly directed shots of my battery were at least one hundred meters off. It's high time that we once again establish communications. Finally, after nearly a full hour, we got there. And just as I was about to relay the firing positions, I saw on the edge of the forest a wide and thick cornflower blue mass materialize. Without any resistance they were moving forward; an adjoining field was shielding them from the eyes of our infantry. The thought that without doubt the enemy wanted to mount their offensive here went through my head at lightning speed. And then I allowed the battery to reposition itself and aim for the new target. A minute later the first round was shot toward them. High above the heads of the blue mass it detonated. "One lower. Break off one hundred meters." Our second greeting fell right into the middle. They sprung apart, so that it looked almost comical. And now it hissed from group to group and each of them found its target. Now there wasn't any additional assault; what didn't fall stumbled back into the forest. So we managed it after all. The remaining parts of the church stood completely engulfed in flames since the time we had so hastily fled from it.

Three blue signal flares over our lines meant that rapid firing was to begin. As it started, the infantry dared to attack. It worked. We saw how the hand-to-hand fighting began, how hand grenades exploded for minutes at a time; then as we observed the fleeing French, we knew that victory was to be ours. Two hundred meters past the enemy's position I laid down barrage fire so no one could escape. Shortly thereafter I saw in front of me the signal flag: "Artillery cease fire—the battle has ended." The resistance was broken; the offensive could now continue.

Lieutenant Fischer took over the command of the battery, and I was his second. As we were about to get going, the brigadier general rode past us by chance and called, "If this can continue through tomorrow night like it has today, fellows, then we will have reached our goal." And it went forth, without any interruption, without stopping. By the twenty-eight of May during the noon hour, we had left the area of the trench warfare. This third advance brought us our largest lead yet of over thirty kilometers. In the early morning hours, we saw Soissons, which lay very close on our right flank, trailing large clouds of smoke. It was very seldom after four difficult war years that anyone wanted to wage an offensive, but now the troops were energized by this prospect in a way I had not thought possible. However, our big win at the Chemin des Dames, and even more so the fact that we now found ourselves in territory that no German soldier had set foot in since 1914, overcame the indifference and exhaustion.

New groups of prisoners, sometimes small squads but then whole troops of them, pulled by and passed us, then numerous pieces of military equipment that belonged to enemy regiments and had been shot to pieces, fell into our hands on a daily basis. Countless batteries, ammunition depots, anti-aircraft stations, and supply convoys that the enemy had abandoned and left lying where it stood. An offensive of such proportions had not even been envisioned by the highest echelons of the supreme commanders. Fifty-five thousand prisoners, eight hundred light and over three hundred heavy artillery, we managed to capture in just the first two days of the offensive.

The French army literally took flight. Should we Germans let this once-in-a-lifetime opportunity slip through our grasp and remain stationed at our original position on the Soisson-Reims Line? If we stayed, the remainder of the enemy would be spared. But if we pushed forward, we might even reach Paris and give the war a different turn. It would be irresponsible to ignore the reawakened fighting spirit of the troops, especially that of the enlisted men, and the command staff reluctantly finally agreed to the advance. But with the continued push to the south toward the Marne, instead of a straight Soisson-Reims line that we had anticipated, we encountered an inlet, comparable to a peninsula jutting out into the sea. This was a great hurdle. Another difficulty lay in the terrain between us and the capitol, which consisted of steep ridges which would make every advance extremely hazardous. These obstacles were known to the generals, but we of course had no idea. The infantry is there to attack and to shoot, both of which we did well, with the result that the enemy continued to retreat. We continued to follow and gave them no rest.

On the fourth day of our advance, the thirtieth of May, we hit the so-called Paris Stand, a natural protective barrier surrounding the capitol. It was here that Foch, now commander-in-chief of all the allied forces and wielding dictatorial power, had amassed all of his reserve troops. This was where he had concentrated his defensive weapons. Here the English, Italians, Americans, and Portuguese had joined the French to stop the German army in its tracks. The result was a battle the likes of which, with the exception of Verdun, had never been seen before. It was staged with such might and power because over there stood refreshed and well-equipped regiments of all branches of the military, who had during peacetime been able to utilize the latest military technology; but here stood the troops who had been stuck in this fire since May 27th, who had two-thirds of their shelters destroyed, who couldn't wage any offensive, who tiredly staggered forth.

Already from about ten kilometers' distance, heavy naval artillery fire was greeting us. Her huge shells ripped entire companies to pieces, but what remained continued to press forward. Numerous squadrons of fighter planes were dispatched and flew over us; our few planes were useless against them. They threw bombs and showed the infantry their targets. We could thank them that they destroyed two of my division's long-range guns before we had even received our firing orders, as we stood motionlessly on the marching line. In between the harnesses of the first guns a direct hit zoomed, and six horses along with their riders were tossed into the winds, ripped into atoms.

Then we galloped over to a nearby hollow through the middle of an open field. But even before we arrived, a new hit had flung our last munitions wagon into the air, filled with personnel. And as we dismounted, we found the torn-off arm of the dead driver Schumacher pinned to the mounting of the fourth gun carriage. We tried to dig in, but the earth was rock hard. What was happening in front and behind us, we didn't know; we only saw the hill that blocked our view entirely. We only heard the crashing around us, and then we discovered with satisfaction that some of it was from our guns that were trying to drive the enemy away from us. It was luck that at least we were free from them, because here the danger of being shot up was less. But unfortunately we had celebrated too soon. As soon as the first group ceased firing, just a scant ten meters behind us another strike broke everything into pieces. We threw ourselves down until the shells could bury themselves. But as we got up we saw that the ammunition handler from the right division and Lieutenant Strachwitz had been mowed down in the middle of the group.

One of them had his lungs ripped apart; the other no longer had a skull. And once again, it hissed around us, but this time the impacts seem to be a bit further away. Could it be that the enemy's fire was satisfied with just these two victims? We kept shooting, continuously at the same target, as we no longer had any communications with the lookout positions; our telephone line must be damaged. A signal balloon was raised high behind us. Three blue signal lights fell from it: "Artillery stop your fire—battle ended." Then we knew: "Paris Positions" were in our hands; the offensive could continue.

And once again we passed the barbed wire and the trenches following the infantry. Mounds of the dead and wounded lay about us, French and German, Italians, English and Belgians, Black and White.[15] We reached the stopping point. Between the fortress there lay the fruits of our labor: gun after gun, everywhere direct hits and damage from our heavy caliber shells. Pieces of protective armor, pulverized positions, torn-up axles, metal and iron tossed about, shattered oak planks, holes as deep as houses torn up by the tusks of our shells, into which man after man was pressed, jumbled together among rocks, wood, and earth.

And on the road, long columns of prisoners with pale and bloody faces. Our victory is huge; but unfortunately so is the sacrifice. The infantry was sliced to bits and there were no more reserves available. A lieutenant of the Pioneers, his arm in a sling, passed us on his way to the regimental medical aid post and declared: "It is pure madness to try to advance any further. We don't have any men left, and the enemy has just received freshly deployed American divisions in order to set into motion a counterattack. I don't even want to think about how this is going to end."[16] He was absolutely correct in his prediction. This day served as the very last day that we would ever win a decisive battle again in this war. What happened later was just a frustrated effort against an overwhelming superior force.

But for the interim the march continued forward. The resistance became stronger. In hand-to-hand battle the enemy was always beaten. Every piece of land needed to be fortified, even though we lacked munitions and the delivery of supplies had halted. We did claim a victory on the first of June at fifteen kilometers' distance. However, the following night we had a turn of fortune. We had come as far as the spread-out forests of Villers-Cotterets, which held the

15. Although two divisions of African American soldiers served in the segregated American Expeditionary Force, none were known to be in the area during this phase of the battle. It is, therefore, more likely that these troops were French colonial soldiers, of which approximately 450,000 served in France. See Richard Fogarty, *Race and War in France: Colonial Subjects in the French Army, 1914–1918* (Baltimore, MD: Johns Hopkins University Press, 2008).

16. The Pioneers, or *Pionieren*, were troops trained in construction and demolition, serving the role of combat engineers.

summer houses of rich Parisians. But in these thick forests with their protective undergrowth the Americans had embedded themselves by the tens of thousands. In this place, all could assemble that we had previously held back. And here in these forests the remainder of our infantry bled out, as they were the first casualties of any battle. It was a wonder that their thinned-out lines were still standing, as they were accosted on a daily basis by the powerful assaults that were now commonplace on the front. Now we understood why our command staff had so reluctantly agreed after much hesitation to continue the march forward past Soissons. For four weeks our regiment stayed in this vicinity, but there wasn't a day that we didn't incur any losses. Then suddenly we were pulled out. We were made to understand that we were to participate in another offensive in a different area that the command staff had worked out. So we secured our guns during the night and proceeded to move backward, while our way was lit up by shell fire.

During this march, a significant change occurred that had larger consequences and meaning for the entire regiment. Our commander, Major van Hamm, had been promoted to lieutenant colonel and was also transferred simultaneously to another post under the same banner. He was already gone by the next day. A general sigh of relief followed him. The staff was said not to be sober for a full two days, and the officers even longer. With his departure the mood rose by at least 100 percent. Soon his replacement, Major Peiker, arrived, who had been the leader of a Guardsman of the Artillery unit, an excellent, benevolent man of good character who quickly became well loved. He was simply astonished that the previous commander had replaced his officers from other divisions while his own first-year graduates, who had stood in the fields since 1914, were still volunteers and non-commissioned officers, or at most were assistant patrolmen. He immediately ordered that the battery needed to receive advancement promotions. One week later I received a promotion to vice constable of the reserve and was on track to be an officer. Well it certainly took damn long enough!

As quietly as we had set off for the Chemin des Dames, we left in the night of the twelfth of July toward our new position. Across to the southwest lay the strong fortress of Reims, a main pillar of the French front. So this was where the command staff wanted us to try and break through? Could we do it? If you took into account the massive amount of artillery we had assembled, you might have had some hope. The problem was the reduced numbers of infantry reservists. But there was probably a good reason for it. Once again, two thousand shells lay next to us, once again the target was theoretically calculated, since test firing at them would have betrayed our attack. The clocks were set exactly. The day could begin.

Under the cover of darkness, on the fourteenth of July, the assault from the trenches from certain infantry positions started. Every position was worked feverishly. The artillery adjusted its calculations, taking into consideration the fluctuations in weather that were necessary for the proper trajectory of the guns. That's because we had just received from the field weathermen the newest updates on wind direction and strength in different altitudes and also the barometer and temperature readings. At midnight "all was in order"; the field mess hall had supplied us with food and warm coffee. At one thirty a.m. everyone was at their posts. The quiet of the spring-like night was broken by a few infantry and artillery shots. Everything as usual. Everyone listened and waited. The leaders as well as the assistant leaders kept looking down at their watches. One minute before two. Now!

With great force the artillery and mortars started opening their gullets. Again the earth shakes far and wide. You only hear crashing and hissing; you only see flashes of light and long snakes of fire. The heavy artillery, whose shells fly more slowly, fired many more projectiles before the lighter ones, because these projectiles needed more time on their trajectory, so that exactly at two a.m. the first shells hit all targets at precisely the same time. And from this point on it howled and thundered without pause at the same strength for hours. The positions of the individual guns are no longer recognizable, because they are shielded by thick smoke rings. It stings the eyes so that they start weeping. But that is now so insignificant.

The enemy answers with a few of his heavy batteries. At a nearby station the ammunition supply flies into the air. In this moment it doesn't touch us, and additionally the shrapnel didn't fall on us either. Suddenly it becomes bright and then even brighter! Daylight is upon us! What will it bring us? We had heard that the Kaiser arrived at the front in order to observe the battle in a very high tower located far from the action. This news, that perhaps under any other circumstances would have made a meaningful impression, we heard, but shortly thereafter forgot about. How could we have reacted any differently? It is now six a.m. We start the fireworks. Every four minutes the sheaf of fire springs forward another one hundred meters. I remembered how it was from the Chemin des Dames. Would we also have to battle alongside the infantry? Let's not think about it. With our binoculars we see our stormtroopers appear up high and then immediately disappear again. Are we now at the point of hand-to-hand combat, or is the enemy lying up there destroyed as it was on the twenty-seventh of May? We continue to shoot. At eight a.m. our scopes are set at seven thousand meters. That is the maximum limit. The two thousand shots have been fired. Our work has ended. The horses advance; we are following the infantry.

I ride out with the battery troops in order to find a new lookout post. We arrive at the enemy's position. It is a pile of debris. Direct hit after direct hit. But it is astounding that the dead are not to be found among this. In addition, there is virtually no military equipment to be discovered. Just then a small group of prisoners neared us. It was led by a wounded sergeant. I asked him how the attack had played itself out. "Good," he says, "because we didn't find any resistance. The French had evacuated the trenches at midnight. The attack was relayed to him just in time." But that is just terrible news. So we just spent six hours firing on an empty target and therefore squandered our diminished ammunition.[17] What was to happen now? We weren't puzzled for very long.

The forest that we had just entered was under heavy fire. I dismounted and sent the horses back and then we pushed forward. We estimated the front was running about one kilometer ahead of us, as we could determine by the sound of mortar strikes. We came upon a small fortification that was full of the dead and wounded. Black troops. But in front of them lay double that amount of our own infantry. Everywhere there was moaning and groaning. A couple of medics were opening uniforms and dressing the wounds of the numerous casualties. They also carried some men together on the same stretchers, in order to have them seen to by an as-of-yet-unbuilt field hospital. But what would be the use of it here? The first shrapnel rounds were already flying over us. We kept running. We saw new enemy trenches come into view that had already been taken. The whole forest was crawling with the wounded that had retreated.

17. This marked the initiation of the Second Battle of the Marne, July 15–18, 1918, the last German offensive. The failed attack was followed by the continuous advance of the Allies until armistice was declared.

I asked a corporal where the headquarters were that I was to present myself at. "It is situated at the forest's edge, if it is still alive," he answered and continued onward as if in a dreamlike trance. It is ghastly listening to the collapse of the trees that were being torn out of the ground by shell impacts.

A shell fragment hits one of my communications assistants in the case that he's carrying on his back. He screams, but when we examined him we found he wasn't wounded. The impact was so strong that he was shaking from head to toe. Finally we locate the edge of the forest. Immediately near the front we detect the enemy's barrage fire. More and more wounded are passing by us. They say, up front, it is pure hell! The command staff was embedded behind a thick oak tree. I presented myself to a first lieutenant, whom I had thought was the aide-de-camp, and then discovered that he was leading the regiment. Just as of one-half hour ago. All of his superior officers are now either dead or wounded. I asked him where my artillery units should fire. He told me the target and then added: "However, if you don't begin firing immediately, it won't do any good, and then we'll all find ourselves on the other side." A heavy shell hit right in front of the oak tree and covered us with sand. There wasn't any use to lay down telephone lines over to the cannons; they would have been destroyed in a matter of seconds. Therefore, all I did was draw out the target on the map and sent the communications assistant back. Hopefully he would arrive safely!

I asked about the situation. The enemy had established itself in its reserve position and we were highly outnumbered. And he had enough prior warning of the assault, so it made it very easy to acquire fresh divisions to thwart any advance. And these were going to arrive at any hour now. We were only able to advance by five kilometers. Now we were stuck here in the middle of this forest, without any knowledge of what was coming for us. Our flight squadrons are useless because they can't tell what's happening with the enemy because the trees block all views. An orderly springs toward us: "At the Second Battalion Second Lieutenant Schmidt just fell due to a shot in the head. Vice Sergeant Mueller has just taken over as battalion leader. Combat strength is sixty-four men." "Thank you," the first lieutenant says curtly. Then the breathless orderly springs up again just as a new attack showers us with splinters and massive amounts of sand.

As we raised ourselves, we heard the hissing of light artillery over us in the direction of the enemy. That could only mean my artillery units. Perhaps our strikes will serve to boost the morale of the infantry and strengthen their resistance. The strikes in front started getting stronger. Machine guns were rattling, mortars crashing, rapid-firing gunshots whizzed by. After five minutes it becomes more quiet and then subsides. The wounded are coming back. One states: "The enemy with about five-hundred-men-strong just started a counter assault. The Third Battalion stopped the advance and is holding its position. Losses: one officer, twenty-nine men. The battalion only has the combat strength of one officer and forty-eight men. Five machine guns are still operable. A new assault cannot be defended." "Thank you," the lieutenant says yet again. Then he sends the messenger back to the infantry leader with a short message. It says the regiment will have bled out in about an hour. Then the French will have an easy time with us.

As darkness fell, we received the order to move back. Under the rapid firing of our artillery, the infantry was to disengage from the enemy. However, the French surmised that we wanted to catch them during the night. Therefore, they changed their direction of fire into the forest and set up a blocking cordon behind our backs. We had to get through this, otherwise we would have been captured. In the darkness you could barely see your own hand in front of your eyes. All around us it was lightning and twitching and gruesome ringing. We just jumped from one tree to another and then threw ourselves down again. Everyone tried to find his own mode of protection.

By calling out to each other we tried to determine if we were still together. We tripped over the fallen and over torn-off tree limbs, we fell into the trenches along with the dead, but we didn't give this much thought. Our only thoughts were to try to get out of here safely. I lose my helmet, now I continue running without it. When we finally reached an open area, we discovered that Corporal Beerbohm is missing. He was later found by the French and buried. Our artillery unit is positioned close to a shot-up farmhouse and is firing its last rounds. I present myself back to the artillery commander. He is waiting anxiously for the cavalry, which should have long ago arrived.

The other division was set upon as it was retreating. Two dead gunners were lying sideways and a few of the wounded have been carted off. The farmhouse is being hit with heavy artillery and we are being pounded by the resulting shrapnel. Finally the sound of horses' hooves! That must be the cavalry. However, only three riders were visible; one of them is Corporal Schueler. He reported that the artillery, in a battle two kilometers to the back, were completely shot up. The intelligence command has fallen. What to do now? Lieutenant Fischer ordered that the supply wagons be left as well as the field kitchen and to gather any available horses and bring them here immediately. Even though under these circumstances the munitions wagons needed to be left behind, at least the artillery could be rescued. The non-commissioned officer rides off quickly. Will he be able to return in time? Then the last of the batteries next to us were being disassembled. Individual infantry units now appeared in the darkness in front of us. We wait. After a time, we again see a couple of shapes become visible. As they passed us, one of them said: "Say, you look like you want to fall into the hands of the French?" "Why?" we asked. Then Lieutenant Fischer established a chain of marksmen on the high ground. Finally, we hear the sound of hoofbeats. Thank goodness! The team has arrived. Within seconds we mounted and were off. Then we retreated in a gallop.

The offensive was wrecked, that was a fact. But even worse was the realization that our infantry was used up and now couldn't be replenished, and behind us stood an enemy, who had at his disposal dozens of fresh and unimpaired divisions that could be used at any time to break through. We had hoped that our regiment would serve as the one to make ground at the front, as we had suffered greatly. My battery lost its permanent staff sergeant Blauk and nine men, and we counted in addition three officers and sixteen men among the wounded. We saved nothing besides the guns. Under these circumstances, could we even still be combat ready? We reckoned not, but the high command had a different opinion.

In these days of great suffering they kept entire divisions that had been reduced to just ten men in the line of fire, not to mention that the artillery only had a total of nine guns! In strongly constructed lines and in great masses and under the watch of a ramped-up artillery, the enemy rammed into our protective lines where they found just one defender every ten meters. Here our front line would be and must be broken. And still it couldn't be done. With a will that bordered on heroic efforts, the rest of the infantry sacrificed itself in a battle that was entirely hopeless. We retreated just one step at a time, and the terrain we covered was just a huge scene of carnage. We were under fire where we stood and directed both by day and night. The third cannon received a direct hit, so that we had to leave it where it was along with four of our dead; the First Battery was laid to waste by fighter squadrons, the division headquarters destroyed and swept away by machine-gun fire. We kept standing and shooting. One entire week long. Then suddenly we saw reserves coming on cars and supply wagons. Young recruits, who had just been drafted, who could hardly understand how to carry a gun properly. Fodder for the guns! They were supposed to drive back the attack. We could account for only half of our supplies and were relieved. I took with me this certainty: that this was the beginning of the end.

The mood was dim everywhere. During this march, the battery leader advised me that my papers were cleared for me to become an officer and that I should be prepared to obtain the necessary uniform. In a little town we came upon our replacements. Now it seemed it was only necessary to be schooled in a bivouac encampment. With anxious eyes the boys looked at us. None of them could have been older than nineteen. They couldn't recognize the individual pieces of artillery gear and knew even less about how to operate them. They now became our burden, but at least they had brought with them munitions and supply wagons as well as horses. On paper, we were now considered replenished and able to fight, but in reality, we were little more than a traveling circus. So, with this in hand, three days later we found ourselves back at the front.

Here we found what we had already anticipated: a weak, thinned-out but tough line of defense that had been able to hold its position in spite of the massive attack of the enemy. But with each passing day, the enemy became stronger in its superiority. It could allow its troops that had stood thirty-six hours in the line of fire to move back for an entire week. However, our people had to stay until all of them had bled out. Whatever was sent forward was immediately counted as dead. It was a wonder that we hadn't been overrun at least one hundred times over already. Very slowly but yet steadily we moved in retreat, sometimes only a few hundred meters per day and sometimes a few kilometers. We are thin and starved and the little food we do get is supplemented by all kinds of substitute items.

However, the shirkers we complained about had become army contract suppliers and in that way had made even more gains for themselves. These thoughts riled us. Where is the right in all of this? Our barrels are shot out. We have too few horses and munitions. Our replacements are the half-grown, and have come to us undernourished and in need of a rest. One thing they do understand is how to die—we all sensed that. The memories of this particular time are very blurry to me, because we couldn't escape the fire. Mortars, aerial bombs, fighter squadrons, blood, and death were all mixed together as one. After one month my regiment was pulled out. The defensive battle between Oise and Aisne had finished it.

Very far behind the front we found leave accommodations. For how long we did not know. We once again received replacements who weren't any better than the previous bunch. This is where I was promoted to lieutenant, together with two other comrades. I celebrated this achievement with a big cocktail party at headquarters. I could justify this expense because I had over eight hundred marks due to me through having had outlays for uniforms and mobilization pay in addition to back pay.

What use was any money if you didn't know whether or not you were going to be alive the next day? One spent it as soon as one had any opportunity to do so. I even bought a few bottles for the non-commissioned officers of my battery to prop up their morale. They were sorely in need of it.

Soon we were alerted. We needed to go back to the front. But this time we didn't have very far to march; the front had advanced very close to us. In the so-called Siegfried Line we built the positions for our artillery. How much has already been discussed about this defensive belt! It was said to be impenetrable, and the enemy was supposed to gnash its teeth in frustration. As we arrived, instead of built foundations we found just a chalkboard under a tree that indicated that the guns should be positioned here. And with the infantry's trenches it wasn't much different. Some barbed wire was laid in front of them, and the shelters and tunnels had not yet been completed. Just some light field fire would destroy them. Even then, it took the English and Americans a full two weeks before they had shot everything to smithereens and felt they could advance.

With unbelievable losses, we were able to deflect it. But evermore fresh divisions pushed forward and stormed us anew. As they finally forced their way in, they found nothing but the dead and dying of the occupying troops that were defending the trenches. And further and further the bloody front retreated. We knew we weren't just being defeated but rather literally being crushed to death. Now the fighter squadrons flew over us in groups of thirty, forty, or fifty planes and dropped their bombs on our artillery, infantry, convoys, and staff headquarters, on trains and munition depots. Their tanks, at first just sporadic and made-fun-of, now dragged themselves continuously over tree limbs, barbed wire, and foxholes and squashed everything they passed over. A few were shot apart but it didn't do any good because now they came snarling at us in groups of fifteen to twenty at a time.

At first it was a furious hatred that gripped each man as he reconciled himself with the fact that courage and persistence were not enough; that he was sacrificing himself, even though it didn't give any advantage to him or to his comrades. And this feeling of futility and powerlessness from day to day robbed him of the rest of his resistance of moral conscience. In the communications center it was said that insubordination now reigned. In the front lines there was no sign of that; that's where one stood for the other, as death was sweeping over all of us. How much longer would it take until we had reached our border and then would battle on German ground? Soldiers back from leave and the wounded, who were returned to us as healed, spoke about the hopeless conditions in the homeland. It might not have been their intent, but they exaggerated their tales and with that threw further unrest into our own lines. But it was impossible to prevent them from talking like this, and otherwise they would have done it behind our backs anyway. The war was lost and the command staff now was reconciled to it. Now all that matters was to be able to broker a peace treaty under the most favorable conditions. As I departed on the first of October for leave, the Berlin Extra announced that Germany had asked the allies for a ceasefire agreement.[18]

In Bromberg, the only ones who still clamored for victory were the über-patriots and the unschooled. Everyone else knew exactly or could imagine how it stood with us out there. There wasn't any use to disguise it. Three weeks later I returned back to the theater of war operations. Just over the border in Luxemburg, in Montmedy, the train stopped. It appeared the enemy's heavy artillery could even reach here. Unrest everywhere. The trains were in the process of loading. Many displaced persons were running around. At the mustering point I found out the site of my regiment. It was three-days' march from here, but perhaps I would find a truck that could take me near there. I was in luck! An assistant doctor, Dr. Burzello, who

18. Germany first asked for a cease-fire on October 3, 1918.

had also just returned from leave, had secured himself a place on a bakery truck convoy, and he made himself small so that there was still room for me. Everywhere we came upon vehicles that were coming back and were loaded with military equipment.

The next morning, we arrived at our destination completely shaken and rattled through and through. The commander quickly advised me of the most recent developments of the regiment. Four officers were dead, nine officers were wounded, seven guns were lost, and of those, five had been direct hits. The losses on non-commissioned officers and men were more than one hundred and fifty. My battery stood in firing position. My valet Jablonksi was waiting for me at the entrance of the village in order to show me a protected route of advance. The whole area was being churned up by heavy strikes so that we needed to wait until cover of night. Then we went forward by leaps and bounds. Two wounded came limping toward us; they were from my division. "It's good that Sir Lieutenant has returned," said the one, "just now the first artillery position has been struck and Sir Lieutenant Krahn was hit. Now we don't have any officers other than the battery leader." Then I kept running.

During this night the lookout vehicle was torn to shreds; the next morning suddenly all communications with the command center were broken. As we searched for the reason, we learned that an aerial bomb had destroyed it. The only one who escaped any injury was the aide-de-camp. That's because he was just on his way to let us know that during the night the regiment was to pull out and join the Fifth Army that was fighting at the Maas.

During this march toward St. Leger, we were informed that the ceasefire had been accepted by the enemy. At the same time, we also found out that our current government had collapsed. Another rumor said that the Kaiser fled the country. In the meantime, all of this talk was just scuttlebutt to us. Then the news became clearer. There was no longer any doubt: the fire in front of us ceased, so at least the part about the ceasefire must be true![19] The commander called the officers to him. He made very short work of it and only read a telegram that had been sent that stated that Ebert and Scheidemann had taken over the running of state business. The troops were still to follow the command of its present leadership. More detailed instructions would follow. With that we were dismissed. We left silently.

19. The armistice was final on November 11, 1918.

Just as I was dispensing this news to my people, I received the order to lead the 985th Light Munitions Division, as the current commander Count von Schwerin urgently needed to return to his homeland. Both officers and enlisted men were overcome with a heavy malaise during these hours. What was to become of us now? Everyone had wished for the war to end, but now that it had finally come, we couldn't celebrate. The unusually harsh conditions that the enemy had already demanded for conceding to the ceasefire made us realize that even greater sacrifices would be required for peace. We stood around in groups and exchanged opinions, but at least universally agreed that to continue to fight this war would be futile. We were at the end of our strength; any further resistance would be suicidal. However, now we had a change of government and that worsened our frustrated position even more, although we understood it. We held it for cowardice that the liberal Leftist Party had taken advantage of the fatherland in order to fulfill their own aspirations. We saw no relief from this suffering and did what we always did under these sorts of conditions: we got as drunk as we could so we didn't have to think more about it.

Two days later the general retreat began. It was overly hasty. The enemy had worked that out so there was no opportunity to return to the many supply stations to retrieve and take the contents with us.[20] It was a pity that we had to watch how hundreds of millions now just fell into the enemy's hands. As long as we pulled through French territory, we were greeted by the tricolored flags that the inhabitants had hoisted. Massive numbers of war prisoners came toward us in order to reach the Allies that were following closely behind us. No one was concerned about them anymore; they could now do whatever they liked. If horses became tired, we had to leave them behind. Immediately mobs of French surrounded them in order to move them into their own stalls and feed them. If a supply wagon broke down, it was overrun within seconds by those who lusted after it.

But during this retreat, one realized the difference between the front and rear lines. The pitiful remains of the infantry regiments

20. Despite the absence of the traditional leadership (i.e., the Kaiser), German troops largely maintained discipline and unit cohesion as they withdrew from the occupied territories. See Scott Stephenson, *The Final Battle: Soldiers of the Western Front and the German Revolution of 1918* (New York: Cambridge University Press, 2009), ch. 5 passim.

marched in tight formation and were led by the music corps with drums beating. The staff officials and transport vehicle drivers and the crew brothers wore red ribbons in their buttonholes and made fun of those who were still showing obedience to their leaders.[21] But until now they were still in the minority. We had been tasked to vote on a soldier's representative for every division, who would be there to support the leader but was not able to give orders. That didn't seem dangerous, as long as people belonged who had experienced both heartache and danger on the front lines in unison with their officers. For the most part they were reasonable people that understood the rank-and-file order of discipline. But it also occurred that the biggest proponents of these trusted positions, once attained, used them to their own advantage to stir up trouble and become insubordinate. Their sinister objectives had to be taken in stride, as there was no way to separate ourselves from it.

So thus we came upon Luxemburg, which had remained neutral during this war, but even so, the citizens approached us in just as unfriendly a manner as the French had. They openly held the view that they had wished for the downfall of Germany all along and now were pleased with the outcome. We traveled over the Hunsrück [mountains] into the gorgeous Mosel [River] valley. Now we had the homeland under our feet, now we saw the German flags festooned with garlands, now we heard friendly calls and were greeted most heartily. How good that felt! It almost seemed as if we were returning as victors, and yet we were a defeated army; however, in battle we had not been beaten.

From the village of Traben-Trarbach I was able to take a happy memory with me. I was quartered together with a cavalry captain in the villa of the wine merchant Kayser. After a very hearty and long-hoped-for dinner, the host of the house invited us to have a taste of his wine cellar. So we sat ourselves down in a snug little corner of his study and waited until a local resident, a teacher at a secondary school, joined us, and then we started the tasting. One bottle after the other was emptied; it looked like there was no end to it and each one was better than the last. Around midnight we had drunk our way to the year 1895. As we finally finished in the early morning hours and decided to immediately depart as well, we had happily made it

21. Red ribbons were a common symbol of support for Communist and other Leftist groups.

to the year 1879. The host told us that we had opened bottles that no one would ever be able to taste again.

Finally we saw the Rhein. With what hopes had I traveled over it a scant eight months ago as I had returned from Russia! Our fatherland in the interim had suffered such a heavy twist of fate! Now for years the enemy would be able to have their horses drink from its waters untouched and unpunished. And for all of this, two million of our best had to sacrifice their lives!

In Rüdesheim we came to a stop. This is where I received my orders that the next morning I was to load my military equipment and on the next day the regiment would follow. The trip took fifty hours; the cars were unheated and they were bitterly cold. On the sixth of December we arrived in Hamburg. An orchestra in full strength greeted us. I stepped forward and put on my helmet; then we marched with beating drums into the city of millions. Thick crowds were packed in all the surrounding streets. You could see red banners and stripes. My horse, who wasn't accustomed to such thick and swarming crowds, started dancing as if on eggs. In this fashion we proceeded until Villenvorort Halstenbek, where we were to be quartered.

The next few weeks brought us a lot of work as the demobilization was carried out at an accelerated tempo. First, I surrendered the munitions wagons and supply vehicles at the artillery depot, then there was a public auction for the horses. They were auctioned off for a pittance, as there was a substantial inventory. I saw many riders with teary eyes as they parted from the animals that had taken them out of danger and trouble. At the end the troops were given their severance pay and then sent home. Only the staff sergeant with his administrative personnel and I stayed behind in order to conclude the remaining accounts and close the books. On the eighteenth of December, even that came to an end. Field Artillery Regiment Number 223 had ceased to exist.

The officers got together one last time for a going-away celebration. We honored those whom we had left behind and buried in Russia and France. Now once again we traded our war stories. Then the commander had the last word. He started with the fortitude and sacrifice that he had always seen in all divisions of his regiment, but he couldn't savor the fruits of these labors, because a dreadful tragedy had sealed the fate of the German people. Very difficult times were ahead. The fraternal strife might still pit us against each other and tear us to pieces. Then we must stand as one for the fatherland and use all of our soldierly skills that had served us so well and for so long. We were the leaders of the people and the leaders of the people we shall yet remain in the future. Everyone must be a bastion of strength and stand against any enemies of the state. Presently we drank our last glass to this, and to that which had bound us so closely together, namely our comradery. Then we went on our separate ways. I made my way to the train station in order to return to my hometown.

6

Battles against the Bolsheviks

From the outside, in the December days of 1918, the city of Bromberg was really no different than those of Hamburg and Berlin. The streets were filled with idle folk who wore dirty uniforms, and only the inevitable red ribbon secured in a buttonhole seemed to be cared for, or perhaps a red cockade affixed to the hat as well. All sense of honor and decency had disappeared, and it almost seemed as though a shabby and therefore rough demeanor was the best proof that one honored the attainment of revolution. It seemed like everything had been turned on its head. With it, the saddest and most miserable figures were those who now could show off the most, as if they were the masters. All of a sudden, they held all the positions of authority and were members of all of the boards; now it was as if nothing would work without them. They were the ones who criticized the past superiors, and now only they alone and only through their holier-than-thou edicts and measures could anything be accomplished.

However, if you had any actual dealings with these people it quickly became clear that they were just a group of shirkers, deserters, and rear-echelon pigs who had brought forth the revolution at home, while at the same time securing good positions for themselves, and all of this while the front still stood in flames.[1] That this rabble now held the power was a testament that our people were not

1. Probably a slang term from the time, "rear eschelon pigs" is Entappenschweine, literally "staging area swine." "Entappen" was used to describe support organizations—such as rear echelon troops serving in logistical support or medical units—whom the "front swine" (i.e., frontline troops) often looked down upon. Stephenson analyzes the sometimes-strained relationship between the various parts of the German army. See Scott Stephenson, *The Final Battle: Soldiers of the Western Front and the German Revolution of 1918* (Cambridge: Cambridge University Press, 2009).

yet ripe for a real political overthrow. Even so, it was thought that conditions should improve and attempts in that direction were being recognized. The vote for a National Assembly had been decided; the independents were forced to resign from government, and now murder and plunder had been avoided. The proletariat appeared to have wearied; its might was shrinking.

But I had little desire to stay here and await the golden age of my fatherland without any prospects of employment and with nothing really to do. Then, at just the most opportune moment, an advertisement fell into my hands that appealed for voluntary enlistments into the "Iron Division."[2] The advertising agency had its office at the Karlschule and would supply more information there.[3] Now this could be something for me! So I went there immediately. A lieutenant who was leading the interviews gave me the details. The Iron Division was embedded near Riga and was tasked with the job of making sure our supply depots that were filled with clothing, equipment, and food would not be plundered by the approaching Bolsheviks but rather transported and returned to Germany.[4]

In the meantime, some large battles had ensued, and although heavy losses on our side had been somewhat misrepresented, we were now hoping to recruit volunteers to close off any further access to the remaining gaps. I didn't spend much time contemplating this offer and almost immediately signed a bond committing myself to a period of four weeks. I solemnly promised to uphold the revolution and to broker peace and order. This torrent of words did give me pause for thought as I found them ridiculous and superfluous, but I was of the opinion that I wouldn't be quizzed about my philosophical orientation toward their revolution.[5] More or less, I wouldn't be engaged in

2. Schiller's memoir reminds the reader that for many in central and eastern Europe, the war did not end in November 1918. Schiller joined what became known as the *Freikorps*, or "Free Corps," a loose aggregation of paramilitary groups and quasi-mercenaries made up in part of discharged German soldiers who fought to maintain Germany's borders in the east. See discussion in Robert Gerwarth, *The Vanquished: Why the First World War Failed to End* (New York: Farrar, Straus & Giroux, 2016).

3. Karlschule was the name of the school where the agency was located.

4. Riga is now the capital of Latvia.

5. While Schiller clearly held no love for Socialist and Communist groups, he is also dubious of politics of the groups he signs on with. He does not align with

these discussions but rather thinking about how I would best be able to protect life and limb from the enemy's hands. When the shots were whizzing about, you had more to think about than politics.

I had certainly learned much of that during the run of the recently ended war. This fact could easily be confirmed. Now I had become a proper mercenary, but presently I wasn't too worried about it. I had found myself a job that paid very well, and besides my war salary I was also getting eight marks extra per day. What else was I supposed to do, anyway? I hadn't learned anything, and the art of war was really the only thing that I had a lot of experience with. Therefore, I was very happy with my decision! With anticipation and in much improved spirit, I celebrated Christmas [1918] with my parents, and then on December 30th I was called back to the advertising agency, where I was told that I would be departing that very same afternoon on an express train to Riga along with Cavalry Captain von Briesen.

I quickly packed my suitcase, then my new valet arrived, who was to accompany me to the train station. The parting was a lot harder for me this time but it was because I was going into unknown and vastly different circumstances, the course of which could not be predicted. In the station lounge the cavalry captain, my new traveling companion, was waiting for me. He made a decidedly rickety impression. He had white hair and seemed to have very mixed feelings about this assignment. A bottle of wine strengthened our acquaintance. I found out that he had filed divorce papers and that it had hit hard emotionally, and now he needed distraction and a change of pace. However, reading between the lines I felt that he had come to an end and was seeking death but was too proud to do it himself. His wish, though, was soon granted.

As the train rolled, we had the cushioned seats made into beds and then promptly fell asleep like the gods. The next afternoon we were already in East Prussia. Then we traveled further to what had been the Russian border. In the twilight we had reached Wirballen, the central railroad station.[6] Now we were in war territory. We already

---

dominant scholarship on the motivations of these paramilitary formations, which focuses on their violent participation in early Weimer Germany, in particular against the political Left. Many were later painted as precursors to the Nazis. See Gerwarth, *The Vanquished*, 70–71.

6. Now Virbalis in Lithuania, on the southwestern border with Poland.

noticed that there had no longer been any civilians on the train, which ran very slowly and carefully and stopped at many local stations for longer periods of time. We asked several men in field gray uniforms, who were standing guard and holding rifles, what the situation was like here. Their answers gave us as little confidence, as did their appearance. They shrugged their shoulders and said they really didn't know what was going on at the front and really didn't want to know either. They had only been engaged in order to secure the passage and safety of the goods and supplies, but not to fight. If the enemy should dare to come nearer, what would they do? And with that they pointed their thumbs behind them, in the direction of Germany. Then I knew that this rabble only stayed here in order to richly line their own pockets, that every pledge to the fatherland or to a sense of responsibility was a foreign concept, and that it would be better for us to chase them away. But where would we get any replacements? And who could be certain that the next crew would be any better than the first? So those were the new comrades! But what more could we expect, since after all we ourselves were mercenaries! I continued to speak at great length with the cavalry captain over these issues, who declared them to be just as hopeless as I had. Then we fell asleep.

As we woke, we were greeted by a new year [1919] and at the same time had reached the train station at Riga.[7] We immediately sensed a distinct frenzy and hasty rushing about. A lot of furniture and crates stood around on carriages, and in between those a lot of agitated people, who seemed to be running to and fro with no real plan and seemed not to be able to get away fast enough. Our first stop was at the command center that was stationed in a government building. Even here everything was completely disorganized! In front of the building, there were many baggage cars that were loaded with huge stacks of official documents; you could hear the sounds of nails being driven into crates from the rooms inside; on the steps you saw the

7. Latvia had declared independence in November 1918 and was promptly attacked by Russia in December. Schiller arrives just in time to experience the fall of Riga to the Bolsheviks on January 3, 1919. The Russians soon declare the Latvian Socialist Soviet Republic, but fighting continued between supporters of the old regime and the Bolsheviks. The Germans not only wanted political dominance in Latvia for its own sake, Latvia and its neighbors could be a useful hedge against Russian incursion into East Prussia.

shapes of people scurrying up and down the stairs. We asked for the division commander, to whom we wanted to introduce ourselves. No one could tell us where he might be found.

Finally, we located an aide-de-camp, who was busy supervising the packing of weapons. After a hurried introduction, we told him we had just arrived and needed to have instructions about our duties. He declared we had come at a very inconvenient time because they were busy with the packing and moving out. He had his hands full and couldn't help us at all. If the commander were here, or where to find him, he had no idea. We continued our search. A general staff officer approached us, identified by his wide red intelligence stripes. He was in just as much of a hurry as everyone else. Once again, we asked for clarification. "Very sorry; I don't have any time," he answered. Finally, a doctor showed us to the offices of the commander. It didn't look any better here than in the other rooms. Closets and drawers were open, papers were strewn about everywhere, and a couple of transcribers were carrying some suitcases out. Is the commander here or will he be returning?, we asked once again. They didn't know; he had ridden off during the night. Where he went no one knew. We weren't any the wiser; it seemed pointless to wait around.

Therefore we decided to find our lodging quarters. Just as we were preparing to leave, an aviation officer appeared and told us that the commander, Colonel Kummer, was expected back at any minute. We learned that the headquarters was being transferred to Mitau because the Bolsheviks were on the march.[8] Yesterday a large battle was waged between the last of our military and the enemy at Gross-Hammersdorf, and it didn't end well for us. Now the enemy was positioned just twenty-five kilometers away from the city. It was doubtful that we could hold the city, especially because inside the city walls there were lots of Bolsheviks to be found, who could start shooting at us any minute! Now I understood the frantic haste around us! The staff of the command center were scared for their lives and therefore could not get away fast enough! It was likely that during the course of the war, they had gotten used to avoiding battles, and that's why the thought of engaging rattled them to their very core.

Finally, Colonel Kummer appeared, as agitated as his subordinates. We introduced ourselves and offered our services to his unit.

8. Mitau is now Jelgava, just southwest of Riga.

He greeted us curtly and declared that he was overwhelmed at present, that he couldn't decide exactly what to do with us, and that we should present ourselves again in the morning. Then he thanked us for our service. With that we were dismissed. Our impression of this unit was not favorable; we anticipated doom and gloom, since its leader seemed to be running about so scatterbrained.

We headed over to the officers' quarters, where our valets had already arrived with our luggage. We were assigned rooms that were outfitted with all the newest comforts. The dining room was even more impressive; its three mighty crystal chandeliers covered nearly the entire ceiling. After we had finished a very hearty lunch, the cavalry captain recommended we take a walk through the city streets in order to observe the goings-on. The news of the unlucky battle and the nearing of the dreaded Bolsheviks seemed to have made its way to the citizens. Everyone, but especially the wealthier classes, was fraught with anxiety and worry. And who could blame them, since they had already become well-acquainted with the bloodlust shown by these Weltbegluecker.[9] In front of many houses you saw trucks that were being loaded with furniture. Now we understood all the frantic activity we found at the train station as we arrived this morning. All that was worth anything and could be transported was on the move back to Germany until the threat had subsided. And good for them who were taking to their heels! At least they could save their own lives. Those who elected to stay and couldn't part from their treasures, however, were for the most part either shot, beaten to death, or sentenced to death by the new regime. It wasn't a good idea to believe in the goodwill of the Bolsheviks, since they had none to spare.

Only a very few German soldiers could still be seen. In comparison, you saw more folks dressed in a gray-blue uniform with blue cuffs on the coat and trim on the caps. In comparison to our troops, they were like night and day. As soon as they came upon a German soldier, they greeted him with an erect posture, and their prominent faces glowed with willpower and determination. I asked who these people were and found out they were volunteers in the newly established "Baltic Military" that was overwhelmingly comprised of

9. Something like "bringers of world happiness," Schiller uses this sarcastic term to refer to those who establish paradise on Earth by attacking and killing off those who disagree with them.

Kurland's nobility. The threatened loss of their lands, which the Bolsheviks would immediately confiscate if victorious, had moved them to join forces and create their own troops. Soon after they formed, they were joined by members of the upper classes as well. And even though they had not yet been properly trained, they had shown great promise during previous battles. Later on, where necessary, whether to force an assault or defend one, the Baltic Corp was at the ready and threw themselves into battle with a fervor just like the very best of our freedom fighters.[10] With these efforts they sustained heavy losses, but they gave it a good run for the money nonetheless. Many of our so-called revolutionary heroes should have taken a lesson from these corps. It was a great pity that by numbers they were too weak to show any lasting success. That shouldn't detract from their heroic efforts, though.

A lot of senseless riffraff was lurking all over the streets. They crawled about as if they were searching for places to loot. Probably hidden in their rags was a revolver or a dagger that would come in quite handy as soon as the opportunity to murder and plunder presented itself. These were undoubtedly the Bolsheviks who lived within the city walls. The aviation officer had told us that so far, they could not yet dare to raise their weapons against us. However, they were just waiting for the moment that we were gone and their comrades could move in, and then they could root around in a bloodbath. As I looked upon them, I began to pity all of those that would yet fall into their hands. At the very latest, by tomorrow morning they would rule this city. Then the rage would begin.

Very depressed, I returned to the quarters with the cavalry captain. Our thoughts were so consumed with the threatening danger at hand that we took little notice of the impressive palaces and monuments that we kept encountering. We wished we could depart immediately for Mitau because we felt as though we were completely up in the air here. We felt entirely abandoned. And it seemed as though we were stuck in the middle of a volcano that could explode at any second and wipe us all out. Still, we had to stay because the division's commander had asked us to present ourselves the next morning. We did not know that during this time Riga had already surrendered and the division was in retreat behind the Düna [River].

10. "Friedensregimenter," literally "peace regiments."

By now it was five p.m.! A deep darkness lay over the streets; they were only sporadically lit by a few lanterns. The cavalry captain had seated himself next to me in the dining room, had ordered a bottle of wine, and we were in the midst of swapping various battle stories. Besides the two of us, there was only a pair of unknown officers a distance away at another table. Suddenly a messenger tumbled breathlessly into the room and screamed: "The Bolsheviks have entered the city!" We sprang up and opened the windows. Faintly we heard the sound of gunshots in the distance. Then a hand grenade exploded; then it was quiet again. Someone ran over to the telephone in order to call the commander for an update. The phone line was dead. Most probably the lines had been cut. A field gray soldier ran by and called: "Everyone assemble at the train station!" With that he disappeared into the darkness.

We hurried back to our rooms and helped the valets pack our suitcases. Since it seemed to take too long, we just threw everything in topsy-turvy. After five minutes we were back downstairs. We went to a gun cabinet and took the carbines and ammunition. Then we opened the front door in order to hurry to the train station. One of the two unknown officers was the first to step out in the open. He had just taken the first step on the stairs when suddenly we saw three or four flashes of light come from the windows of a house across the street. "I've been hit!" he was still able to call out to us before collapsing. We had to leave him there, slammed the door shut, and bolted it. Cavalry Captain von Briesen suggested we take cover to wait out the attack. Before that we turned off the lights, so that the enemy wouldn't be able to see us. But as soon as one of our group neared a window, numerous shots from across the street were fired. To defend the house seemed useless, as we were only three officers and ten men, and at any rate we were cut off.

We held a quick council of war. We decided to try to escape through a back door and then reach a street that way. Our attempt didn't go the way we expected. We came upon a narrow alley and chose a path at random. From the train station we could hear the sounds of machine-gun fire. That served to give us direction. Suddenly, right in front us, we saw a fiery glow. What could that be? We didn't have long to wait before we knew. The Bolsheviks had ignited the German theater, located right next to the train station, in order to secure a better view of those defending the station. They sat in all the windows and on the roof and were firing across the entire perimeter of the train station. We were in a troubling position. There was no use in running any further; we were sitting ducks. It was only from the other side that we might still be able to reach the train station. A park was located there and it was pitch black. We looked for the darkest streets, so that we wouldn't be seen, but even so an enemy patrol spotted us.

Suddenly we saw three people coming toward us who were speaking very loudly in Russian. Quickly we pressed ourselves into a doorway. The footsteps came nearer. Then we suddenly noticed that a window was opened and a voice called out to the men. It was certain that they had been warned not to go further, because they stopped in their tracks, pressed themselves against a wall, and secured their arms for firing. Now we were absolutely certain that these were Bolsheviks. We had to break forth and outrun them immediately, otherwise they would just bring in reinforcements and we would be lost. We broke free and ran quickly forward. Three shots were fired upon us, from not even ten meters away. Then we returned fire with our rifles, which we fired while running. Two of the fellows collapsed; the third attempted to flee. A corporal kneeled, positioned his rifle barrel, and fired. At that same second the escapee tumbled to the ground and wasn't going to get up again. Only then did we notice that one of our people was lying in a doorway. As we quickly ran back there, we saw it was Cavalry Captain von Briesen. He was dead. Shot right through the stomach. The Bolsheviks had taken excellent aim. I quickly grabbed his briefcase, then we hurried along, because the shots had likely put this entire enemy rabble directly onto our heels. We were in luck. Without any further confrontations, we reached the train station.

Captain Graf von Zeppelin was in charge of the command center. He had gathered all those who were still remaining after the fall in Riga. He told us that the division's retreat order was to have been delivered by messenger because the telephone line had been disabled. But this messenger giving us the necessary notice never arrived. Perhaps he was waylaid on his way and beaten to death or he could have fled himself by quickly boarding a refugee train that was heading in a direction that was much safer.

We were about two hundred men defending the train station. In addition, there were almost fifty nurses and the wives of German citizens whom we needed to protect. Except for a very few, they were gathered, anxiously crammed into the basement of the National House. A long train with the emblem "D-Train" was at the ready on the rails. It would depart as soon as the battle subsided a bit and as soon as we could determine that no more stragglers were to arrive. There were two dead people lying right next to the entrance of the tunnel. The panes of the large glassed-in waiting room rattled whenever a shot was fired at it. Then the glass shattered and clattered all over the concrete floor. There weren't any lights on; only the flames from the burning theater illuminated things, and occasionally we saw light flashes from guns. In this manner, about two hours passed. Then suddenly the Bolsheviks broke free from their cover and in a huge mass and with wild screaming ran toward the train station to capture it. But they hadn't figured upon our vigilance. A hailstorm of bullets whistled toward them, struck them head-on, so that they fell in droves. Then the rest fled faster than they had arrived.

Graf von Zeppelin used this second of general confusion and moral depression on the enemy's part to his advantage and ordered us to step onto the train. Just a few minutes later, the wheels started slowly rolling away. That was when the Bolsheviks discovered our blessed plan. But for them it was already too late; we got away. In a terrible rage all they could do was lob their gunfire at the disappearing train. However, soon a new enemy was upon us, firing shots from the rooftops. And even though we traveled with no lights on, in the moonlit evening our train cars were a good target. Too many times the bullets pierced through the thin wood walls. It was very bad luck that we had to go so slowly; however, along the way we had to collect the station's sentry men who had been protecting the rails. We were completely jammed together in the hallways and compartments of the long carriages and kept firing back at the Bolsheviks just to scare them, since we couldn't make out any targets in the pitch-black darkness.

Finally, we passed the last houses of the city. In front of us lay the two-kilometer Düna Bridge. If we could get across it then we had saved ourselves, because according to the news we obtained, no enemy had yet tried to fight past the bridge. Then all of a sudden, we heard loud calls from outside in broken German: "The bridge is set to blow up, as soon as you reach the middle!" Breathless anticipation followed. I felt the shivers go down my back. Could it be that death was going to catch us after all? Were we few people worth so much to the Bolsheviks that they would destroy something worth millions just on our account? The next few minutes would tell the tale.

Far below us the fearsome currents rushed by. You could hear the breaking of the mighty ice floes beneath us that were being shattered by the pilings. The thought of finding your own grave down there was a decidedly unpleasant one. At a snail's pace, the train crawled along. Two nurses in my compartment were praying softly while holding their crucifixes. The seconds seemed like a lifetime. We calculated we might have made it to the middle of the bridge but couldn't reach a consensus. Finally, we no longer heard the rushing of the big ice floes and then even the little ones, and soon we felt we were back on firm ground. We had made it.

In the early morning hours, we arrived at Mitau. Despite the early hour, everyone was moving about. I saw the same street scene as in Riga. Everywhere furniture was being loaded into wagons in order to travel backward into security. It was already well known that in the next few days even this city would be surrendered, as it wasn't easy to protect. The streets and squares were full of baggage carts that didn't look as though they had any destination. A few officers were swearing that nothing had been organized. Numerous field gray soldiers were lounging about as if they were waiting to see just how things would pan out. They didn't seem to belong to any particular unit. Their character was insolent and arrogant, and their facial expressions made them look like professional criminals.

I announced myself once again to Colonel Kummer and informed him that Cavalry Captain von Briesen had fallen yesterday. At the same time, I handed him his briefcase, so that it could be delivered to the proper authorities. I received the order that, along with a Captain von Borke, we were to form a new battalion. In the Russian barracks I met up with my new boss, a gentleman who was in his mid-forties. He greeted me in a very friendly fashion and offered that I should serve as an ordinance and provisions officer on his staff. I only too happily accepted this assignment, especially because there would be a lot to do. I have never regretted this; we got along famously during this entire military campaign.

For the next days I was completely buried in work. If I was able to sleep for three or four hours a night, then it was a blessing. I was responsible for many things: for the timely acquisition of weapons and munitions, for vehicles, field commissaries and horses, for telephones and dishes, for gear and entrenching tools, for feed for the animals, to meals for the troops. The difficulties I encountered everywhere were huge. The mobilization of a troop during peacetime is already an undertaking, even though the conditions in the cities and depots were known and even though business was more or less was regulated. But now the conditions had changed dramatically. There were no telephone communications, so I had to personally ride over to every person's duty station. When I finally arrived, I discovered they were in the midst of packing and balked at giving anything up that had already been put away. Either that happened or I had just missed the bureaucratic official in charge.

One order chased another; I must arrive here, now I needed to go back and settle something else there. It all seemed to be in a complete panic, wherever one looked. I quickly learned that long negotiations were useless. Therefore, I decided in the future to have a lot of staff personnel accompany me and then had them occupy the entire depot until our trucks had been loaded. This was tantamount to robbery, but it was the only way to get anything done. The main office wasn't in agreement with my harsh tactics. They complained loudly and asked me what justification there was for my actions. Therefore, I decided to go straight to the commander and painted him a picture of the sorry circumstances that were making it impossible to form a new battalion. If I hadn't been so forceful and seen things through, our troop would exist in name only, but now they were battle-ready. I didn't mince my words and told him we had achieved the assigned goal, and with that Colonel Kummer gave his blessing to the entire operation. The next order of business was that the complainers were to be relieved of their duties. That was my first success in the Iron Division. I was very happy.

The people we cobbled together were for the most part wretched associates who could only be carefully tolerated. They were very careless regarding the safety of their sidearms and daggers. There were fights daily, with corresponding injuries. However, these were people who had nothing to lose. It was enough that they at least carried out the orders given by their officers. However, in battle they turned out to be excellent fighters. At the time we were just satisfied that we had soldiers, weapons, and ammunition. However, if we were to gain any measure of success, we would have to first educate this motley crew for at least three weeks. And now we wouldn't be able to do it because the division had to retreat further until the Windau. In an army dispatch it was declared with heavy hearts that the wealthy town of Mitau, with its population that had roots and feelings for Germany, would be surrendered to the Bolsheviks, as it had been surrounded on three sides, and the enemy had a force ten times the size of ours. As soon as they could get new formations in line then Mitau would immediately be attacked.

On the tenth of January we departed the city. Captain von Borke received the order to leave with his staff ahead of us in order to secure accommodations. Our battalion was assigned to become part of another troop, but it was only for the duration of the march. That was a rare exception, but with the confusion of the division commander's staff, it was understandable. We traveled by train to Murajewo, let the Polish vacate our quarters, and waited for the rest. After a few days we were told we needed to go to Libau because the line of retreat had been changed and our present location was not in any danger.[11]

In Libau we were greeted by disappointment. Our carefully cobbled-together battalion had been divided, and most of the comrades were in another free corps. Complex tactical reasons were given at this critical moment for taking this measure. In taking into account all that had been demonstratively proven in the formation of our battalion, this division was especially recognized. In Libau we were now to become a new troop. Even though these words were nicely said to appease us, we still couldn't get over our resentment. Especially when we thought about our comrades, who had been taken from us as soon as the majority of the work had been successfully completed. We wanted to throw down the gauntlet and just return home. However, we were mercenaries, and we had signed a bond that was effective until January 31st [1919]. Until then, we had to follow orders. So now we had to start fresh and canvas for supplies. Once again, the grueling activity of a newly organized unit set in. At least now we had had some practice at it. That worked.

In very little time we managed to get three hundred men, whom we divided into two field companies and the command staff. The leaders were Captain Vorkampf-Laue and First Lieutenant Luettgenhaus, as well as a second lieutenant. Luettgenhaus took over the Second Company, and he was an extremely competent and considerate officer who had been recognized for leading large-scale battles on the Western Front. He was circumspect, and even in the most dangerous situations analyzed them correctly. Because of his admirable personal bravery, he was always someone we could all count on. Although a very strict disciplinarian, he had the full confidence

11. Now Liepāja in Latvia, on the Baltic coast.

of his people, about whom he cared deeply. He was a natural-born leader. Unfortunately, though, he was forced to deal with a lot of egotistical personalities who caused significant friction within the command staff. The staff consisted of Captain von Borke; myself; the aide-de-camp, Lieutenant Krause, who was an unapproachable and withdrawn character; and Lieutenant Vogee, who through his sense of humor gave us many happy hours. It was during this time that I engaged a new valet, a growing boy from Saxony by the name of Roemer, who epitomized all the strengths and weaknesses of his tribe. He was as loyal as could be and stayed with me until my service in the military ended. It was hard to look at him at first, because he was so terribly cross-eyed, but after a while I even got used to that.

We were given three weeks' time for training here, and then we were to be embedded at the Windau line. This sort of reprieve was made good use of. The men we assembled at Libau soon learned that in this new battalion good character and sharp discipline reigned. Most notably, the Second Company often had many onlookers as they marched through the streets. They marched in strict formation led by drums and whistles through the streets to our parade ground. We could be well-satisfied with the fruits of our training. We were quartered in a villa, and after a hard day's work brought many a bottle back there. Afterward we played poker games that started with a bid of four marks and ended with bids of up to twenty marks. We went through hefty sums but were being paid very well and didn't really know what to do with it anyway. We were a party of five, consisting of the Captains Borke and Vorkampf, the First Lieutenant Luettgenhaus, the Second Lieutenant Krause, and myself. That was a good consolation in the case of any losses.

In the meantime, an important change of command occurred in the Iron Division. The commander, Colonel Kummer, resigned from his post and Major Bischoff, just arrived from Germany, took over. We looked at him quite skeptically at first. A major and a division commander? That was quite unusual. Usually such an important position would be only be filled by a general! But soon it was shown that the change had been worth it. Now we had a man who was going to restore order. He was an older general command officer, and his first order of business was to assess the troops and make a real fighting machine out of them. With unabashed zeal and ardor, he went forth.

All of those who had no appetite for battle, those who couldn't take orders or who made themselves unpopular, were placed into custody and transported back to Germany under watchful eyes. All the various disposable units were dissolved and transferred to the infantry. It didn't fare any better for the many little outpost commanders. The strength of the staff needed to be reduced by half and even the train station positions needed to be redirected to the front. It only took three weeks to conclude this vast undertaking. It was true that the division was by numbers much smaller, but at the same time we were no longer carrying any slackers with us. We now consisted of people who were at the ready and competent to take up the battle with the enemy. One by one the new commander now replaced the leadership positions. He didn't take into account an officer's rank, but rather his level of service. Many older majors and captains suddenly lost their battalions and free corps. They were replaced by younger and stronger leaders. It was only as soon as all of that was completed that the division was worthy of attention and assault-ready.

Our preparedness for battle had been severely weakened. The Bolsheviks had dared to approach until they were at the Windau River, but despite their overwhelming numbers were still too cowardly to attack our front line. The little river with its steep embankments offered very good defenses. We took this time of cease-fire to better our defenses and restock our supplies and munitions, as well as regulate the flow of replacements. There wasn't really a clear line of battle, as we had previously laid in the east and the west; we didn't have enough personnel to stretch that far. The distance between the individual battalions was in some parts thirty kilometers or more and was only secured through the use of small cavalry regiment patrols. For the time being this was enough though, as long as the enemy didn't launch an offensive. It didn't seem as though they had that intention, because it seemed as though they had overrated our strength. Little ventures in moving forward by the enemy only served to reinforce the idea that it would be a long haul for them.

By the end of January, we were transferred, rode until the station at Wainoden, and then we marched until we reached the village of Niegranden where we were quartered.[12] The command staff and the First Company stayed in the manor house; the Second Company

12. About seventy kilometers (about forty-four miles) inland from Libau, now Nīgrande in Latvia, near the border with Lithuania.

proceeded about two kilometers further toward the east and positioned themselves directly on the river. To strengthen them, another battery was set up with two cannons positioned side by side. Besides that, an engineer's locomotive was placed on a neighboring railway bridge. That was the entirety of our fighting force that we commanded. The distance to the right flank unit was nearly forty kilometers, the one at the left over thirty kilometers. We would have thought that we had been floating in the air if we hadn't known that the other parts of the front were equally sparsely equipped. Captain von Borke satisfied himself with the fact that he could have the companies maintain several important strategic posts that were just far apart enough so that they could still see each other through binoculars. During the day this strategy worked very well; however, at night it clearly was inadequate. Even though we constantly patrolled the perimeter, completely unaware to us, the Bolsheviks were still able to raid our supply wagons on any number of occasions. The attending personnel were shot or beaten to death before we could get there to help, and the robbers had made off with the horses and the contents of the wagons and had disappeared into the night. We were just left out in the cold.

It was very disconcerting that the opponent didn't wear a defining uniform but ran about in their civilian clothes. The only sign of recognition was a small red armband that could easily be thrown away as soon as danger threatened. Only the regiment commanders, a sort of high leadership, distinguished themselves by wearing a red sash that reached from the right shoulder and went down to the left hip. Unfortunately, we rarely caught a glimpse of these people, as they seemed to exhibit a certain shyness about showing themselves to the other side.

In Niegranden we led a very comfortable life. We were quite well-fed and cared for and were able to hunt in the thick forests that yielded rabbits, and sometimes deer, which added additional richness to our meals. In the evenings the mandatory card games were played in the dining room, since the commander was very fond of these. A few times we were needlessly disturbed by gunshots, so we grabbed our rifles and ran out in the darkness, only to return and immediately resume our interrupted game. Incredible amounts of grog were consumed, as this stuff was easily procured and it was bitterly cold. We weren't in need of anything and we were satisfied, as were our men. However, after we had led this kind of life for five weeks it began to become monotonous and boring. People started voicing their opinion that we should think about moving ahead, and we felt strong enough to take on the battle in grand style.

Through our patrols, we discovered that the enemy had nestled itself in small forest villages that were approximately fifteen to twenty kilometers from our position. I had already accompanied such a cavalry patrol a few times before in order to get a better picture of our position. From afar we came upon a couple of Bolsheviks, who were carelessly traversing the perimeter on horseback. We tried to cut off their return route, but they recognized us just in time and headed for the hills. We sprang after them, but they got away, as their horses were better than ours. My bet to capture one of the enemy alive and bring him back home was lost. That cost me five bottles of wine and highly increased my rage against the Menschheitsbegluecker.[13]

In the first days of March it was finally time for the march forward to begin. In a large conference with all of the battalion commanders in the division, the assault was outlined and discussed in great detail. The end result was that we were going to liberate the city of Mitau and take it back. At six a.m. we were to get started. The two days we still had left were used to prepare for the assault. An appeal to the troops showed that personnel, horses, and vehicles were in good order.

Captain von Borke himself promptly led the battalion forward. I was ordered to stay behind and then in two hours follow with the supply units. A bitterly cold wind swept over the bare snowfields as I stood at the head of my convoy of thirty-two wagons and field commissaries and started moving out. In thick furs and coats, the personnel sat huddled on their seats. I didn't think I was going to have any encounters with the enemy, but nonetheless I sent three people out ahead who were to serve as lookouts. This precaution was well worth it.

We followed our companies in pretty much a carefree mood. They should be arriving shortly at their appointed location, the knight's estate at Pampeln, and appeared until now not to have encountered any opposition because we had not heard any thundering cannons or small infantry fire.[14] Perhaps the Bolsheviks had the intention to retreat into the dust without initiating battle. I was comfortably

13. Related to "weltbegluecker," "bringer of happiness to humanity," again tongue-in-cheek.

14. Pampeln is now Pampaļi, around fifteen kilometers (about 9.3 miles) northeast of Niegranden.

smoking my cigar and out of habit had put the reins on the neck of my mount, in order to bury my hands in my pockets.

The unobstructed tract of land was ending and a pine tree forest was coming into view. The lead riders had just disappeared between the first thicket. Suddenly a shot rang out. A second later the entire forest's edge had lit up. An ear-deafening crackling set in; shots by the dozens whistled by; within a moment we were covered by fire. Right at the first shot my horse spooked and with one leap sprang over to the side and threw me off. That saved my life. One glance backwards convinced me of the fact. The personnel had jumped off their wagons and were seeking cover. Two or three shapes broke through and ran toward the rear. I crawled back and ordered that a defensive line be established and had the wagons seek cover behind a bank in a field. A number of vehicles had to be abandoned, where horses had broken down wounded, and we had to leave them where they fell.

While we were still developing our defenses, the Bolsheviks broke free. I estimated at least two hundred men. They didn't get far, though; our rapid-firing weapons chased them back. A group threw themselves forward and fell, but the rest hid anew back in the forest. I allowed us to move forward in fits and starts. A number of people were screaming, but we didn't have any time to attend to them. After the third jump forward, I realized it was useless to wage any kind of assault here. The enemy had too much protection and outnumbered us. The only solution for us was to find a way to bypass their flank. I commanded a sergeant to select from the horse handlers a group, and with these launched a surprise break. As soon as I heard him shout "Hurrah!" I then would commence my own assault. I was hoping that the opponent wouldn't engage in any hand-to-hand combat; until now he had always tried to avoid it.

I was not wrong in my assumption as to the courage of the Bolsheviks, nor to the bravery of my sergeant. He was able to move undetected with his group until he was very close to the left flank. With his bayonet readied and with hand grenades he now started to roll up the flank of our adversaries. We heard screaming and increased gunfire. Then individual enemy combatants sprang forth and ran to the aid of their fallen comrades. This unrest and commotion on the other side we quickly used to our advantage. I ordered sidearms to be loaded, and a moment later I called: "Spring forward—march—march." So we rushed forward as quickly as we could.

Individual shots hit our lines, but we didn't allow this to hinder us. By the time we had advanced to fifty meters, we suddenly discovered that the Bolsheviks had hurriedly disappeared into the undergrowth. We immediately followed. It took a lot of effort; the undergrowth was thick and obscured vision. Therefore, I was only able to establish a few security posts and searched the battlefield. The enemy had left behind twelve dead and ten wounded. Of my men we lost three lead riders and another man; five were wounded. We couldn't afford a time-robbing burial, as we had to reach the battalion. We carried the dead and piled them up and covered them with foliage. The wounded we loaded onto the wagons. Then we proceeded further. Around noon we arrived at the Pampeln Manor, where our company had already taken up quarters. They were extremely surprised when they saw the wounded and then heard what had transpired in this first push. Immediately the entire edge of the forest was searched, but the enemy was gone and didn't show himself. His plan had been well-thought-out, though. He didn't dare assault the battle-ready combat troops and therefore allowed them to pass by peacefully. With the hapless supply convoy, he believed that he had an easier target, and besides, the enemy was lured by the spoils of war. But this time we were able to thwart their plans.

That evening the forest cavalry arrived to let us know that we had been ordered to remain here for the next few days. So we settled in and did housekeeping chores and would have been very happy if we could have discovered the hiding place of the opponent. But it appeared he had just vanished into thin air. However, it was evident that even though not seen, he was stationed all around us in this forest and at any time was prepared to engage in battle. We established lookout positions everywhere and constantly roamed around the entire area.

Two days later, Captain von Borke sent an officer along with twenty men with the order that we were to start searching neighboring areas. As soon as this was finalized, the lieutenant was to present himself back at headquarters. When he hadn't arrived by late evening, we began to get worried. However, by the next morning, still with no news, we knew for certain that he and his troop had encountered a serious misfortune. That's when the commander decided, along with both of his companies, to conduct a full-fledged search for the missing. It took a long time, but he found them. They lay in a ravine. Dead! The bodies were badly mutilated, their ears and noses were cut off, their eyes were gouged out, and the officer had both of his arms cut off. Maybe some of them had even still been alive as this savagery was inflicted upon them. It appeared as if the troop had made a rest stop here and then was raided by complete surprise. No one survived. Drag marks showed that during this battle the Bolsheviks likely had wounded or dead men that they hauled away. And here, at the sight of the mutilated bodies of their comrades, the volunteer battalion of von Borke vowed that from this point on they would no longer take any prisoners. Then everyone swore a pledge to this solemn oath.

In the meantime, we had notice of the status of the other groups that had marched forward.[15] Some had marched forward with absolutely no opposition; however, most of them had been engaged in serious battles. Major Doin's battalion suffered the worst casualties, as he was to storm Murajewo. It lost its leader and half of its men and despite these losses didn't advance an inch. Because the artillery had not been positioned there, the city could not be taken. So now that was the position of the front in the south. The Baltic military had achieved greater successes in the north. The opponent had been overthrown everywhere. They chased him nearly fifty kilometers backward. Still, the Bolsheviks outnumbered us, and our situation was critical, especially because the populace was very fond of the Soviet Star, and one felt threatened by their position behind. Luckily, a bigger transport of replacements from home was in the process of arriving. It was only when the weak areas of our defense had been reinforced that we could even think of waging another assault. Because of these circumstances, the division decided to halt any further advances and tried to reinforce the front line. The approaching time of peace and relaxation I used to my benefit in order to travel back home to Bromberg.

I arrived just in time to celebrate the silver wedding anniversary of my parents, but then just as punctually I traveled back to my battalion on the nineteenth of March [1919]. I didn't return to my previous quarters because the march forward had been ordered earlier than anticipated. Through heavy combat, the Iron Division had made its way to Mitau. With three fresh divisions, they still had to get into the

15. March marked the initiation of a major German-Latvian push against the Russians along the entire line.

doors of the city, as the Bolsheviks had attempted a counter-assault. Then the Baltic military, in a hastened forced march, seized the opponent at just the right time at the left flank.

Now there was no stopping him. Many were driven into the Ar River and drowned, many were captured, and many more were killed. But the Iron Division had suffered badly. This was the reason we were content with taking Mitau and then establishing a fortified position ten kilometers east of the city for the time being. The citizenry was still in a frenzied excitement when I arrived. The Germans were received with open arms because they had brought liberation from this terrible chokehold. But how did the once-beautiful city look now? The Bolsheviks had only lived here eight weeks, but that had been enough to wreak untold havoc. Charred remains of walls marked the places where the houses of the wealthier inhabitants had been standing. Their owners had been led to the prison and disappeared without a trace there. Now their charred corpses were found. The murders had been part of the order of business. Whoever was just even suspected of disagreeing with the Bolshevik teachings forfeited their lives, and neither women nor old men were spared.

The higher class of citizens had been chased from their homes and were only allowed to seek shelter in a basement or on the streets, their former dwellings now given to the proletarian families. If someone dared to grumble, then he was considered a public enemy of the state and summarily executed by a firing squad. About three hundred people were killed in this manner during the short horror the Menscheitsbegluecker wrought upon them. The shops were barren and desolate since the enemy had immediately seized all the goods and distributed them to its workers. Everyone started feeling the hunger now because new edibles could not be delivered since the whole of Russia suffered from lack of food. So the little that still remained was rationed.

Even that did not help. Finally, the only thing that was delivered was flour. The population was divided into three classes. Those who openly wore the Soviet Star received one hundred grams. The middle classes received seventy-five grams and the rest fifty grams of flour per day, per head. The consequences of this were massive death tolls: the victims were the sick, the weak, and the elderly. Dogs and cats were slaughtered, and after they had been eaten, rats and mice were next on the menu. The scope of the misery could best be shown by the fact that even in early March, twenty rubles were paid for a crow and fifty for a mouse. Death circled over the city, and the desperation reached a peak. Then the Germans appeared! No wonder that our liberation of these tortured and martyred people came as such a release that they could hardly contain themselves with gratitude and joy. Our food supplies were also affected, as now our portions had to be reduced by half in order to feed the many hungry mouths in Mitau. However, the sentimental gratitude we received was ample compensation for the restrictions that we had to endure. It took weeks until the worst traces of the Bolsheviks began to blur.

Meanwhile, Major Bischoff had also set up his headquarters in the city. A new energetic assistant arrived, Major General Count von der Goltz, who had already made a name for himself in the liberation of Finland and was now the supreme command of all armed forces, including the Baltic states. His main focus, though, continued to be the Iron Division. He had been given the difficult task to maintain and protect the largest and most important sector of the front.

I met up with my battalion about seven kilometers east of the city limits in Telemuende. The command staff was quartered in an inspector's home; one company stayed in the starved and half-burned-out castle; the others were in a thick forest about two thousand meters toward the enemy and had established a couple of observation outposts. Unfortunately, these were spread so far apart that contact between the two was not possible.

During this period, we received significant reinforcements from a Latvian volunteer regiment. Whether the Latvians were worth anything as field soldiers we did not yet know, because no one had ever fought shoulder to shoulder with them before. The name of their leader definitely had a good ring to it. Amazing stories were told of the courage and ability of Lieutenant Colonel Kolpak. There must have been some truth to it, otherwise no colonel in Czarist Russia would be entrusted to lead a division on the Caucasus front. Soon we officers had the opportunity to get to know this magical being. He visited us. He made a poised and stately appearance, and with his flattering fur hat he stood over two meters high. He smiled engagingly as he approached us. His fine, striking soldier's face spoke of wisdom; his clear and sharp eyes betrayed willpower and bravery. He carried his left arm in a sling because recently he had received his seventh wound. His appearance was firm and sure, his manners amiable and free of even a little hint of condescension toward comrades of another nation, as was usually displayed by the higher-ranking Russian officers. He might have been between forty-eight and fifty years old.

So now he became our comrade for several days; he also quickly became our friend. His regiment was located north of us and was following our battalion, but to push on the outermost edge, you had to trot almost two hours at a steady pace. The unoccupied space was secured by patrols. Often, the Latvian leader joined this patrol in person and arrived at our position. Soon he became a well-known, respected, and admired personality by our people. We had heard that this man Kolpak could alone do what it would take a whole regiment to accomplish, but none of us had ever witnessed any acts of his courage. And not any of us had yet been convinced of his military acumen. It was almost as if anyone who ventured near him became hypnotized. The only thing we knew was that his people idolized him down to his bootstraps even though he maintained iron discipline. After having heard these tales, it was clear we were in great anticipation and looking forward with excitement to his first acts. This opportunity was not long in coming.

We soon realized the enemy was moving its troops, and it became clear to us that the Bolsheviks had begun preparations for a major attack. From a prisoner we had learned that a stronger division was planning to push itself between us and the Latvians in order to disturb our direct line of communications during the night. This could not be allowed. Colonel Kolpak and our commander agreed that the two troops should ready themselves for battle under cover of night, and at the first dawn the enemy would be attacked from two sides at the same time. This well-executed plan could leave no doubt of its successful outcome.

Promptly at four a.m. our two companies and the machine-gun section were at the ready to leave. An icy-cold chill permeated all at such an early hour. A lieutenant with his column held the foremost position, at a distance of six hundred meters the majority followed, and at the end were the machine gunners and the military equipment wagons. On the crunching snow we walked into the darkness and had no idea that so many of us would never return from this morning's expedition.

While the first part of our journey traversed over open land, at about five a.m., we came upon a wooded area with a small and crippled looking stand of trees. The lack of cavalry was now sorely felt by all of us; we had already had to stop quite often and hold back, but now it was even more necessary. Gradually the darkness began to fade and dawn began, but unfortunately dense fog had settled over the entire area and made it impossible to see anything. If the advance continued at this pace, we would not possibly begin our attack at the right time. The hated enemy would have saved himself once again in this case. That went against our honor. In no way could we Germans fail the Latvian commanders and give ourselves a black eye; we had to be on time.

Therefore, the commander gave me an order to ride to the front and tell the leader about the necessity of speeding up the march. No sooner had I delivered this notice and once again joined my unit than in front some shots were fired that were immediately followed by a raging rapid fire. In a split second we had dismounted from our horses, thrown our valets the reins, and quickly had the battalion form a circle. We put one company to the right and the other to the left and placed the machine gunners in the middle. A few more were used to strengthen the outermost flank. Just a few minutes later this plan was executed. Very slowly the troops worked themselves forward, while the sheaf of fire had already resulted in the first losses.

Before us in the fog four or five figures appeared. Were those already the Bolsheviks on the attack? No, that was all who were still alive from our front column. Completely stunned and half in disbelief about the bloodbath that had been encountered and that they escaped they now told the tale: at about a fifty-meter distance they had made out the fur hats of the enemy but had thought at first they were just the first of a small patrol and opened their fire slowly. The result was a sudden and highly destructive firing on them by the Russians. As many were wounded, they were sent back to the aid station.

The command staff decided to fire back with its machine guns. At an ever-increasing pace the bullets hit us all over and took their victims. We had not even been able to shoot fifty rounds because in the thick fog we didn't even know where we were shooting. As we felt the massive firepower and the effects of it, we realized that the enemy's numbers were many times superior to ours. Meanwhile, we finally received a message that our two flanks had encountered the front of the enemy's firing line. They had been able to approach within a hundred meters of the enemy but had suffered significant losses. There was nothing to see. We could only fire in the general area by our own estimation.

Suddenly the fog began to lift for just a moment in front of our section, and very dimly in the distance we could see our firing positions. We immediately positioned six machine guns, set up our gunners, and into the yonder began to lob our iron seeds down their throats. The dead from our front line lay directly in front of us. With courage and desperation, the enemy now fought back. We are not used to such a fierce fire fight from this enemy. But we feel it and then it becomes less noticeable as we slowly gain the upper hand due to our excellent machine-gun firing. The enemy was now so covered by our own fire that he couldn't position himself to fully shoot back. Now if only the Latvians could intervene from the other side in this fight! Then not one of these Bolsheviks would escape!

Then—all of a sudden—the fog disappears. We were amazed at the suddenness with which this happens and can hardly understand it. We now clearly see the enemy positions that are very close in front of us. Very clearly, we see how the furry heads are pressed deep into the ground to provide protection from our hail of bullets. This is now the signal for assault! We grabbed all the rifles and machine guns and filled them with all the ammunition they could hold. But now the last enemy heads have disappeared. It would have been suicide, if anyone had dared to stand up for even a moment or had just shown a few centimeters of himself. But even behind their shelters we heard the outcries that bore eloquent testimony that we still knew how our missiles would find their targets.

Suddenly during the rapid and inexorable destruction of fire that rockets into the enemy's lines, we see a figure warning us with an outstretched arm. It stands there as though made of molten steel. Each line on its serious face is visible. We think we've seen a ghost! There's only one here of this size, of this herculean yet so lithe physique, and only one that holds such a cold-blooded contempt for death. We are not mistaken; it's Colonel Kolpak in person, the high white-gray fur hat with the silver crest of Latvia he is holding up high in his right hand. A few seconds, maybe even less, he stands there. Then he collapses in the hail of bullets.

But these few moments were enough; every one of our people immediately recognized that this hero was our ally. As if each individual shooter's hands suddenly freeze, as if the mind is paralyzed, all stops at one communal stroke without any command to cease this insane fire. It is as quiet as the grave. And while we stare at each other in complete disbelief, still in shock and dismay, the rest of the alleged enemies jump up and make themselves known. They are indeed our allies from the Latvian regiment. Just a few steps and we arrive at the point where the blood of the brave colonel already has stained the snow a bright red. At once we see that all hope is fruitless. The person we are facing has already passed over to the other side and joined the many of his comrades who had already died that day. Ten bullets had given him death, and one of them had pierced his George's Cross and embedded it deep into his chest. It was as if fate wanted to imply that this highest Russian bravery medal was never worn by one worthier of it. His fine face was destroyed almost beyond recognition. Both Germans and Latvians together carried his corpse to a combat supply wagon and placed him there upon a bier. We all stood around this bed for the last time as a Latvian and a German officer spoke a short prayer, offered a farewell and thanks. Only very seldom have I seen seasoned field soldiers get teary-eyed when they attended a poignant scene, but here it was the case.

During this service an aide tenderly placed a coat over Colonel Kolpak's human remains and many were likely thinking about how this incomprehensible tragedy could have occurred. Was it at all possible that the man who had been so highly revered and admired above all else by our people was shot dead following a fatal misunderstanding between ourselves? And of how many other comrades on both sides uselessly lost their lives today! How many would now have to run around as cripples in the future? How was it possible that a friend had stood against a friend today?

A perfect storm of events was to blame. The Bolsheviks' west flank, which we had gone out in the morning to annihilate, had during the night changed to a new position between us and the Latvians in the immediate vicinity of the future battlefield. Based on their excellent intelligence-gathering, the Soviets had been warned in time of our nocturnal march and of their danger of encirclement. Rightly recognizing that only speedy withdrawal could bring the main force to rescue, the leader had to move the majority of his troops. Only a small mounted rear guard was left with the command to engage in any serious fighting. The Latvians, who were now joined in their advance on this rear guard, had indeed done their best to assemble quickly for action, but despite all of their haste, they had soon realized that the moving enemy had escaped them. Immediately all steps were taken to follow. Then they believed they had captured the escaped opponents again, because they heard the clash of weapons, and as they looked into the mist vaguely defined shapes began to appear. Everything fell to the ground. The alleged enemy, who was none other than our own flank, had now already opened fire.

However, our vanguard could not be reproached. They knew that between them and the Latvian division the enemy was positioned, and they knew who they were supposedly to meet first. Now they suddenly saw in the fog the typical Soviet fur hats. Confused by the blur, they didn't realize the hats were worn by Latvians. They also saw how these wearers of fur hats immediately threw themselves to the ground and formed a skirmish line. This could, therefore, only be the sought-after opponents! And so the battle began against nearly invisible blurred objectives. When then the fog lifted so surprisingly and quickly, Colonel Kolpak was the first to recognize this terrible mistake. He saw his own people lying pressed deeply into the earth; he saw the devastating effect of our machine guns on their own ranks. Every second meant more death among the soldiers entrusted to him. How should you make your presence known to the friends firing from over there? He felt that this duty was his alone, because only he could be recognized, then the error would be corrected, the fire would be silent, and many of his followers saved. So then he jumped up and then so did he fall, giving new legend to himself, true to this oath, sacrificing himself for the sake of his comrades.

He, who had been chosen as the creator of the young army of the new state of Latvia was buried in the state capital with full honors. In the tomb of the great cathedral, he rests from his deeds. He has become immortal. His zinc coffin is embellished with a gold medallion and the inscription: "For you, our great role model—from the army of Latvia." The Second Latvian Infantry Regiment was then named in his honor.[16]

With more than fifty dead and wounded, and substantially weakened,

16. Still considered a national Latvian hero, Oskars Kalpaks was born in 1882 and was a highly decorated Russian soldier during the Great War. He shifted allegiance to Latvia (or remained loyal, depending on your viewpoint) after it declared independence in November 1918 and was put in charge of the new Latvian military. His death in the incident described took place on March 6, 1919. This account is one of the few extant. Something is amiss with Schiller's time line, however, since he claims before this to have returned to the field on March 19. He may be telling this tale slightly out of order. He does begin the entire Kolpak episode with "During this period . . ."

we moved back into our old position. We urgently asked for reinforcements now that the one company only had sixty; the other only counted seventy heads. And with only these weak forces at hand, we were tasked to hold a section of over forty kilometers. And most of this section was located over difficult forest terrain. Quite rightly, the commander rejected all responsibility, as the Bolsheviks could easily overrun us at any opportune moment. The unfortunate circumstances of our battle and the great losses had now become public knowledge, and because of the countless spies swarming about, it was obvious the enemy was also informed about our present lack of strength. Nonetheless, the division always had boots on the ground, and even with no reserves, still staffed other parts of the front weakly. They failed to see that all the enemy would primarily have an interest in was the recovery of the great city of Mitau, so that our battalion, which was the only defense of this city, would have to be exposed to the first line of attack.

To make the Second Company as strong as possible under the leadership of Lieutenant Lüttgenhaus, who had spent most of his time occupying the outposts, Captain von Borke ordered that the machine-gun division be dispatched and likewise sent them forward. What remained of the First Company supported the castle and at the same time also secured the neighboring farmhouse. That was all we could do for the immediate future.

But then the inevitable happened. In the early morning hours of April 6th, our outposts were surprise-attacked at the same time on all sides by a tenfold superiority. Of the five guard posts, the two outermost could only hold the stampede back for a short time and were killed; two others fought with prolonged resistance and retreated only when half of its people had been taken out due to death or injury. Still they did not get far; the attempted escape to the rear failed. Soon they were surrounded. They all died, but they fought mightily to the death, and the battle cost the enemy dearly, as later on we found three times the number of Bolsheviks lying next to them. Only one post did not fall and that was commanded by Lüttgenhaus himself. He only had ten men and one machine gun available, but he managed to get as far as a small forest and then proceeded to set up a defensive line. Four times the enemy attempted an assault by a massive onslaught and four times was thrown back in retreat. The enemy's dead lay in heaps in front of the fences. Lüttgenhaus himself was everywhere. As a flaming arrow hit a roof, he himself put out the flames and while doing so was shot in the shoulder; as the machine gunner was hit and collapsed, he then took over himself on the weapon. A new hit in the left arm was the result. From then on, he took out his Mauser pistol. He had only four men left, but he held out until help could reach him. Thanks to him for holding the first line of defense, the day was not a catastrophe for us and hence for Mitau.

What was happening to us at the staff level in the meantime? Unwittingly, we had laid ourselves to sleep the night before. As the sun rose in the east with the dawn of a new day, we suddenly heard a few alarm shots fired from our outposts. We jumped up, seized our rifles, and rushed into the yard. We were greeted by a hail of bullets that surrounded us and came from the direction of the forest. I looked at Lieutenant Krause's valet, who held his arms high and then toppled down. We ran back into the house and positioned ourselves by the windows. We saw the First Company quickly and safely exit from the castle. We supported them as we swept the forest with our fire. Then I heard the commander call for me. I found him in a skylight, just as a machine gun was brought into firing position. From here you had a good view of the whole farm. He said: "The telephone line to the division naturally was cut by the bandits, so I cannot make any announcement that we are surrounded here and the outposts apparently are lost, but I must have help; otherwise we're finished here. Try to ride along with a few others to Mitau; there you will request unequivocal and immediate assistance. I will make myself a decoy and try to draw the attention of the Bolsheviks to the other side of the front. This moment you must gallop away from us. Good luck and on to victory!"

And that's how it played out. The horses were quickly saddled. We pulled into the courtyard and waited anxiously. Then we heard the reinforced fire, then hand grenades, and last of all the "Hurray!" cries. I sat with my four men ready at the saddle and galloped off. When I reached the exit, it flashed right and left between the trees, barely one hundred yards away. I saw individual characters, who wanted to run up to the other side, stand, put rifle to cheek, and then shoot down on us. At the whistle of bullets, I realized that they would largely pass over us. Behind me a horse fell, which had to have been hit; the rider was a dead man lying on the ground, sure to be massacred because he who lay here would be killed by the Bolsheviks. We could not help him; here it was life and death for all of us.

These moments were among the worst I had been through during the war. But after two minutes we had managed to penetrate the circle of the enemy and break it. Bathed in sweat, I arrived at division headquarters. He was sitting at the coffee table. My message was received like a bomb blast. Major Bischoff realized that immediate assistance was the only possibility of salvation for our battalion. If we could not establish telephone communications, then not only was Mitau lost, but no one could even imagine the further consequences. He turned immediately to the only reserve that was in the city and they were the stormtroopers of the Baltic country's defense, led by Baron von Manteuffel. With astonishing speed, he had his people together despite the early hour. Vehicles and wagons were brought in an accelerated tempo to the enemy's door.

The glowing forces of the Baltic troops once again saved the day. Not only did they liberate Captain von Borke from his dangerous position, but they chased the stronger opponents back past the forester's lodge, which Lieutenant Lüttgenhaus still held. A counterattack by the Bolsheviks failed in a bloody attempt and robbed them of the rest of their fighting spirit. In the evening, all the outpost positions could once again be manned. The sacrifices made on April 6th were costly. Our already very weakened battalion had to sustain a loss of thirty-two dead and almost as many wounded. Some people were still among the missing. They were later found slain in the woods. Thus, the battalion was effectively wiped out.

We were subsequently moved out of the front and were to be provided with replenishment of forces by once again advertising for new replacements. It did not succeed. The flow of volunteers had stopped because in Germany a newly guarded border had been erected against the Poles, and that took away a lot of available manpower. So now there was nothing left for us here except for a losing battle. Therefore, the division broke up our unit and distributed the rest of the remaining men to the other units. I was offered the position of supply officer on the staff of the Second Infantry Regiment of Kurland. The place certainly called to me and promised some nice perks that so far I had never before experienced. I was just about to accept when Captain von Borke asked if I wanted to set up a new command force at home together with him. I could not decline this offer, which spoke of a lot of confidence in me, and accepted. Two days later, the train carried three members of the Iron Division back to the German border. It was Captain von Borke, my valet Roemer, and myself.[17]

17. Schiller leaves the Iron Division right before the Germans and pro-German Latvians overthrow the Latvian government in mid-April before going on to retake Riga in late May. During these ensuing actions, the Freikorps were responsible for mass killings of Latvians, precipitating a split between the Germans and Latvia. Assisted by Estonia and the Allies, Latvia prevailed, and Germany's designs in Latvia were thwarted by midsummer. Both the Freikorps and the Bolsheviks were responsible for mass killings and murders throughout the Latvian campaigns. Schiller may have left before the worst of it on the Freikorps side, but this remains an open question.

7

Protection against the Polish at the Border

After I had recovered for two weeks at home from the exertions, I was once again mentally rested enough to think about my future plans. They lay in uncertainty before me. Captain von Borke's plan to set up a new battalion could be regarded as a failure, because all the command posts reported back that they were unable to accept new personnel based on the fact that they were already overstaffed, even though with people who had little capability for efficiency. If new volunteers offered to enlist, they would be assigned to the existing body of troops. There was no model in place to establish any new volunteer corps. So that's how it was with the border guards against the Poles! I was not encouraged by this news, but one day Captain von Borke surprised me by personally appearing in Bromberg. I somewhat resented the fact that I had followed his enticements, rather than accept the post offered in Kurland. Now it was too late. Captain von Borke quickly departed again and I remained behind, newly annoyed. What was to become of me now?

Suddenly I received a card from my old boss, sent from Kreutz an der Ostbahn.[1] He asked if I would be willing to come and work with him there. He had established a new command unit and urgently

1. "German Cross Railway," a major railway junction and town, which is now Krzyż Wielkopolski in western Poland. Poland declared independence in November 1918 after the armistice but was still occupied by Russian and German troops. As the Germans withdrew, the Russians advanced, until Poland began an offensive against the Russians in February 1919 while the Germans continued to withdraw to fulfill the terms of the armistice. The Poles were much more preoccupied with the Russians than the Germans after this. Though there is some ambiguity here, Schiller's role in this new posting was much more connected to the official duties of the German military than his role in Kurland.

needed an officer to become his aide. Of course, I did not hesitate in the least but sent off an acceptance telegram at once, indicating I should be arriving by the next afternoon. Once again, the old field suitcase was packed, and once again off I went to the train station. The train carrying me to my destination had now reached Nakel. It showed clear signs of a violent struggle during the nation-building that had just recently raged around its perimeter. We closely hugged the right bank of the Netze River, which also formed the border between the German and Polish line.

The railway junction at Kreutz offered an impressive sight with its many large and small houses, numerous workshops, locomotive, freight sheds, and countless bars. You would have thought you had arrived at a big city and yet this village was comprised of just barely four thousand inhabitants. At the exit, two border guard soldiers stood with rifles slung over their shoulders, and on the platform itself another dozen were running up and down, holding all disembarking passengers to a rigorous screening. Due to the military presence everywhere, you could tell the importance of the place and of its proximity to the front. Anyone who wanted to leave the station first had to get permission to do so from the headquarters. I was about to go there myself and was looking toward a path completely congested with people when I caught the portly presence of Captain von Borke. He was followed by a gray-haired civilian on foot. On his arm he wore a white band with the inscription "Bürgerwehr Kreutz a/O."[2]

Thus, my field suitcase was handed over for further transport. I asked who this man was and received a smile for an answer: "This is the orderly of my present military unit." Why does this man wear no uniform? Because the vigilante home guard, whose command he had taken, generally perform their service in civilian clothes. These were the people, he added, who would have the task of relieving the troops stationed at the front line, so they could set the stage for peace and order. They were here primarily to serve and protect the city of Kreutz. Although they were equipped with rifles and stood sentry, they would be considered as only a last resort to be called into combat service. Since they were several hundred men strong, guidance among them would be very difficult. Therefore, I was to support Captain von Borke most strenuously.

2. "Kreutz Civilian Militiaman."

I cannot say that I was uplifted by this introduction. In my eyes, this strange military apparatus comprised a kind of factional troops for which I have never had any confidence. I shared this view with the captain, but he dismissed my concerns. I later came to find that I had unjustly condemned the members of Kreutz's vigilante corps by thinking so badly of them. They turned out to be harmless, good-natured fellows who wanted to protect their land but did not want to be excessively militarily coached. They also took in a nice side income because the state paid them like real soldiers, recognized them as a military auxiliary formation, and demanded absolute obedience.

Meanwhile, we had reached our future quarters. It was a villa that was located in a large park on the exit of the town on the Kreutz-Dratzig Road. The garden was well maintained. A lot of ornamental plants, flower beds, garden benches, and tables gave it a distinctive look, which was further accentuated by arbors and birch trees. The villa itself was built in the Swiss chalet style, decorated and renovated with all the advantages of modern times. Balconies, electric light, steam heating—in short, everything that was near and dear to a person's heart was available. I jumped with delight that I should have such lavish quarters as well as an aristocratic landlord. That would be ample compensation for the disappointment I had just experienced due to the fact that now I was forced to take a hybrid position in between a soldier and a civilian.

Soon, though, I received a shock. Although my room upstairs had a fantastic porch, it was otherwise barren. An iron cot with two blankets, a chair, and a table were the sum of its furnishings. When I saw this chamber set up like this in the house, I had to look at the chief questioningly. He guessed my thoughts and told me gently that the villa had been uninhabited and that the necessary furniture therefore could only gradually be obtained in order to live in comfort. He himself had also fared no better. I was crestfallen! Farewell, comfortably furnished lodging, farewell to homemade stews by the old friendly landlord, farewell to sweet notions of living well, luxury and comfort. I only found words again when the chief summoned me to his adjoining rooms and set before me coffee and fresh butter rolls, which were very rare at that time. I then ordered my valet Roemer to immediately procure and then set up, within twenty-four hours, a comfortable room, or I would need to go elsewhere. And he did just that. The local commander, Lieutenant Berg, proved to be a friend in need. He delivered what he had available in stock.

Although it was not much, it was enough to satisfy my modest demands. Then I oriented myself concerning the general situation and layout in this section. The northern front lay exactly east to west, its left flank on the Weichsel [river], the right we built here at Kreutz. At this point our line turned sharply to the south and reached the Silesian border. The front was divided into individual sections, which had an area of twenty to thirty kilometers and were usually occupied by three to five companies of infantry, a battery, and a squadron. In addition, a few armored trains and outposts were available. That was all. The total number of border guards ranged between forty and fifty thousand men. The Poles were superior to that number by five times but had little artillery and lacked suitable leaders. That gave us a very small measure of confidence. The fiercest battles were over and yielded the result that we had held all of our positions. At the time we were experiencing a skirmish détente that was broken only by individual local incursions from both sides on just a few occasions. What was anticipated to happen here, though, was a presumed major attack, since we held the important Kreutz railway junction and that stuck in the craws and haunted the minds of the enemy. With this capture they would dominate the connection between Berlin and East Prussia. We had to be on guard constantly, because there were only four weak companies of Border Battalion Number Seven, a battery, and an armored train.

I shared the villa with the commander of the division, Major Davids. Upon my initial visit with him I found him to be an upstanding, basic, honest, and benevolent boss who might have been just a little too old for his rank but otherwise immediately inspired confidence. He greeted me warmly and was glad that he had secured a new officer for his district. We became the best of friends and spent many an hour drinking together as well.

My service duties were very easy, as I only had to control the posts and guards. So I had plenty of time left to familiarize myself with the local flavor of the land. After I had satisfied myself of that, the job became a bit boring. I complained to the captain of my plight. He then suggested that we jointly visit the troops at their individual positions. We made a pilgrimage to the village of Dratzig that was three kilometers away and lay directly on the river Netze. Similar to the Iron Division, they also had no continuous and connected line, and the companies were widely dispersed without any real communication. I saw nothing of a firmly developed and gigantic frontline position. Very near to the enemy and in front of the village a few security guards were stationed; the rest were embedded in the farmsteads and only came forward if sounding the alarm. I thought that this strategy was very reckless and emphasized it and said as much to the young company commander. However, he laughed this off and replied that the Polish were five or six kilometers away and were doing exactly the same thing. In a way they both seemed to be acting according to some sort of tacit agreement. However, that didn't mean that they weren't surprised occasionally by random acts of an unpleasant nature. Nowadays, of primary importance was to keep the team in a good mood, and this mood was present as long as they were left alone as much as possible. Therefore, even the building of any trenches had been excluded. He then recommended it would be best for us to drown all sorrows in alcohol. So that being said, shouldn't we accompany him on a visit to his favorite pub? Of course, we wanted that. We drank until darkness set in.

One day Major Davids sent for me and told me that I should become both his orderly and court officer. The aide-de-camp had so much work to do that the job had outgrown him; he needed a second in command; my service with the civilian guards would probably not be necessary. The latter I could affirm with a clear conscience. So I transferred to headquarters. It felt very right to me because now I felt I had become a real soldier once again.

For the time being I had a real job in front of me. Left there lying unattended were mountains of files and paperwork. I had to work both day and night just to sift through everything. Only when that was completed was I able to start the real job. Mostly it consisted of court hearings and matters of discipline. Then came a slew of crimes and misdemeanors! Assault, theft, rebellion, insubordination, everything you could possibly think of was well represented. This gave me pause for thought that we really were not a peacetime army because such acts would have been unthinkable on such a large scale otherwise. I also got an overview of the human element that comprised the Border Patrol. One part consisted of the dark men of honor whose previous life for the most part had to be covered with the Cloak of Love; on the other hand there were those who had taken up weapons in the true German nationalistic attitude to protect their homeland.[3] They were in it both in heart and soul and would have

3. "Cloak of Love" (*Mantel der Liebe*) is a German idiom, here meaning that these men were trying to either redeem themselves for, or cover over, past deeds.

preferred if the High Command had ordered them to stage a major attack immediately. With such unevenly inclined journeymen, friction inside of the divisions was inevitable. That was the reason why I could not get out from under the most basic part of my job, because as soon as one thing was done then promptly I had another new task that soon became more interesting than the last.

For the days' pleasures and annoyances, I was then well compensated by the cozy evenings that I could spend with Major Davids. He loved socializing, light entertainment, and a good drop. It was always the same core group that gathered together—the major with his inseparable pipe in his mouth, sitting in the sofa beside him the portly Captain von Borke with a real Havana [cigar], in a cane chair the eternally tipsy leader of the Border Battalion Number Seven, Captain Goerke, next to him the Section Adjutant Lieutenant Bunk, who was my work colleague and whose companionship soon united us in friendship. Besides these, I was also included in this group. The necessary libations were always plentiful because money was readily available and there was plenty of wine to buy. Rarely did we ever part before midnight. It was a carefree time. The enemy behaved decently and very seldom bothered us, and we likewise returned the favor.

We were sitting together one evening, once again in a merry mood. This time we were quite happy, as we had been paid our salary the day before. But in the middle of our finest drinking and storytelling we were bothered by the ringing of the field telephone. Without any worry our host picked up the phone, thinking that at the least it would probably be one of the usual messages that were irrelevant. But we realized that after just the first few words this time there would be more serious explanation. "Hold the position at all costs; I will immediately send help and will stay here so you can reach me." That was the urgent conclusion of the call. We soon knew what had transpired.

The enemy had executed a surprise attack. We jumped up. The old man was as if electrified and called to us, "Enough for now, gentlemen. The company in Dratzig has just been attacked by a superior enemy force. Individual houses are already in Polish hands. The sounding of the alarm systems did not work. The company commander has only a handful of people. Collect whatever teams you can immediately rustle up here in Kreutz. You, Captain Goerke, rush over to Dratzig and take the lead. God bless you." "Yes, sir," said Captain Goerke, clicked his heels together, and ran off, but before he did so he drained the rest of what was left in his bottle down his throat. Perhaps in doing so, he would gain a better advantage on the battlefield. Captain von Borke had already lowered his glass as he received this unexpected news with shock. His somewhat blurry eyes suddenly lit up with an energized glow. He thought of his civilian vigilantes and that he might still die a hero's death this day as their leader. When we tore a window open, we already heard the machine guns. A moment later our battery began to fire. Our people were readily at hand and were not like those in Dratzig, who were likely to be found lying about pubs while the Polish got the best of them. The recklessness of company leaders and Lieutenant Hautschke would now have its consequences. He alone was to blame for this.

While we quickly buckled on rifles and revolvers, shots could already be heard crashing close to our home. Even the guard who stood sentry at the park entrance now fired his weapon in rapid succession. A view from the window informs us that in the town itself the struggle must have already started because there are flashes everywhere. No doubt the enemy, under the cover of night, crossed over the Netze and then attacked Dratzig with one division and Kreutz with the other. But it is incomprehensible to me how he could have been able to advance so far without being noticed. Our sentry guard posts must have been sleeping, otherwise it is not conceivable. It was critical for me to first reach the city and go to the office in order to save the military maneuver plans from the Polish. My valet Roemer suddenly appears in full combat gear in the doorway.

Together we race down the stairs. We come to the park. It is hard to see your own hand in front of your eyes. We slowly feel our way to the entrance. Suddenly it flashes before us and shots are driven into a tree trunk. We throw ourselves down. A new shot is the result. Quite clearly we hear the rattle of a machine gun at the station. We do not know, is it one of us or has the enemy already established its position there? Incessant gunfire rolled through Dratzig. This is proof that the citizens will defend themselves to their skin and bones. From the direction of the park entrance, from where we have just been shot at, we now hear voices. There are Germans. So this cannot be the enemy. So I call: "Here is Lieutenant Schiller. Who's there?" Answer: "Here civilian militia of Kreutz." We jump up and the next moment we have reached the doorway. We meet up with two excited fearful figures with gray hair. I ask why they fired on us. No answer. The fellow is still quite puzzled. I ask again. Because they believed that the Poles already had occupied the villa and that the officers were captured. When they heard our footsteps, they were of the opinion that we were also enemies. Suddenly Lieutenant Bunk appears. I tell him what just happened, outraged, but there is no time to reflect, as at this moment there is no time for further introspection. As a precaution, however, we take the cartridges from our infamous snipers. Otherwise they might have mowed the commander down and that would have been quite the shock.

The firing upon the main train station has become more intense by the minute. In the streets you hear the bangs and crashes that are so loud you cannot make out your own words as you speak. We discuss what we want to do. Bunk proposes that we advance to the city to determine the situation. I agree. Roemer remains with us. His squinting cross-eyes sparkle as the light flashes; he is fully aware of the scope and severity of the moment. We first run to the Einsiedler Bridge that is by the national building. When we come within a hundred yards of it, a deep voice shouts from above: "Who goes there?" Before we can answer, we hear the command: "Fire."

Once again the bullets are whizzing around our ears, and once again we are being bombarded by our own people. This time they have blessed us with a full volley. The deep bass voice belongs to the master tailor Krählich. We know him. It drives us to distraction. We immediately jump from the road and into a ditch and then roar as loudly as we can: "Do not shoot; we are German border guards." But either they do not hear us or they do not understand us, because up there on the bridge they proceed to switch to firing single-weapon discharges upon us. My valet suddenly cries out. Bunk, who lies close to him, bends over him. He asks if he has been hit. But the honest Saxon has already collected himself and railed off in his dialect: "The cursed band of sows has shot up my carbine. The shock of the strike electrified my entire body." And then he transforms into quite a primitive man and swears his bloody revenge. He will roast the bums alive who wanted to promote their own comrades to the afterlife. Slay them, stab them, he will eat them alive. Despite the seriousness of the situation, we have to laugh out loud about so much anger and rage. But how long are we still going to have to lie here?

A white signal flare rises straight ahead into the air. The firing stops. In any case, Mr. Krählich still wants to convince himself about how strong the "enemy" is and where he is lurking. This moment Bunk used to our advantage, as he jumps up and shouts:

"Here is Lieutenant Bunk." And while he is still calling, he runs in long strides toward the bridge. We follow him. We meet up with a dozen civilian militiamen. Mr. Krählich, the commander, emerges. He wants to proffer some sort of an excuse but is so aghast that he initially lacks the language. I yelled at these folks as never before to any subordinates. Only Mr. Krählich was spared. He, however, got his measure from elsewhere. We left him in the hands of Roemer to berate him. Although he broke his vow and did not roast or eat him, nonetheless the conversation he had with him was anything but polite and was teeming with zoological terms, among which donkeys and livestock were the more delicate.

I quickly discussed our other plan with Bunk. I wanted to walk into town and there put an end to further shooting and he would try to reach the train station. From the direction of Dratzig, slowly but steadily the fire has died down and the artillery had become quiet. It had long been clear to me that not a single Pole may have been in Kreutz or even its vicinity, but that our hardworking defenders of the civil militia had been shooting at each other. So I walk through the streets and grab a couple of real soldiers who have just crawled out sleepy-eyed from under their covers. Therefore, they do not know what is really going on and are at a loss but are at the ready with carbines in front of their quarters. They are quickly oriented on the situation and given orders that also provide for the termination of this battle. They spring apart quickly and are off in all directions. As I near the marketplace, an honest citizen is holding his firearm at me from his window. I hiss at him and advise him to hang his weapon back behind the mirror, as soon as possible. Otherwise failing to do so he would make acquaintance with my revolver. Wherever I asked why they were shooting I would always get the same answer: "The Pole has invaded the city." But then no one had actually seen him. That I can well imagine.

Finally, after an hour, peace has resumed. It is now even as still as it was at the time when we were still sitting together in a relaxed atmosphere and thought neither of war nor of bullets. Soon the roads became busier. Now that it is no longer dangerous, the citizens wanted to satisfy themselves and reveled in curiosity. A couple walking arm in arm in front of me, in love and oblivious to danger, just like on any other night, is the best proof that the coast is now clear. Just then the clock strikes three o'clock in the morning from the church tower. From the east, the first glimmer of light breaks through and will help clarify what errors had occurred the night before. I go to the station and on the way meet up with the major. He is beside himself and is boiling over with rage and anger. He already knows that the vigilante civilian militia is to blame for the whole incident. Therefore, his remarks concerning them are in line wholeheartedly with those of my faithful Roemer, only to hear them come from his mouth is less scary. The battle is over; we leave the battlefield and go back to our quarters.

The next morning, I did some actual legal work in my capacity as a court officer, namely to determine the main culprits. It was not hard to figure them out. It revealed the following facts: a stronger enemy patrol that had some light weapons with them had actually made a surprise attack on Dratzig. One of our sentry guards had been treacherously killed before he could sound the alarm; a second post had detected the enemy and thrown a few hand grenades at his feet. This good effect gave the company commander time to gather a few people and grapple with the Polish in the outermost villages. But since he lacked any overview of the strength of the enemy and reckoned on an overall attack, Lieutenant Hautschke requested the artillery set barrage fire into action. The quick volleys of artillery from the back and the rifle fire in front had laid the foundation. This served to make the guards of the militia, which were at their Kreutz posts, so excited and it brought them to confusion; they were of the opinion that the enemy had already broken their barriers and was now before them. So they just started firing all they had in the city at what they thought was coming from the direction of Dratzig. As they were interrupted from their restful slumbers, the other respectable citizens had jumped out of bed, taken their guns, and stationed themselves at the windows of their apartments. If someone had the misfortune of rambling about during this time, he was at great risk, as this rumor immediately made all the rounds and had the consequence that anyone who showed up in the dark on the road was regarded as an enemy and was immediately covered by a hail of bullets.

It was a miracle that despite the amount of ammunition fired, only one soldier and a civilian were injured. But that bore witness to the "excellent marksmanship" of the vigilante civilian militia of Kreutz. This night they had more than adequately proven that this division was not up to the task, and that instead of helping, they could even be extremely dangerous. The major then proposed the dissolution of the division and provided detailed descriptions of the reasons for it.

It wasn't long before the related general staff command came to the same conclusion. This was now the cause of the many long faces in the general civilian population, because now their little side income had vanished, and it also meant it was back to the monotonous routine of everyday life. I collected the civilians' rifles, cartridges, and armbands and then sent all of the weapons of war to the fortress at Königsberg, where they would hopefully land in more worthy hands.

Our reserve company was sent to Kreutz in order not to leave the guard stations and posts that had previously been provided by the vigilantes unattended. It was only when a regular military had taken control that we could be reassured. Certainly, the Polish had been fully informed and knew about the idiotic episode.[4] This time they truly had a right to relish this fact. However, for them, there was a drop of melancholy in it, as not a single man had returned from their patrol stations after Dratzig. Captain Goerke had formed a perimeter around the area immediately after his arrival. And, fortified by the last great gulp from the wine bottle, that also helped him to determine a good take on the situation. Unfortunately, we were now going to lose one of our regular customers, Captain von Borke. He had become redundant after the dissolution of his "troops." He was discharged from the army and went back to his family in Berlin. The rest of us had to go on celebrating without him. He had left a big hole in our group; the amiable sociability in its old form was now gone.

And again, the days and weeks went by without anything special occurring. A couple of times I went riding out with the major to the individual companies to visit them, and several times smaller skirmishes were reported. But a serious struggle had not presented itself. The Peace Treaty of Versailles had been adopted and cosigned by Scheidemann, without whose hand it might have withered.[5] The entente now was the supreme word in Germany and we only had to obey. It was ordered that the Polish institute a cease-fire and there

4. What we render here as "idiotic episode" is "Schildbürgerstreich," a German idiom based on a collection of folk tales from the sixteenth century, referring to idiotic actions by government bureaucracies. A loose parallel in English might be "SNAFU."

5. Philipp Heinrich Scheidemann of the German Social Democratic party (SPD) made the official proclamation in 1918 that Germany was now a republic. The Treaty of Versailles was signed on June 28, 1919, and went into effect on January 10, 1920. At this point in the narrative, Schiller is referring to the earlier date.

was also a neutral zone created within which no soldier was allowed to show himself. And yet, one day, some of our hotheads invaded the neutral zone anyway. They were immediately dismissed and later even judicially held accountable. This example alone served to work better and was clearer than any instruction or explanations for the people.

The peace treaty also forced us to terminate the border guard. In order that the officers and men were not immediately put out of work, the division took on the title of the Defense Ministry before reclassifying all the troops of the Eastern Front. Major Davids, and with it Bunk, Battalion Number Seven, the armored tank division, and the batteries, were demobilized and partially incorporated into the already existing German military formations. The only one who initially remained in Kreutz was me and that was because Lieutenant Berg had taken his leave, so the local headquarters was in need of a new leader. I applied for this position and got it, to my utmost delight, because I was now going courting. A few months ago, during a little soirée that was given by the company commander of the staff command troops embedded in Neuteich, I was introduced to a certain Miss Margarete Zeisler. On September 17th [1919], we became engaged. From that time on I had an urgent need to show myself more often in Neuteich. This can well be understood.

We now eagerly awaited what would become of the new Reichswehr battalion that had now been formed.[6] It had to occupy all the positions in general that had already been held by the Border Patrol. In Kreutz itself, only the staff remained quartered. It consisted of Major Bertold, a closed-off and less accessible gentleman who had many quirks and was therefore not particularly well thought of; the adjutant, Lieutenant Schicke; and the aide-de-camp, Lieutenant Dickers. With the latter two I soon became better acquainted, so that a nice relationship developed between us. The chief doctor and the purser hardly made their appearance; they went their separate ways,

6. Schiller is probably referring to the new German military, limited by the Treaty of Versailles to one hundred thousand men, and which was primarily concerned with defending the borders of the new Weimar Republic (Reichswehr = realm defense). There were, however, several "Black" Reichswehr formations, illegally funded and controlled by the German government and used for various operations against foreign and domestic targets. See for example Matthias Strohn, *The Germany Army and the Defense of the Reich* (New York: Cambridge University Press, 2010).

and I didn't mind at all. I now changed my accommodations and moved into the home of a man of independent means, who was also a shoemaker and whose apartment was directly above my local headquarters. There I found a comfortable home, as I had always wanted. The people in the neighborhood saw to it by their best endeavors that I should feel at ease.

I like to think back on that time fondly. This part of my service was quite bearable and even left a lot of free time. I was to provide for the accommodations of the military, as well as for safety and order in the city. I also had to process permits that allowed civilians entry into Poland. Only those that were in possession of a valid permit could be transported under guard across the border. Of course, first the applicants had to be vetted most thoroughly before any permits were granted, because it had been revealed that individuals who had been sentenced in Germany to imprisonment were trying to escape their punishment by fleeing and emigrating to Poland. Others had formerly served as spies of the enemy and had informed the enemy commanders in great depth and through communications on our presumed strength and positions. It was not in Germany's best interests to allow such people to leave the Reich. Hence the strict control. I was able to make some good catches in the process.

At my suggestion, a provisional officers' club was set up in one room of the town hall where now we could eat our lunch together. We had our food delivered from the field kitchen, not because it tasted particularly good but because then the teams would see that we were not getting anything more or different than they were. After conclusion of the meal, the major usually disappeared very quickly, but that did not stop us from staying for an hour more over a glass of beer and a cigar together. We got to know each other much better that way, and then it became significantly easier for us all to cooperate.

When winter came, the stream of immigrants died down considerably. Then at the same time, the activities of the local headquarters were also reduced. That gave me the opportunity very often to ride to Neuteich to my bride to spend the afternoon and evening there. The only uncomfortable part of this day was the way back home, because it took me nearly five kilometers through an unsecured area that was more often than not patrolled by the Polish. But only once did I make such a contact. It was almost midnight and I trotted forth unsuspecting and carefree. Suddenly, I was covered on all sides by close range fire. Three shots! My steed, who was otherwise sluggish and slow, was just as frightened as his rider. He broke to the left across the ditch and took off in a full gallop across the fields. I had never before returned to Kreutz as quickly as during that night. It was fortunate that the moon had not seemed particularly bright, otherwise a bullet between the ribs would certainly have taken me down, and then the state would have owed me no further compensation. I immediately reported the incident, and a troop went to sniff them out. Of course, by that time the Polish were long gone. Only six rounds left on the ground that had been fired indicated their location. This was the last time that I found myself in mortal danger during the course of the war.

Shortly after Christmas, my old valet Roemer left me. I felt sorry for the poor guy. He suffered from a broken heart. When I had first told him of my engagement, he grinned and had shaken his head disapprovingly, raised a greasy forefinger, and said: "Now, now, sir, that's asking for trouble. These broads are all good for nothing." All of his attempts at courtship had thus far been unsuccessful, and he claimed that he possessed enough experience in it. However, that had not prevented him from pursuing a local Kreutz girl and then a few months later also making a marriage proposal. However, not unexpectedly, he had come up short once again. Now all he thought about was getting away from here. He didn't want to see the place that had brought him this disappointment again. But as I myself could not leave on his account, he had no choice but to separate from his position. I dismissed him from his military service well compensated. He went back to his beloved Saxony, from which he apparently expected more luck than had been given him here. With him, the last well-known face disappeared from the old lively border protection time under Major Davids.

Soon after the ratification of the treaty, the Polish occupied Danzig and the entire surrounding area up to the Netze River.[7] Our troops had previously been withdrawn on the day before, just before those of Kreutz. But we were not long in staying here, because a special agreement stipulated that Germany should leave no divisions within the first six months that were closer than within five kilometers from the new border. As our town was still in that zone, it had to be evacuated. This also explains why a local headquarters was now

7. In 1920, Danzig, now Gdansk in Poland, was declared a free city under a League of Nations Mandate.

unnecessary. I received an order from the command of the division that all must be dissolved by the twentieth of February [1920]. I was now to become part of the first battery of the Reichswehr Artillery Regiment Number Forty-Two that was stationed at Flatow. In gratitude for my services in border management, I received a letter from the division commander, the Exzellenz von la Chevallerie [award] and was granted permission to carry a sword with the inscription "Grenzmark 1919."[8]

My new military unit was quickly found. There was a dashing streak in it, so that the service was fun. I had to settle in slowly to this position because since November 1918 I had not belonged to any battery unit. The leader, Lieutenant Moeglich, had already become an officer at the outbreak of war and understood his business. I became closer to him and soon saw that we were philosophically inclined and tolerably suited each other well. He had a terrible relationship with the second lieutenant named Sattler, who would have liked to pull me over onto his side. I tried to act as a mediator and effected some reconciliations, but then at the next opportunity, the two leaders fought each other again and all reconciliation was cast to the winds. After that I gave up. Incidentally, all three of us were later transferred to the police and currently hold [in 1928] the rank of police captain. Moeglich and Sattler were both sent to Berlin and finally learned to tolerate each other. Their increased age and therefore maturity, along with their knowledge, insight, and good sense, may have largely contributed to this. I couldn't have been happier with this outcome.

About three months still remained for me where I was permitted to carry on a fresh and unbounded soldier's life. Then the effect of the peace treaty was felt by all of us. Our regiment had to be demobilized earlier than planned. It was a painful feeling, as we had to return guns, horses, and other military equipment to the military training area in Gragow near Stettin.[9] The majority of the officers and men and all the reserve officers were relieved, and we received our farewells on May 31st, 1920. From that day on there was only the

8. "Grenzmark 1919" was likely an indication of his service on the border. Grenzmark, or "borderline," was part of the name of the Grenzmark-Posen-Westpreußen area after the armistice.

9. Now Grabowo and Szczecin in western Poland, respectively.

very numerically limited Reichswehr. With a recognition and letter of thanks from the Defense Ministry in my pocket and with resentment against the dictates of Versailles in my heart, I went to Neuteich. Thus my military service had ended.

Index

www.ingramcontent.com/pod-product-compliance
Lightning Source LLC
Chambersburg PA
CBHW051940230125
20765CB00014B/406/J